Architecture and the Housing Question

Architecture and the Housing Question examines how the design and provision of housing around the world have become central both to competing political projects and to the architecture profession.

How have architects acting as housing experts helped alleviate or enforce class, race, and gender inequality? What are the disciplinary implications of taking on shelter for the multitude as an architectural assignment and responsibility? The book features essays in the historiography of architecture and the housing question, and a collection of historical case studies from Belgium, China, France, Ghana, the Netherlands, Kenya, the Soviet Union, Turkey, and the United States. The thematic organization of the collection, interrogating housing expertise, the state apparatus, segregation and colonialism, highlights the methodological questions that underpin its international outlook.

The book will appeal to students and scholars in architecture, architectural history, theory, and urban studies.

Can Bilsel is Professor of Architecture at the University of San Diego where he served as Chair of the Department of Art, Architecture and Art History, and the founding Director of the Architecture Program. He holds a PhD from Princeton University, SMArchS from MIT, and a B.Arch from METU in Ankara, Turkey. Bilsel has written and lectured on modern architecture and archaeology museums, and on the changing political contexts and audiences of architectural conservation. His publications include *Antiquity on Display: Regimes of the Authentic in Berlin's Pergamon Museum* (Oxford, 2012), "Crisis in Conservation: Istanbul's Gezi Park between Restoration and Resistance" (2017), "Our Anatolia: Organicism and the Making of the Humanist Culture in Turkey" (2007). He is currently working on a series of essays on urban protests, resistance and memorialization.

Juliana Maxim, Associate Professor and Chair of the Department of Art, Architecture and Art History at the University of San Diego, is an art and architectural historian whose work focuses on the history of modern aesthetic practices – from photography to urbanism – under the communist, centralized states of the Soviet Bloc. She completed her PhD dissertation in the History, Theory and Criticism of Architecture at MIT in 2006. Maxim was a recipient of the National Council for East European and Eurasian Research Award (2008–2010) and was an American Council for Learned Societies post-doctoral fellow (2012–2013). Her book titled *The Socialist Life of Modern Architecture: Bucharest, 1955–1965* (Routledge), explores the remarkably intense and multifaceted architectural activity in postwar Romania and the mechanisms through which architecture was invested with political meaning.

Routledge Research in Architecture

The *Routledge Research in Architecture* series provides the reader with the latest scholarship in the field of architecture. The series publishes research from across the globe and covers areas as diverse as architectural history and theory, technology, digital architecture, structures, materials, details, design, monographs of architects, interior design and much more. By making these studies available to the worldwide academic community, the series aims to promote quality architectural research.

The Architect and the Academy
Essays on Research and Environment
Dean Hawkes

Architecture of Threshold Spaces
A Critique of the Ideologies of Hyperconnectivity and Segregation in the Socio-Political Context
Laurence Kimmel

Pyrotechnic Cities
Architecture, Fire-Safety and Standardisation
Liam Ross

Architecture and the Housing Question
Edited by Can Bilsel and Juliana Maxim

Mies at Home
From Am Karlsbad to the Tugendhat House
Xiangnan Xiong

For more information about this series, please visit: https://www.routledge.com/Routledge-Research-in-Architecture/book-series/RRARCH

Architecture and the Housing Question

Edited by
Can Bilsel and Juliana Maxim

Routledge
Taylor & Francis Group

LONDON AND NEW YORK

Graham Foundation

This publication has been supported by a grant from the Graham Foundation for Advanced Studies in the Fine Arts.

Cover image: A splash pool in Novye Cheremushki. 1964 © John Reps Papers, #15-2-1101. Division of Rare and Manuscript Collections, Cornell University Library

First published 2022
by Routledge
4 Park Square, Milton Park, Abingdon, Oxon OX14 4RN

and by Routledge
605 Third Avenue, New York, NY 10158

Routledge is an imprint of the Taylor & Francis Group, an informa business

British Library Cataloguing-in-Publication Data
A catalogue record for this book is available from the British Library

Library of Congress Cataloging-in-Publication Data
A catalog record has been requested for this book

ISBN: 978-0-8153-9602-4 (hbk)
ISBN: 978-1-032-18186-8 (pbk)
ISBN: 978-1-351-18296-6 (ebk)

DOI: 10.4324/9781351182966

Typeset in Sabon
by codeMantra

Contents

Figures

Contributors

Can Bilsel is Professor of Architecture at the University of San Diego where he served as Chair of the Department of Art, Architecture and Art History, and the founding Director of the Architecture Program. He holds a PhD from Princeton University, SMArchS from MIT, and a BArch from METU in Ankara, Turkey. Bilsel has written and lectured on modern architecture and archaeology museums, and on the changing political contexts and audiences of architectural conservation. His publications include *Antiquity on Display: Regimes of the Authentic in Berlin's Pergamon Museum* (Oxford, 2012), "Crisis in Conservation: Istanbul's Gezi Park between Restoration and Resistance" (2017), and "Our Anatolia: Organicism and the Making of the Humanist Culture in Turkey" (2007). He is currently working on a series of essays on urban protests, resistance, and memorialization.

Daria Bocharnikova is a historian of modern architecture and urban planning. She received her PhD in 2014 from the European University Institute in Florence and was a post-doctoral fellow at Harvard University. Her research interests lie at the intersection of urban studies and history of state socialism. In 2012, she started teaching in the Faculty of Liberal Arts at St. Petersburg State University and launched the international collaborative project "Second World Urbanity" (http://www.second-worldurbanity.org/) together with Steven E. Harris that explores the history of urban planning, and lived experience in socialist cities across Eurasia and beyond. In 2016, she moved to Brussels where she began to work at the Center for Fine Arts BOZAR as institutional advisor and curator of Russian Turn program, while continuing to collaborate with different universities, including KU Leuven and the Free University of Berlin.

M. Melih Cin is Research Assistant and PhD candidate in the Department of Architecture at the Middle East Technical University. Cin received his Master's degree in Urban Regeneration at İzmir Katip Çelebi University (2016) with a thesis titled, "Urban Regeneration Strategies for Supporting Social Sustainability of Roma Community: İzmir-Ege

Neighbourhood Urban Regeneration Project." His current research focuses on urban sociology with particular emphasis on the urban spatial practices of marginalized, underserved, and subaltern groups.

Miles Glendinning is Director of the Scottish Centre for Conservation Studies and Professor of Architectural Conservation at the University of Edinburgh. He has published extensively on modernist and contemporary architecture and housing, and on Scottish historic architecture in general: his books include the award-winning *Tower Block* (with Stefan Muthesius) and *The Conservation Movement*. His current research is focused on the international history of mass housing, and he has just published the first comprehensive global overview of this topic: *Mass Housing: Modern Architecture and State Power – a Global History* (Bloomsbury Academic Press, February 2021). His other planned books include a history of public housing in Hong Kong (Routledge; likely publication 2023) and a history of postwar housing in London.

Kıvanç Kılınç is Associate Professor in the Department of Architecture at Kadir Has University (KHAS). He previously taught at Izmir University of Economics and Yaşar University, and at the American University of Beirut (AUB) as Visiting Assistant Professor and Associate Professor where he also served as the Architecture Program Coordinator (2019–2020). Kılınç received his PhD degree (2010) from State University of New York at Binghamton, and Master's degree (2002) from Middle East Technical University. His current research focuses on the transnational connections and their consequences which shaped contemporary social housing practices in Turkey and the Middle East. Kılınç has published extensively in academic journals as well as in edited books and is the co-editor of *Social Housing in the Middle East: Architecture, Urban Development, and Transnational Modernity* (Indiana University Press, 2019). He also serves as managing editor of the *International Journal of Islamic Architecture* (IJIA).

Samuel Y. Liang is Associate Professor of Humanities at Utah Valley University, where he served as the Director of the Humanities Program. He previously taught at University of Manchester and MIT. He received his PhD in History and Theory of Art and Architecture from Binghamton University (2006). He has published extensively on Chinese urbanism, architecture, and cultural history, including two books: *Remaking China's Great Cities: Space and Culture in Urban Housing, Renewal, and Expansion* (Routledge, 2014); *Mapping Modernity in Shanghai: Space, Gender, and Visual Culture in the Sojourners' City 1853–98* (Routledge, 2010). His current research explores urban housing developments that feature Chinese players across national borders.

Reinhold Martin is a historian of architecture and media, and Professor of Architecture in the Graduate School of Architecture, Planning, and

Preservation at Columbia University. His books include *The Organizational Complex: Architecture, Media, and Corporate Space* (MIT, 2003); *Utopia's Ghost: Architecture and Postmodernism, Again* (Minnesota, 2010); *The Urban Apparatus: Mediapolitics and the City* (Minnesota, 2016); and *Knowledge Worlds: Media, Materiality, and Making of the Modern University* (Columbia, 2021). Martin was a founding co-editor of the interdisciplinary journal *Grey Room*; from 2008 to 2021 he directed Columbia University's Temple Hoyne Buell Center for the Study of American Architecture.

Juliana Maxim, Associate Professor and Chair of the Department of Art, Architecture and Art History at the University of San Diego, is an art and architectural historian whose work focuses on the history of modern aesthetic practices – from photography to urbanism – under the communist, centralized states of the Soviet Bloc. She completed her PhD dissertation in the History, Theory and Criticism of Architecture at MIT in 2006. Maxim was a recipient of the National Council for East European and Eurasian Research Award (2008–2010) and was an American Council for Learned Societies post-doctoral fellow (2012–2013). Her book titled *The Socialist Life of Modern Architecture: Bucharest, 1955–1965* (Routledge) explores the remarkably intense and multifaceted architectural activity in postwar Romania and the mechanisms through which architecture was invested with political meaning.

Patricia A. Morton is Associate Professor in the Department of Media and Cultural Studies and Chair of the Urban Studies Program at the University of California, Riverside. She is the author of *Hybrid Modernities: Architecture and Representation at the 1931 International Colonial Exposition in Paris.* Her current project, *Paying for the Public Life*, focuses on written and built work by architect Charles W. Moore and his collaborators to examine the formation of publics and counterpublics in postwar United States. She has lectured and published widely on architectural history and race, gender, and identity. She is a past editor of the *Journal of the Society of Architectural Historians* and currently serves as First Vice President of the Society of Architectural Historians

Ijlal Muzaffar is Associate Professor of Modern Architectural History at the Rhode Island School of Design. In addition, he has taught at Columbia University, Toronto University, and MIT. He holds a PhD from MIT in the History, Theory, and Criticism of Architecture and Art, a Master of Architecture from Princeton, and a BA in Mathematics and Physics from the University of Punjab in Lahore, Pakistan. His work has appeared in edited volumes, biennale catalogues, and peer reviewed forums like *Grey room, Future Anterior,* and the architectural collaborative, *Aggregate,* of which he is also a founding member. *His book,* which looks at how modern architects and planners played a critical role in shaping the discourse on Third World development and its associated structures of power and intervention in the postwar era is soon to be published by University of Texas Press.

Sandra Parvu is *Maître de Conférences* of Landscape and Urban Planning in the Department of Architecture at the University of Paris. She is a research fellow at the Centre for Housing Research (CRH-LAVUE). Her book *Grands ensembles en situation: Journal de bord de quatre chantiers* (*Public Housing in Situ: A Study of Four Building Sites*, 2011) explores the conflict between architects and French administration over public housing construction at the end of the 1950s. She is the co-author with Alice Sotgia of a chapter entitled "Building by Ear: Boyle Heights, Los Angeles" in Naomi Stead, Deborah van der Plaat, and Janina Gosseye (eds), *Speaking of Buildings. Oral History in Architectural Research* (Princeton Architectural Press, 2019). Her current research examines how the development of specific visual tools of representation enables landscape architects and French administrators to establish and implement landscape policies.

Anooradha Iyer Siddiqi is Assistant Professor at Barnard College, Columbia University. She specializes in histories of architecture, modernity, and migration, centering African and South Asian questions of historicity and archives, heritage politics, and feminist and colonial practices. Her book manuscript *Architecture of Migration: The Dadaab Refugee Camps and Humanitarian Settlement* (Duke University Press) analyzes the history, visual rhetoric, and spatial politics of the Dadaab refugee camps in Northeastern Kenya, as an epistemological vantage point in African and Islamic worlds. Her book manuscript *Minnette de Silva and a Modern Architecture of the Past* engages the intellectual and heritage work of an important cultural figure in the history of Ceylon/Sri Lanka, one of the first women in the world to establish a professional architectural practice. Siddiqi directs the Columbia University Center for the Study of Social Difference working group, *Insurgent Domesticities*.

Alice Sotgia is *Maître de Conférences associé* of Human and Social Sciences in the National School of Architecture Paris-Malaquais. She is a research fellow at the Architecture, Culture, Society Lab (ACS-AUSser). Her book, *INA Casa Tuscolano* (2010), deals with a public housing neighborhood in Rome that is considered a model for Italian modern architecture: it deconstructs the multiple temporalities, practices, narratives, and forms that constitute this neighborhood through time and questions the idea of conservation. The book received the Anci-Storia prize for the best Italian book of the year in the field of urban history. Her current research focuses on the effects of territorial narratives on the image and development of nonmetropolitan areas.

Shannon Starkey is Assistant Professor of Architecture at the University of San Diego. He holds a PhD in architectural history from UCLA and a BArch from WIT. His research focuses on the intersections of architecture and capital especially in California. He is the co-author of *House of the Future* (A+U, 2016) that examines the history of the future of domesticity from the early twentieth century to today. Starkey is the associate or co-curator of numerous exhibitions including "The New Creativity: Man and Machines" (MAK Center West Hollywood, 2015), "Deborah Sussman Loves Los Angeles" (WuHo Gallery, 2013), and "Everything Loose Will Land," Getty Pacific Time Initiative (MAK Center, 2013). His current book project looks at the relationship between architecture and land speculation through the postwar master-planned development of California City.

Acknowledgments

This book is an outcome of a collaborative project that began in March 2015 when the editors convened "The Housing Question: Nomad Seminar in Historiography" in San Diego. Our special thanks to Reinhold Martin who delivered the keynote, and Carmen Popescu who gave the impetus to the Nomad seminars. What began as a working group in the historiography of architecture and housing grew into an international conference, thanks to the strong interest elicited by the call for papers. Emrah Altınok, Nandini Baghchee, Daria Bocharnikova, Sheila Crane, Kenny Cupers, Andrew Herscher and Daniel Monk, Kıvanç Kılınç, Ana María León, Michael McCulloch, Clare Robinson, Sabrina Shafique, Anooradha Iyer Siddiqi, Şebnem Yücel, and Kimberly Zarecor presented papers. Sylvia Lavin, Daniel López-Perez, Patricia A. Morton, Michael Osman, and Susanne Schindler were among the respondents. We owe thanks to the critical discussion offered by the participants in this event, during the authors' workshop in September 2018 and a public lecture hosted by Panayiota Pyla. We are immensely grateful to our authors and interlocutors for their patience and hard work despite the loss and hardship many experienced during the pandemic. The editors wish to thank especially Patricia A. Morton, Manuel Shvartzberg Carrió, Sandra Parvu, Anooradha Iyer Siddiqi, Ijlal Muzaffar, and Sally Yard for offering their insights during the writing of the introduction.

We received a generous publication grant from the Graham Foundation for Advanced Studies in the Fine Arts. Continuing support from the University of San Diego has been crucial in every step of this project. Our thanks are to Dean Noelle H. Norton of the College of Arts and Sciences, members of the Faculty Research Grant Committees, and our colleagues and coworkers in the Department of Art, Architecture and Art History with special thanks to Alexandra Mundt and Joseph Yorty. Our student researchers Julia Norman, Jordan Readyhough, Sou Fang, and Paul Short provided practical assistance and critical insights during the early stages of this project.

This book would not have been commissioned without the support of Grace Harrison. At Routledge we wish to thank Trudy Varcianna and Caroline Church, and all assistant editors, designers, and anonymous reviewers for their care and for subjecting the manuscript to scrutiny. Many thanks must go to Assunta Petrone and the team at codeMantra for copyediting and for guiding us through production. We sought the help of Karen Jacobson editing the chapters of our international scholars, and in translating key concepts into English.

Numerous publics contributed to the development of ideas presented in this volume as we learned from housing justice advocacy groups, tenants' unions, neighborhood organizers, "friends of architecture," and public comments in Southern California's city planning commissions and city councils where the housing question continues to be intensely debated.

Can Bilsel and Juliana Maxim

Introduction. Architecture and the Housing Question

Specific Histories

Can Bilsel and Juliana Maxim

Spaces of Inequality

The chapters gathered in this volume are part of a collaboration of scholars whose work examines the intersections of architecture and the housing question. We recognize housing as a program and an ideological project that exerts its force on our thinking about architecture and about the architect. By *the housing question* we refer to a historically recurrent problem: how have the design, provision, and management of shelter for large numbers around the world helped alleviate—or conversely—justify inequality, be it classed, racialized, and gendered? And what have been the disciplinary implications of taking on housing for the multitude as an architectural assignment and responsibility?

We further connect these questions to urgent issues of the present. What does it mean to read and write about architecture and housing in our historical moment? How do we incorporate the experience of the recent global crises and the shocks that accompany them into new ways of conceptualizing the housing question?

The COVID-19 pandemic has exacerbated the stark lines of inequality that divide the world. In California, where we write these lines, a housing crisis is underway. The uneven economic fallout of prolonged lockdowns combined with high housing costs threaten to produce new waves of evictions and mortgage defaults. This crisis comes fast on the heels of the "subprime" mortgage meltdown of 2007–2008, which amplified decades of systemic racism and inequality.[1] If the pandemic has made painfully concrete the degree to which housing protects bodies from disease, the mortgage crisis and the ensuing cycles of recession and austerity have exposed the complex global economic abstractions that underpin shelter and its unequal distribution. Neither of these catastrophes should be considered independently of the climate crisis and the mass displacement and homelessness that accompany it. Taken together, the events of the last decades have turned a spotlight on the many ways in which housing is implicated in the creation of poverty and inequality.[2]

DOI: 10.4324/9781351182966-1

As the world has lurched from one crisis to another, it has become harder to retreat to the safe remove of academic specializations and to accept housing as the object of seemingly apolitical forms of historical and technical expertise. What, then, can the histories of architecture and the housing question as proposed here tell us about possible ways forward? How can we mobilize the deliberate pace of history writing to address the urgency of now?

Recent scholarship has linked rising inequality with the emergence of an interconnected global space under "neoliberalism." As many have observed, the top-down application of neoliberal policies across the world since the 1970s amounted to privatization, deregulation, dismantling of the social safety net (especially in health and housing), de-unionization, and the precarization of labor, to count only a few effects.[3] After 1989, accelerating divestment from welfare state and public infrastructure has gone hand in hand with the expansion of a government apparatus geared to reduce "regulatory costs," increase supply, and streamline the functioning of large capital financial markets across the globe. Global financial capital colonized urban spaces in "the emerging markets" of the Global South and postindustrial North alike, leaving behind wastelands of urban redevelopment and mass displacement.[4]

A growing interdisciplinary critique has pointed to the mechanisms that produce, perpetuate, and accelerate inequality on the global scale. Thomas Piketty's two-volume analysis of macroeconomic data, for one, tracks how inequality has increased in all regions of the world since 1989. Although Piketty describes "modern inequality" to be mainly socio-economic, rather than racial, gendered, or neocolonial, he infers that it has triggered a global chain of reactions. Connecting the dots on the map, across a global space, Piketty invites readers to ponder about the lives of migrants lost crossing the Mediterranean alongside the plight of "the homeless, immigrants, and people of color."[5] Recently, critical multi-media and architecture collectives have taken up counter-cartography, mapping evictions, dispossession, colonization, mass displacement, and climate crisis across the world. Throughout the pandemic GIS-generated maps have pinned disease and death daily on a perilous planet.[6]

The urge to think of inequality as "global," as evidenced in scenes of human catastrophes on social media, and quantified by big data, naturalizes the idea of a world as one homogenous space interconnected by capitalism. Rather than taking for granted the constructs of local and global, connectivity and exclusion, centers and peripheries, this book engages with the granularity and spatial contingency of *spaces of inequality*. Mapping inequality across the globe is meaningful when it matches a critique of the political economy with knowledge produced from specific spaces, and with histories from below.[7] The emergency order to "shelter-in-place," issued during the COVID-19 pandemic, reveals not only the general condition of inequality between those who have access to shelter and those who don't, but also the lived experience in specific spaces. Under these conditions, spatial contingency marks the difference between health and disease, life and death.

We take Otay Mesa Detention Center in Southern California as an emblematic illustration of how a discussion of housing equality requires us to attend to specific spaces and global relations at once. Located southeast of San Diego, on the US side of the US-Mexico border, in a vast expanse of shipping containers, warehouses, a state prison, a juvenile detention facility, and other campuses surrounded by chain-link fence and barbed wire, Otay Mesa Detention Center "houses" some of the tens of thousands of immigrants detained in the United States. Many of the detainees are asylum seekers who presented themselves legally at the border, others have lived and worked for decades in America before being apprehended.[8] US Immigration and Customs Enforcement (ICE) regularly raids working-class neighborhoods and rental apartment complexes and delivers detainees to Otay Mesa using a fleet of unmarked SUVs, thus connecting seemingly disparate housing geographies (Figure I.1).

In Otay Mesa, the Federal government has partnered with a private corporation for incarcerating individuals whom it excludes from its sovereign territory.[9] To suggest that a privately operated detention center for immigrants and asylum seekers is integral to today's housing question is not merely to take the US government at its word.[10] Following the logic of neoliberal governance, the US government is contractually obligated to pay private corporations for a minimum number of "detention beds," ensuring that private contractors operate at a profit. The critics call the guaranteed minimums that each detention center receives "local lockup quotas," arguing that they create an incentive for ICE to round up more immigrants to fill the quota.[11] Most detainees spend months or years in Otay Mesa awaiting to be "processed" and to appear in court. They all risk deportation.

Otay Mesa Detention Center's location near the US-Mexico border, on formerly confiscated indigenous Ancestral Kumeyaay Territory, is essential to its function in circuits of global mass migration.[12] It is only one node in the sprawling government and for-profit-prison-industrial complex, which enforces labor exploitation, mass incarceration, and climate crisis-induced displacement, and which amplifies the legacies of settler colonialism, American exceptionalism, and structural racism. All these are thinly veiled by a corporate discourse of service, efficiency, and professionalism shared by the Federal Government and the for-profit corporation, a veiling to which the architectural profession contributes its own expertise. Otay Mesa Detention Center boasts a "LEED Silver certificate" in recognition of its "leadership" in "environmental design," energy performance, and user satisfaction.[13] Organizing a series of protests, and sharing testimonials, the abolitionist collective Otay Mesa Detention Resistance has effectively exposed the conditions of incarceration and enclosure inside the facility, calling the sprawling complex during the pandemic a potential "death trap."[14]

Figure I.1 Otay Mesa Detention Center operated by private contractor CoreCivic near San Diego, California. In the background US-Mexico Border and Tijuana, Mexico. The abolitionist collective Otay Mesa Detention Resistance is organized to free the immigrants, refugees, and asylum seekers detained in Otay Mesa, and toward building self-determination for the migrants criminalized by the state. Photo by Juliana Maxim and Can Bilsel.

In the way it "houses" a marginalized population, Otay Mesa encapsulates many of the questions raised in this book: the intense relation between specific locales and political and economic global frameworks, the role of housing in transfers of capital from the public to the private, the possibility of resistance in the face of oppressive systems, and, finally, the role of the architect as technical expert. As several authors in this book show, conceiving and complying with technical design standards is always a political act, even when architects and planners approach it as neutral technique. Architectural expertise obfuscates the greater political question—unless the expert discourse is turned against itself by "specific intellectuals," as Reinhold Martin argues in this volume.

* *

The authors whose work is presented in this book each approach the housing question from their respective specializations: American architecture, the socialist architecture and the city, architectures of European welfare capitalism, housing in the Middle East, critiques of "Third World" development and humanitarianism, history of architecture and urbanism in China. This book is but one outcome of the conversations between them, through which we have sought to overcome the traditional peer-review categories that too often replicate the geopolitical logic of area studies.[15]

It is thus both by choice and necessity that our use of *architecture* describes a broad field of cultural production with fluid and open borders. Each case presents a specific history. No universal ideological project— welfare capitalism, Anglo-American liberalism, "really existing socialism," or "Third World" modernization—has been translated into housing in a predictable way. As Miles Glendinning shows in this volume, European welfare states gave rise to different housing architectures. Words and forms crossed borders and acquired new meanings. "Welfare housing" in Post-Maoist China means something different from what it means in Western Europe, just as the "neighborhood unit" evolved significantly in its definition and application in the Soviet Union. Yet, the dialectic of modern housing has emerged and persisted across the world.

The Dialectic of Modern Housing

The belief that housing is an act of improving the lives of impoverished and marginalized populations has persisted in the European and North American imagination. The English word *housing* (large estates for collective living) preserves the meaning it acquired during the nineteenth century, when recurrent cholera pandemics ravaged through the globe, hungry and unemployed masses flooded the metropolis, and when unmarried working men and women converged in "common" houses prompting government intervention, such as public health measures, social assistance, and housing.

In England, early housing legislation regulated the extent to which government and its local representatives could intervene in the lives and property of individuals in order to ameliorate public health and moral character. "Whereas it would tend greatly to the comfort and welfare of many of Her Majesty's poorer subjects if provision were made for the well-ordering of the common lodging-houses," asserted the preamble of the Shaftesbury Act of 1851.[16] The "common lodging-houses" needed to be registered and inspected by physicians and the police, sexes segregated, public morality and hygiene upheld. By the end of the nineteenth century, "housing" had evolved to refer more specifically to the living conditions of "labouring classes" whose demographic was delineated in English law. Since then, housing has remained a means for ordering and policing the lives of the poor.

Modern architecture and town planning developed as part of a repertoire of supposedly rational solutions to the nineteenth-century outcry over the living conditions of the working class. Housing came to constitute a domain in which progressive reform was imagined, debated, and implemented, and where social values, political projects, and new forms of collectivity could be tested and shaped. This view is consistent with the idea of history driven by technology, whereby the architect and planner, along with social scientists, combat poverty and disease.

Yet from the outset some critics noted that modern architecture and modern housing, like the entities that commissioned them, could fail to help and even hurt marginalized and impoverished people. Since the nineteenth century, multiple voices have denounced the ways in which housing has helped maintain and reproduce a regime of social inequality, and has provided a means for ordering and policing the lives of the poor.[17] The regulation of housing relied on a paternalistic, gendered, and racialized administration of labor both on the factory floor and in domestic spaces.[18] Far from being a panacea for inequality, housing made inequality manageable.

Friedrich Engels was one of the first to point out the fraught relation between housing and the social question in his *Zur Wohnungsfrage* (*The Housing Question*). In 1872 Engels published a series of articles offering a sharp critique of two opposing movements that led housing reform in the nineteenth century: utopian socialism and conservative philanthropy. The first part of Engels' exposé aimed to rebut a non-revolutionary brand of socialism which he associated with the influence of the French thinker P.-J. Proudhon. By trying to alleviate the housing problem of the working classes, Engels argued, the utopian socialists mistook a symptom for the disease. What the members of the proletariat needed most was not access to housing but awareness of the root causes of their misery: capitalism. The scope of Engels' *The Housing Question* went above and beyond a defense of "scientific socialism" against a rival left-wing faction. By the 1870s a conservative philanthropic movement across Europe had turned its attention to housing reform. Engels intervened in the larger discourse about the social question by arguing that attempts at providing sanitary and affordable housing for the working classes was one means the bourgeoisie used to maintain its control of the economic system and its grip on power. Engels contended that conservative philanthropy, not unlike utopian socialism, would produce mortgage-carrying homeowners out of the proletariat who would find themselves in a new bondage of labor to land, and subject to another form of oppression.[19]

Engels' essays initiated a critical discourse on housing, but they also established the terms of a critique of ideology in architecture by marginalizing architecture's role within larger political configurations. He was skeptical about the early experiments with modern architecture and town planning, and of their claims to achieve social justice or engineer a better society. For Engels the working class was the agent driving history, and reformist housing, in the service of "bourgeois ideology," could only delay the workers on their revolutionary course. The housing question would be solved not through architecture and planning, nor the massive provision of social housing, but as a consequence of the redistribution of wealth that a proletarian revolution would bring about.

Revisiting Engels' text in 1934 in *Modern Housing*, Catherine Bauer recognized its power: "As a biting and eloquent criticism of the aristocratic reformers and their works, and as a devastating analysis of the home-ownership ideal, no better piece of work has ever been done."[20] Yet Bauer argued that both the ideology of housing reform and its Marxist critique were similarly embedded in the social conditions of the nineteenth century. For Bauer, Engels' critique was of little use to understanding the working-class–led initiatives of non-profit, cooperative housing since 1900, or the expansion of the government role in housing in the 1920s and 1930s, which, she argued, were inevitable responses to the failure of speculative housing markets.[21] Thus, Bauer subjected Engels's sweeping attack on housing reform as middle-class ideology to the limits of its own historical circumstances:

> Strictly of the nineteenth century, too, was Engels' conviction that all the pressing aspects of the housing problem could readily be taken care of merely by redistributing the existing dwelling-space on the morrow of revolution. Beyond this (so strong was the reaction of 'scientific socialism' against Utopianism of Owen and Fourier) he offers not the slightest notion of what sort of environment the social revolutionists might be fighting for.[22]

As Anooradha Iyer Siddiqi shows in this volume, Engels' descriptions of spatial inequality and violence in Manchester reveal an emancipatory, democratizing, and yet "othering gaze" that privileges a Eurocentric and masculinist perspective. With the exception of a discussion of the "backward" homesteads of Germany, and a footnote about the living conditions of workers in America, Engels' *The Housing Question* focuses on the European metropole. In the second German edition, Engels mentions a letter he received from Eleanor Marx in 1886 describing "miserable little wooden huts" near Kansas City. Yet his reading misses the legacies of colonial dispossession, slavery, and racism.[23] Engels' overarching thesis that housing reformers "put back the clock of world history" by making workers into "slaves of their employers" overlooks other forms of historical oppression based on race and gender.[24]

Engels' *The Housing Question* forms a point of departure for this volume because his attacks on the housing reformers of his day introduce us to a negative dialectics, in which modern housing and the rationalities that have made it possible have often produced historical and cultural forms of oppression despite the emancipatory and egalitarian political projects they were meant to serve. Recent histories have shown that racism, sexism, and classism are not merely deviations from rational thought, isolated transgressions against the public, but rather persistent features of the institutions, policies, and technical discourses that define the social—including modern housing.

We thus return to the questions we asked at the beginning: how can history writing go beyond a critique of reformism and help recognize the critical potential of architectural interventions that mobilize positive change? As David Madden and Peter Marcuse recently wrote in their *In Defense of Housing*: "every emancipatory movement must deal with the housing question."[25] We argue here that a historical critique of housing must take seriously both the oppressive and emancipatory potentials of housing as an architectural project.

Part One: Whose History? Rethinking the Expert

The authors in this book investigate permutations between architecture, expertise, state, racial marginalization, colonialism, and regimes of land and property of the last fifty years. The diversity of the case studies provides at once an answer to Engels' open challenge to architecture's political relevance, and loosens the conventional associations between types of housing and particular political or ideological agendas.

Part One tackles the dialectic of the housing question by investigating the many-fold manifestations of the architect and their possible alignment with anti-hegemonic forces.

Reinhold Martin's "Housing and History" draws our attention to the formation of a class of experts that includes and extends well beyond architects, and whose domain of knowledge and action includes housing: social scientists, urban planners, civil engineers, psychologists, medical doctors, social workers, the juvenile court judges, and the police. It is against this vast "housing apparatus," the tutelage of experts who govern the social field, that Martin revisits the housing question. In reading the housing question posed by Engels through Foucault, Martin asks what a critical practice of architecture may consist of today. He explores the figure of the "specific intellectual" proposed by Foucault in 1977, as an expert who exercises authority within a technical, disciplinary apparatus and yet who chooses to work toward the emancipation of the oppressed from within that very apparatus. Martin probes the ways in which the specific intellectual is at once involved in forms of power and can make visible the relations of power implicit within forms of expertise.

Anooradha Iyer Siddiqi's contribution, "Humanitarian Homemaker, Emergency Subject: Questions of Shelter and Domesticity," challenges both Engels' dialectic of the housing question and the arrogation of expertise within a Western tutelary apparatus. This chapter examines housing in the UNHCR refugee camps at Dadaab in Kenya on the Somali border. Rather than writing a history of humanitarianism and of the technical and administrative organization of the humanitarian building complex, Siddiqi describes the work of Shamso Abdullahi Farah, a homemaker, caregiver, and worker who acquires the skills and expertise of homebuilding in a putatively transient environment. Exploring how the spatial politics of emergency and domesticity have created a new subject-builder, Siddiqi challenges the customary protagonists and narrators of architectural history.

Sandra Parvu and Alice Sotgia's chapter problematizes the epistemological gap between housing understood as a social, political, and economic project, and housing as architecture, a gap which the question of historic preservation makes especially acute. If, for Engels, architectural form was inconsequential to the housing problem, Parvu and Sotgia suggest a reverse process in which architectural form, needing to be preserved, has become the frame through which to rethink housing in social and political terms. Through the act of historic preservation, the consensus that had helped build the social housing projects in France in the 1960s and 1970s recedes in favor of a different definition of the "social." Parvu and Sotgia define the "social" as produced through individual memories, lived experiences, and "lived histories" of the inhabitants. Their definition brings forward dwelling as a relation between a person and a place over the abstract notion of the public. They offer as compelling examples the work of a number of architects who practice preservation with the case-by-case attention of a "country doctor."

Part Two: Housing and the State

Over the past decade architectural historians have come to understand postwar housing as the nexus between modern architecture and the organization of the modern state. A series of monographs have examined how architects working for state bureaucracies transformed the way ordinary citizens lived, and how architecture conditioned the experience under the modern state in the Soviet Union, Czechoslovakia, Romania, Hungary, Yugoslavia, France, and the UK.[26] Together, these studies amount to a sea change in the way histories of architecture have been written, by moving away from a narrative of the Modern Movement (the select works of a group of avant-garde architects) to an investigation of broader architectural networks and forms of production.

Part Two begins with Daria Bocharnikova's study of the way the institutional and discursive practices inside state agencies (such as the All-Union Academy of Architecture and the Special Architectural Design Bureau, SAKB) shaped the architectural profession's approach to housing in the Soviet Union from the 1940s to the late 1950s. She reveals the extent to which a decade of research and experimentation, rather than top-down political pressure, allowed the architects to formulate a body of ideas and principles that guided the planning and construction of housing following Khrushchev's call to industrialize and accelerate housing construction. Bocharnikova's analysis reveals how 1950s Soviet housing practices (prefabrication, the development and use of type designs, the distribution of an apartment to each family, and the planning of housing into microdistricts, or *mikroraion*) were the outcome of decades-long experimental work and fundamental architectural research that proceeded collectively, with the support of the state, and through the study and critique of Western developments. Soviet architects saw capitalist urban growth, particularly the neighborhood unit, as producing disconnected zones dominated by the car. In response they reconceived the neighborhood unit by integrating it into an urban whole and reinforcing the city's cohesion.

Integration, in this case, of peasants into urban production environments, was also the concern of the Maoist state in the 1950s. In "Production First, Living Second," Samuel Y. Liang argues that Maoist China reinvented "the primitive rural dwelling" as a model for the new socialist way of living. The first "welfare" housing projects were rural collective work and living spaces. Minimum existence mass housing research started in China only as urban forces managed to weaken Maoism and its ruralist policies. Assessing this history, Liang contends that the primacy of the "work-unit" system in the production of housing in Maoist and post-Maoist China deprived those who didn't have access to work units from accessing social housing. The disparities between different work units also caused social inequities. In Liang's view, the Chinese case offers a paradox: after Mao's rule, state policies that engendered unequal access to housing prevented the emergence of the working class and, instead, helped create a privileged middle class.

"In Pillars of the Welfare State," Miles Glendinning examines the corporatist, hierarchical, or "pillarized" models of society in Belgium and in the Netherlands, each of which gave rise to very different results in architecture and housing. The private homeownership discourse in Belgium curiously resembles the ideological formulation of "the American Dream."[27] In the Netherlands, by contrast, the Catholic Pillar's coalition with the socialist alliance produced different architectural outcomes. Glendinning examines how the socially pillarized welfare state works and to what extent its organization translates into the organization of modern housing. The Netherlands offers a compelling case: the changing political coalitions, the competing visions of national and municipal authorities, and architectural expertise codified in regulations, standards, architectural manuals, and other documents pose a challenge to the oft-assumed connection between a political regime and modernist housing. Glendinning shows that modern housing developed over a long period of time despite changes in governing parties and cross-pillar coalitions.

Part Three: (De)segregation and the Housing Enclave

Part Three examines urban housing projects from distant parts of the world, each responding to the problem of urban stigma and the marginalization and racialization of an underserved urban community. One of the recurrent questions that we engage in this volume is the failure of the efforts since the 1960s to desegregate the city and to overcome urban blight. Why have many urban renewal and public housing projects failed despite the best efforts of policy experts, planners, and architects? Shall we conclude, along with Engels, that architecture is powerless in the face of adverse real estate market forces, and, as many authors have recently shown, enduring structural racism?[28]

Kıvanç Kılınç and Melih Cin's chapter, "Housing People Who 'Lived Free'," offers an analysis of the Ege Neighborhood Social Housing Project (ENSHP) in Izmir, Turkey. In the late 1960s, Izmir's municipal authorities sought to improve the living conditions of the "Tin-Can Neighborhood," predominantly inhabited by the Roma community. Paradoxically, the segregation and stigmatization of the Roma temporarily "saved" the community from displacement and dispersal, contrary to the dominant tendency in Turkey and across the world to eradicate low-income inner-city neighborhoods and move their residents to urban fringes. Kılınç and Cin's analysis reveals that Izmir's municipal architecture office designed an alternative set of plans for ENSHP, which departed from the normative spatial organization of mass housing in Turkey. The integration of the blocks with the texture of the neighborhood facilitated their appropriation for ceremonies, festivals, and forms of socialization associated with the Roma community, and a non-conforming way of life. Kılınç and Cin contend that as a result of the integration of the blocks into the culture and fabric of the neighborhood, the project has been understood neither as modernist nor as architecture. As Kılınç and Cin show, the municipal architects' willingness to learn from, and contribute to a non-conforming way of life, and the local community's appropriation of modernist housing did not remedy the marginalization of the Roma. The neighborhood remained physically separated from the rest of Izmir's inner city, and its residents suffered from territorial stigma, discrimination, and mass unemployment.

In "Public Life and Public Housing: Charles Moore's Church Street South," Patricia Morton offers a compelling account of the discourse around public housing and urban renewal in New Haven in the 1960s. The history of the Church Street South development offers a cautionary tale about the limitations of architectural solutions. Mayor Richard Lee's urban renewal program in New Haven was a leading beneficiary of federal funding after 1954, at a time when a complex system of public subsidies replaced government-owned "towers in a park." Morton shows that the program exemplified a new model for public housing that depended on government planning and subsidies while being operated by non-governmental organizations. The architects, Charles Moore and William Turnbull, sought to recast an alienating housing environment into a "place," by using supergraphics, coloring, texturing, and various attempts of customization. The architects' assumption that designed environments can change human behavior led them to define the common areas as owned and defended spaces. In Moore's words, "you have to pay for the public life." Morton shows that the Church Street South failed not despite, but perhaps in part, because of the way in which the design interventions posed individual possession of spaces as key to architecture's success, and inadvertently turned the housing project into an isolated enclave.

Part Four: Land, Property, Colonization

Understanding housing as an individual's right to property reduces housing into an aggregate of entitlements. The privileging of the figure of the "possessive individual" over a racialized community becomes a fundamental tenet of the regimes of colonial governance and real estate in mid-twentieth century.[29] Examining contexts as distinct as West Africa and California, Part Four documents how housing imaginaries embedded in planning and architecture services legitimized the appropriation and financialization of formerly colonized or settler-colonial lands.

In "Landing Architecture: Tropical Bodies, Land, and the Invisible Backdrop of Architectural History" Ijlal Muzaffar reads British architects, Maxwell Fry and Jane Drew's *Village Housing* of 1948 against Frederick Lugard's earlier book *The Dual Mandate in British Tropical Africa (1922)* to highlight what is often ignored in the readings of both: the reshaping of land rights. The Dual Mandate, Muzaffar argues, was the Crown's solution to shape a separate system of land inhabitation for indigenous populations in which rights over land coincided with rights over people. Implemented through a network of "native chiefs" in the name of cultural preservation, the Dual Mandate allowed the Crown to move large populations from the field to the mine to the factory, depending upon the needs of the colonial economy. Fry and Drew's proposals in *Village Housing*, as well as latter proposals for new towns like Tema, were intimately tied to this logic of land management and rapidly transforming laws around it. By looking at tropical architecture in relationship to the history of land, Muzaffar unpacks the overlapping regimes of coerced labor, property, introduction to a global economy of exchange, and the imposition of patriarchal gender roles ushered under the rubric of tropical architecture from colonial to postcolonial eras.

Shannon Starkey's chapter on California City (1955–1972) is a history of the efforts to develop a large city in the Mojave Desert. In its rise and fall, California City has the makings of a Brechtian epic, including the hubris of Nathan Mendelsohn, a developer who amassed over 80,000 acres of formerly indigenous lands from the government and private parties by paying cents per acre; American architects and planners who envisioned a master-planned community in the Mojave Desert; a sustained visual discourse that marketed a mirage to thousands of investors. This "total design," a master plan controlling all aspects of a city, eventually collapsed like a Ponzi scheme. In Starkey's history, California City epitomizes the larger historical process of the financialization of housing in postwar America. His archival research shows how the creation of a surreal oasis in the desert—complete with modern architecture, an artificial lake, and an asphalt highway laid on the sand—ultimately amounted to a mechanism for shifting financial responsibility from monopoly capital to public debt.

***

By bringing together these histories, this book maps a multipolar and surprising world in which the old fiction of center and periphery no longer holds. The chapters go beyond the geopolitical binaries of welfare/socialist, formal/informal, suburban/mass housing, and beyond the Cold War view of a world order historically divided between American capitalism and European socialism. The authors examine with care exceptions, accidents, and failures, rather than understanding modern architecture through models of diffusion of expertise from West European and North American metropoles toward colonial/postcolonial territories. Put together, their writings show how the housing question of one place can no longer be divested from the legacies of racial capitalism, racialized and gendered labor, and the colonial regimes of land/property and dispossession in other places.

The architectural histories we have gathered here examine housing as specific spaces where inequality is crystalized, where local configurations intersect with global networks, expertise, and techniques, and where, precisely due to the heterogeneity of these spaces, the possibility of local resistance and international solidarity emerges. By bringing these histories together we wish to respond to, and contribute to various spatially contingent, localized, and historically specific attempts of reconstituting the public—an emergent/insurgent public sphere.[30]

The work of Otay Mesa Detention Resistance, whose goal is to shut down a particular prison complex and to "create spaces of transition" and "self-determination" for the imprisoned migrants, offers a compelling example of the attempt to reconstitute a public. It is by casting their attention to specific spaces and to the ways of decolonizing them that the Detention Resistance collective, alongside anti-eviction and rent strike movements across the world, offers an entry into a "universal" vision: "We want to live in a world that is anti-capitalist and decolonizes the paradigm of the nation state powers."[31]

If architecture is to address the social question today, and reimagine the public, it is by recognizing the historical potential of housing in bringing together disparate emancipatory movements, and build solidarity against inequality and oppression. Our aspiration for this volume is to provide a context for new constellations to emerge, and to lend the weight of collective writing to potentials within histories of housing which *per force* remained underdeveloped. What is needed is not merely an explanation of how we got here but of how it might have been and still could be different.

Notes

1 As Keeanga-Yamahtta Taylor has pointed out, the seemingly neutral term "subprime" conceals how building, real estate, and financial industries have profiteered from market bias against African Americans and other racial minorities. See Taylor, *Race For Profit: How Banks and the Real Estate Industry Undermined Black Homeownership* (University of North Carolina, 2019). After 2008, borrowers of color lost their homes at twice the rate of white households, see https://www.responsiblelending.org/research-publication/lost-ground-2011.

2 Reinhold Martin, Jacob Moore, and Susanne Schindler write:

> Yes, it does seem today that everyone is talking about inequality. But perhaps that is because inequality is everywhere. Political standoffs between incentivized luxury development and rent regulation run parallel with a litany of racial violence that, in turn, reflects the role of both race and space in determining economic outcomes.

The Art of Inequality: Architecture, Housing, Real Estate (New York: The Temple Hoyne Buell Center, 2015), 11.

3 See for example David Harvey, *A Brief History of Neoliberalism* (New York: Oxford University Press, 2005). For a critique of Left intellectual movements after 1989, which, despite rejecting all "grand narratives," have adhered to "'the market' as if it were a universal and inevitable law of nature..." see Ellen Meiksins Wood, *Democracy Against Capitalism: Renewing Historical Materialism* (London, New York: Verso. 2016), 1.

4 For a critique of how global investment colonize urban spaces see Brenna Bhandar "Property Abolitionism: Race, Colony, Body, Land," May 19, 2019, https://thedisorderofthings.com/2019/05/10/property-abolitionism-race-colony-body-land/ - _ftn7, accessed on April 19, 2020.

5 Thomas Piketty, *Capital and Ideology* (Cambridge, MA: The Belknap Press, 2020), 2. See also the earlier volume, *Capital in the Twenty-First Century* (Cambridge, MA: The Belknap Press, 2014).

6 Eyal Weizman and Fazal Sheikh, *The Conflict Shoreline: Colonization as Climate Change in the Negev Desert* (Göttingen: Steidl, 2015); see also Naomi Klein, "Let Them Drown: The Violence of Othering in a Warming World," *London Review of Books*, vol. 38, no. 11 (June 2, 2016). For "political equator" see Teddy Cruz and Fonna Forman, "Unwalling Citizenship" in *And Now: Architecture Against a Developer Presidency* (New York: The Avery Review, 2017).

7 See for instance the Anti-Eviction Mapping Project, whose contributors insists that data, in order to be meaningful, should be combined with on-the-ground knowledge of specific communities. A grassroots project outside academia, it describes itself as "a data-visualization, critical cartography, and multimedia storytelling collective documenting dispossession and resistance upon gentrifying landscapes," https://antievictionmap.com/about, accessed December 23, 2020.

8 Juliana Maxim, "Regarding Immigrant Detention," *Architectural Theory Review* (2020), DOI: 10.1080/13264826.2020.1805009.

9 As Peter Camejo noted in 2003, those the government deems "illegals" are among the "lowest paid workers in California who work the hardest" and "are children of indigenous people of this continent": it is not they, but the border that "crossed" them. "Full Transcript of California Gubernatorial Recall Debate," *Washington Post*, September 24, 2003.

10 According to the US Immigration and Customs Enforcement (ICE), detainees are "housed" in the "Otay Mesa facility." See also ICE statement: "We strive to provide quality service to people in our custody, their family, friends, and to their official representatives." https://www.ice.gov/detain/detention-facilities/otay-mesa-detention-center-san-diego-cdf, accessed April 25, 2021.

11 "Banking on Detention: Local Lockup Quotas and Immigration Dragnet" (Detention Watch Network, 2015), https://www.detentionwatchnetwork.org/sites/default/files/reports/DWN%20CCR%20Banking%20on%20Detention%20Report.pdf, accessed July 12, 2021.

12 The US-Mexico border serves as a conduit for migrants from Mexico, Central America, Haiti, Russia, Ukraine, and various African countries.

13 CoreCivic, the private prison company, has announced that Otay Mesa is the second of its detention centers to be awarded a LEED (Silver) certification: "LEED requires not just energy efficiency, but also making sure a building's occupants are satisfied and comfortable." https://www.corecivic.com/news/corecivic-forges-sustainable-path-with-leed-certifications, accessed April 25, 2021.

14 The Otay Mesa Detention Resistance contends that—as of October 2020—"San Diego's Detention Center ... has the most Covid-19 cases of any immigration facility in the US" and calls for freeing all detainees before it becomes a "death trap." https://www.detentionresistance.org/freethemall. A heavily redacted, pre-COVID report by US Department of Homeland Security Office for Civil Rights and Civil Liberties documented the understaffing of medical personnel, and inhumane isolation cells. The US Department of Homeland Security Office for Civil Rights and Civil Liberties Report of April 25, 2018, https://www.dhs.gov/sites/default/files/publications/otay-mesa-expert-memo-04-25-18.pdf, accessed April 25, 2021.

15 The participants in the conference, "The Housing Question: the Nomad Seminar" of March 12–13, 2015, and the authors' workshop funded by the Graham Foundation, "Architecture and the Housing Question" of September 14–15, 2018 generously contributed to the development of the positions presented in this volume.

16 *Lodging Houses Acts: The Common Lodging Houses Act, 1851, and the Labouring Classes Lodging Houses Act, 1851, with Plain Directions and Forms for Putting Them into Execution, adapted by Robert A. Strange* (London: Shaw and Sons, 1851).

17 See for example Jacques Donzelot on how "the social question" reproduced the social inequalities it was called to alleviate, *L'invention du social: essai sur le déclin des passions politiques* (Paris: Fayard, 1984); see also Peter Marcuse, "Housing Policy and the Myth of the Benevolent State," in J. Rosie Tighe and Elizabeth J. Mueller, eds. *The Affordable Housing Reader* (Abingdon: Routledge, 2013), 36–52.

18 For a critical history see Gwendolyn Wright, *Building the Dream: A Social History of Housing in America* (New York: Pantheon Books, 1981).

19 Frederick [Friedrich] Engels, *The Housing Question* (English translation of the second German edition of 1887), ed. C. P. Dutt, Marxist Library volume XXIII (New York: International Publishers / Co-operative Publishing Society of Foreign Workers in the USSR, n.d. [1935]).

20 Catherine Bauer, *Modern Housing* (1934) (Minneapolis: University of Minnesota Press, 2020), 95.

21 Bauer, 96–97.

22 Bauer, 96.

23 In a footnote of the Second German edition of 1887, Engels quotes a letter from Eleanor "Tussy" Marx, English socialist, writer, and translator, and third living daughter of Karl Marx and Jenny von Westphalen (Engels refers to her as "Eleanor Marx-Aveling"), sent from Indianapolis, Indiana, on November 28, 1886. In her letter Eleanor Marx writes:

> In, or near Kansas City we saw some miserable little wooden huts, containing about three rooms each, still in the wilds; the land cost 600 dollars and was just enough to put the little house on it; the latter cost a further 600 dollars, that is together about 4,800 marks [£240] for a miserable little thing, and hour away from the town, in a muddy desert.

Engels presents Eleanor Marx's observations as further evidence that "In this way the workers must shoulder heavy mortgage debts in order to obtain even these houses and thus they become completely the slaves of their employers..." in Engels, 35. See also Yvonne Kapp, *Eleanor Marx: A Biography* (London, New York: Verso, 2018); and Reinhold Martin, "Notes on the Housing Question" in *The Urban Apparatus: Mediapolitics and the City* (Minneapolis: University of Minnesota Press, 2016), 109–113.

24 Shortly before he quotes Eleanor Marx's description of workers huts in Kansas City, Engels writes: "Proudhon only forgets that in order to accomplish all this he must first of all put back the clock of world history by a hundred years..." Engels, 34.

25 David Madden and Peter Marcuse, *In Defense of Housing: the Politics of Crisis* (London, New York: Verso, 2016), 9, 12.

26 See Kenny Cupers, *The Social Project: Housing Postwar France* (Minneapolis: University of Minnesota Press, 2014), Miles Glendinning and Stefan Muthesius, *Tower Block: Modern Public Housing in England, Scotland, Wales, and Northern Ireland* (New Haven, CT: Yale University Press, 1994), Steven E. Harris, *Communism on Tomorrow Street: Mass Housing and Everyday Life After Stalin* (Washington, D.C: Woodrow Wilson Center Press, 2013), Vladimir Kulić, Timothy Parker and Monica Penick eds., *Sanctioning Modernism: Architecture and the Making of Postwar Identities* (Austin: University of Texas Press, 2014), Juliana Maxim, *The Socialist Life of Modern Architecture: Bucharest, 1949–1964* (London: Routledge, 2019), Virág Eszter Molnár, *Building the State: Architecture, Politics and State Formation in Post-War Central Europe* (Abingdon: Routledge, 2013), Sandra Parvu, *Grands ensembles en situation* (Geneva: Métis, 2011), Mark Swenarton, Tom Avermaete, Dirk van den Heuvel eds., *Architecture and the Welfare State* (London: Routledge, 2015), Kimberly Elman Zarecor, *Manufacturing a Socialist Modernity: Housing in Czechoslovakia* (Pittsburgh: University of Pittsburgh Press, 2011).

27 See also Hilde Heynen "Belgium and the Netherlands: Two Different Ways of Coping with the Housing Crisis, 1945–70," *Home Cultures*, vol. 7, no. 2 (2010), 159–177.

28 See for example Charles L. Davis II, "When Public Housing Was White: William Lescaze and the Americanization of the International Style," in *Building Character: The Racial Politics of Modern Architectural Style* (Pittsburgh: University of Pittsburgh Press, 2019), 171–210, Paige Glotzer, *How the Suburbs Were Segregated: Developers and the Business of Exclusionary Housing, 1890–1960* (New York: Columbia University Press, 2020), Keeanga-Yamahtta Taylor, op. cit.

29 As Cheryl Harris argues in her essay "Whiteness as Property," the failure to overcome the legacies of racism is in part due to the "dialectical contradiction" in the law. The courts recognized racial group identity when it comes

to racial exploitation and subordination in the past, yet refused to recognize group identity as the basis of continuing inequality. Thus, the economic disparities between racial groups, such as the gap in their access to public investment and infrastructures, are normalized into the "neutral" status quo of a liberal society. Harris observes that the approach that reduces equality to equal treatment of individuals under law, and to anti-discrimination, is built upon a fundamental tenet of liberalism that rights are vested in an individual and not in a group. It replicates the Lockean idea of autonomous individual who *possesses* freedom and of property. See Harris, "Whiteness as Property," *Harvard Law Review*, vol. 106, no. 8 (June 1993), 1707–1791. For "the ideology of possessive individual" and "racial regimes of ownership" see Brenna Bhandar, *Colonial Lives of Property: Law, Land, and Racial Regimes of Ownership* (Durham, NC and London: Duke University Press, 2018).

30 See Andrew Stefan Weiner on "emergent public sphere" in "Universality and Entanglement: Aesthetics, Politics, and Publicity across the Arab Spring" in Anne Kockelkorn and Nina Zschocke eds., *Productive Universals, Specific Situations: Critical Entanglements in Art, Architecture, and Urbanism* (Berlin: Sternberg Press, 2019), 384–405.

31 Detention Resistance, https://www.detentionresistance.org, especially "Our Vision," accessed April 25, 2021.

Part I

Whose History? Rethinking the Expert

1 Housing and History
The Case of the Specific Intellectual

Reinhold Martin

Honored as I am by the invitation to address the crucial question posed by this collection of chapters,[1] I join some likely readers in saying: I am not a housing expert. This is not to justify the lacunae in my account, or to pre-empt inevitable objections, but rather to qualify certain fragments of intellectual history in hopes of forcing together two great lineages of critical thought as they pertain to our subject. I say this also to point out the preponderance of duly certified expertise that has attached itself over the years to what this book calls, after Friedrich Engels, the "housing question." Housing, as a subset of architecture and urbanism, a social policy, an economic nexus, a tangle of infrastructure, a commodity, a locus of desire and power, a home, a space, a luxury, a site of exploitation, a prison, or a utilitarian response to utilitarian concerns, tends to call forth expertise, and to demand a scientist's—or a social scientist's—trained eye and cautious hand whenever its vagaries, dilemmas, or histories are discussed. Expertise of this sort populates today's joint centers, institutes, think tanks, advocacy organizations, NGOs, foundations, and—yes—academic departments and academic publications. Historically, the deployment of such expertise in the great metropolises of Europe, and eventually throughout the world, bears some relation to what has been called the "rule of experts" in Europe's colonies and, especially, in its later articulation among the community of nation-states.[2] Just as with today's globalized histories, we cannot simply add new contexts or cases to the current hegemony; instead, we must examine that hegemony's organizing principles, and gather counterhegemonic forces from within it, as well as from without.

Sometime during the middle of the twentieth century, a different kind of expert also emerged. It may seem a monumental non sequitur to name the dissident nuclear physicist J. Robert Oppenheimer in this regard. But perhaps you recognize the reference: Oppenheimer is the rather surprising example given by Michel Foucault in response to a question posed to him in 1977 regarding the role of the intellectual in everyday political struggles. In a written response to his Italian interviewers, Foucault proposes replacing the intellectual as the custodian of universal reason (he likely had in mind his compatriot, Jean-Paul Sartre) with the "specific" intellectual, a

DOI: 10.4324/9781351182966-3

strategist who deploys expert technical knowledge in an oppositional fashion at carefully chosen points within the dominant system. As Foucault says of the transition:

> Intellectuals have got used to working, not in the modality of the 'universal,'... but within specific sectors, at the precise points where their own conditions of life or work situate them (housing, the hospital, the asylum, the laboratory, the university, family and sexual relations).[3]

To illustrate he cites Oppenheimer, a leader in the wartime Manhattan Project who later vocally advocated arms control and opposed the development of the hydrogen bomb, and suffered personally and professionally as a result. Foucault argues that expert dissidence within a specific sector of knowledge, and particularly techno-scientific knowledge, can reach well beyond that sector, provided that it connects its specific concerns to a society's "regime" or "apparatus" of truth, including the power relations thus entailed. Hence, for Foucault, "it is necessary to think of the political problems of intellectuals not in terms of 'science' and 'ideology,' [he is referring to Louis Althusser, and to Marxism in general] but in terms of 'truth' and 'power.'"[4]

And so we have our conundrum: as posed by Marx's colleague Engels in 1872, the "housing question" comes down, as we shall see, to a critique of housing as ideology. This critique pertains equally to utopian socialists and to the bourgeoisie, against whose daydreams Engels asserts the universality of the class struggle and of scientific Marxism. About a hundred years later, rejecting that very same universality, Foucault insinuates housing among the local, strategic sites in which, as he says, specific intellectuals gain "a much more immediate and concrete awareness of struggles."[5] We will deal with this concrete awareness in due course. For now, I want to ask: in what ways and at what levels might these two quite distinct and possibly antagonistic positions, one occupied here by Engels (and by extension, by Marx) and the other by Foucault, be reconciled, if at all?

If at all, the "housing question" may be as good a place as any to start. But first, we must establish what that question is. Even before which, we must ask: what, after all, is housing? Surely among other things, housing is an architectural type, a species of building that branches into a variety of subspecies and groupings: perimeter blocks, high-rises, low-rises, *Siedlungen*, planned-unit developments, single-family houses, projects, gated enclaves, slums, favelas, barrios, squats, condominiums, cooperatives, and so on. Nonetheless, housing seems to be a very special building type that bears the burdens of society as a whole; in it appear all the antagonisms, the hopes, the failures, and the contradictions of modernity. It is exactly this burden, this apparent proximity to history that confers upon housing its aura of specialization. Since the European nineteenth century, a seemingly direct connection to a society's aspirations, to its contradictions as well as to its productive forces, has qualified housing as a distinct object of expert study and administration, alongside (not coincidentally) those other building types studied by Foucault: prisons, asylums, and hospitals. What is more, and closer to the frame around our book, in the realm of architectural historiography, where meaning is generally taken to be multivalent, the cultural meaning of any given housing project is quite readily treated as functionally and symbolically transparent to its social world.

I have in mind first of all the tendency, visible in architectural scholarship since the 1970s, to treat the history of housing as principally a form of social history, as in the ground-breaking work of Gwendolyn Wright, Dolores Hayden, Dianne Harris, and numerous others;[6] or, barring that, to treat the architecture of housing as ideological projection, rather than as a productive intervention in its own right. In contrast, there does exist a different, minor historiography from within which, I believe, the housing question may also be posed. This, more properly architectural approach treats buildings and their discursive surround less as documents of social processes or as ideological datum lines or archetypes than as *technical infrastructures* whose workings have been buried under layers of over-interpretation. Provisionally, we can call such an approach archaeological. With respect to housing, among its most able practitioners, and one whose work has sometimes been identified with Foucault's, has been the historian Robin Evans.

Mainly, I have in mind a short, influential article published by Evans in *Architectural Design* in 1978 titled "Figures, Doors and Passages."[7] There, Evans locates a shift in European domestic life that corresponds to the gradual disappearance of rooms arranged *en suite* or *enfilade*, with multiple doors making multiple connections, and the emergence of the corridor as a planimetric and spatial device, with one door per room. Evans explores his floor plans with customary finesse. His conclusion, however, is disarmingly simple: that the isolation of rooms or apartments along a corridor has, during the course of four or five centuries, led to an impoverishment of the sensual, convivial sociability, or "carnality," that he finds built into plans like that of Raphael's Villa Madama with its interlocking rooms, begun in 1518, and in paintings of human figures—they tend to be holy families or fragments thereof—like Raphael's *Madonna dell' Impannata* (1514), with bodies intertwined, almost skin to skin.

Unfortunately, this thinly disguised postmodernist critique of functionalism undermines the originality of Evans's approach. Strip it away and you get what matters most: a pre-typological encounter with the architectural thing—let's call it here a house—that takes a given pile of documents (floor plans, paintings, texts, as well as the thing itself) as literally as possible, and attempts to make sense of them in the manner of a detective who assumes that something has happened but is not sure what. Although his architectural examples are mainly aristocratic or bourgeois, Evans makes clear that he is really writing a history of modernist mass housing. He trains us to see changes in an actual rather than a projected social world, arranged *enfilade* or lined up along a corridor, uncovered by painstaking analysis. Without Evans actually saying it, we recognize that the most basic unit of that social world is the family, holy or otherwise. The family is the figure—the social body—that is transformed by the rearrangement of doors and passages that "Figures, Doors and Passages" discovers. Which is not to say that Evans has discovered social reality inside the house. It is to say that he has discovered the entrails of the housing apparatus.

Foucault used the term *dispositif,* which is usually (if controversially) translated as "apparatus," throughout his career. But by his own admission he only began to favor it rather late, during the 1970s, in the midst of a slow but decisive shift away from the early emphasis on language in works like *Les mots et les choses* (*The Order of Things*) and *The Archaeology of Knowledge.* The book that has exercised the most influence on architectural discourse, *Discipline and Punish* (*Surveiller et Punir*), from 1975, is the one that marks this turn most clearly. There Foucault shows Jeremy Bentham's panopticon to be an apparatus of sorts, but only insofar as it is linked, through a series of relays, to a wider and more diffuse set of disciplinary practices and procedures that encompass education, medicine, and other realms of social reproduction. These all amount to what Foucault calls "the carceral," or "carcerality," in which a dispersion of texts mixes with physical cellularity, panoptic perspective, light and shadow, and spatial confinement. The carceral, then, consists in an irreducible materiality that, although present, was less active in Foucault's earlier works.

In the first volume of the *History of Sexuality*, published one year later (1976) and titled *La Volonté de Savoir*, or *The Will to Know*, Foucault refers to sexuality, too, as an "apparatus" that, beginning in the eighteenth century, Western societies deployed, or rather "superimposed" on the networks of familial alliance—kinship, names, possessions, and the like—that defined the older, classical order. Foucault's purpose is to challenge what he calls the "repressive hypothesis," which holds that bourgeois modernity placed human sexuality under a series of prohibitions or prudish silences associated with juridical power. Architecturally, we can recognize a version of this "repressive hypothesis" in Evans's claim that the modern house calcified or repressed planimetric "carnality." Foucault argues the contrary: that the new power nexus was productive rather than repressive, and that, rather than censorship, "when one looks back over these last three centuries... around and apropos of sex, one sees a veritable discursive explosion."[8] This explosion comes to light when we understand sexuality as something that has been deployed in a strategic fashion, as "an especially dense transfer point for relations of power: between men and women, young people and old people, parents and offspring, teachers and students, priests and laity, an administration and a population."[9] What Foucault calls the "family cell" is its main site, which suggests that the housing question may not be far behind.

In an interview with a group of psychoanalysts published in 1977, Foucault is more precise about what he means by the *dispositif* (or apparatus) of sexuality, and by a *dispositif* in general. He says:

> What I'm trying to pick out with this term is, firstly, a thoroughly heterogeneous ensemble consisting of discourses, institutions, architectural forms, regulatory decisions, laws, administrative measures, scientific statements, philosophical, moral and philanthropic propositions—in short, the said as much as the unsaid. Such are the elements of the apparatus. The apparatus itself is the system of relations that can be established between these elements.

Foucault explains further that he aims to specify particular relations among particular, heterogeneous elements that form a strategic response to an "urgent need," as in the assimilation of an uprooted "floating population" under a mercantile economy and then under industrial capitalism, into regimes of "madness, mental illness, and neurosis."[10]

Although Foucault generally said little about housing, a bit further on in the same interview, in response to a challenge that his approach downplays the agency of human subjects in favor of anonymous strategies, he responds with the example, during the late 1820s, of "definite strategies for fixing the workers in the first heavy industries at their work-places." Factory towns like Mulhouse, in northeastern France, saw the deployment of various tactics: "pressuring people to marry, providing housing, building *cités ouvrières*, practicing that sly system of credit slavery that Marx talks about, consisting in enforcing advance payment in rents while wages are paid only at the end of the month."[11] Out of this complex of relations emerges the "discourse on philanthropy and the moralization of the working class," by which Foucault means both the elaboration of techniques for associating sexuality with the home, and, simultaneously, attaching that home to the moral programs of the philanthropic societies that had sprung up in France, England, and Germany during the middle of the nineteenth century. These philanthropic societies, along with some of the larger industrial concerns like Krupp or Lever Brothers, were responsible for the majority of purpose-built worker housing during the mid-to-late-nineteenth century. But Foucault's point was that such housing, in turn, belonged to a more general, strategic response to the need of the factory system to manage its workers. His interviewers press him on this. What role does class play? Is not what he is describing better explained by the class interests of the bourgeoisie in developing and maintaining the means of production? To which Foucault replies: no, it is not. Or rather, this "moralization" *produces* both the working class and the bourgeoisie and places them into a relation of subordination and dominance. To which he adds:

> But what I don't think one can say is that it's the bourgeois class on the level of its ideology or its economic project which, as a sort of at once

real and fictive subject, invented and forcibly imposed this strategy on the working class.[12]

This is as clear a summary of Foucault's relation to Marx and to Marxism as we are likely to get. In it, the housing question meets the housing apparatus. Even as Foucault rejects the historical a priori of a collective subject, like the bourgeoisie, who act strategically to advance their class interests, he says that, in the subordination of workers within the power relations of philanthropy, such an objective "was accomplished because it met the urgent need to master a vagabond, floating labour force. So the objective existed and the strategy was developed without it being necessary to attribute to it a subject which makes the law."[13]

As instruments for managing what Marx and Engels called an "unemployed reserve army of workers" or a "floating population," we can therefore add the philanthropic housing estates that arose in Europe and North America during the nineteenth century to the list of "other spaces," or heterotopias, that Foucault had already compiled in his influential address to the Parisian Architectural Studies Circle in 1967.[14] We can also add the dossier on "machines à guérir," or curing machines, that a group of French architectural and urban historians published together with Foucault in 1979, which established the "origins of the modern hospital" as a corollary to the housing apparatus around which we have been circling. In his contribution to that volume, Foucault rehearsed the points of contact: an emphasis on childhood and the medicalization of the family, the rising importance of hygiene and of medicine as a form of social control, and the emergent dangers and usefulness of the hospital itself.[15]

But we find our most direct interface with the housing question, as well as the inflection point in my argument, in the work of Foucault's colleague, the urban sociologist Jacques Donzelot. In *The Policing of Families*, which appeared in 1977 with an introduction by Gilles Deleuze, Donzelot describes the transformation, in France, of the family, "the smallest political organization possible," an institution that had been governed but which also possessed its own laws, into the inner circle of a governmental "apparatus."[16] According to Donzelot, this transformation occurred along three vectors associated with the philanthropic societies and, later, with the administrative state: moralization, in the form of counseling and advice rather than charity or alms; normalization, in the form of hygienic, sexual, and behavioral norms transmitted through schooling; and contract and tutelage, in the form of philanthropic and state institutions that took the place of the family in the care and custody of troubled or disadvantaged children. During the early twentieth century, these roles were consolidated into the figure of the social worker, who occupies the center of what Donzelot calls a "tutelary complex" enclosing the family within a whole array of normalizing judicial, psychiatric, and educative practices.[17]

Despite the fact that one of his most telling examples involves the trial in juvenile court in Lille of Ounadjela Boubaker, "a fourteen-year old Algerian adolescent," Donzelot refrains from addressing directly the legacies of French colonialism as reproduced by the tutelary complex. Still, the case he describes is punctuated by racially coded discourse, including the judge's vulgar taunt in response to inconsistencies in Boubaker's psychiatric evaluations: "Are you really an imbecile, or just pretending to be one?" Notably, the young Algerian's dwelling space also features. The police accused Boubaker of theft, though the money in question belonged to his mother. Having been deemed inaccessible to education, Boubaker was therefore at risk of conviction and imprisonment but for the resourcefulness of his state-appointed defense attorney, who proved to be an able representative of tutelary normalization. Boubaker was alleged to have stolen the money from his stepbrother's room in their shared dwelling. The judge, presuming walls and doors, declares this evidence enough. But only a curtain separated the rooms. The attorney: "Was this curtain drawn or not? It's too much to bear, from a judicial standpoint, these North African families with their extended sense of family relations, their custom of living in houses without doors!"[18]

Such "houses without doors" were overexposed to tutelage, even as they evaded its norms. Similarly, the patriarchy reproduced by the tutelary complex addressed women as both emancipated household managers and, like Boubaker's mother, points of contact with the state.[19] In his preface to the English edition, Donzelot finds this ambiguity exemplified by the alliance, during the late nineteenth century, between militant feminism and social philanthropy.[20] Deleuze's foreword, titled "The Rise of the Social," allows the constitutive, contradictory role of gender to remain implicit. He emphasizes instead that in the juvenile court, Donzelot finds "a different organization of space," in which "a whole circle of tutors and technicians... press closely in upon the 'liberalized' or shattered family."[21] In the floor plans decoded by Evans, we can see this space extending into the home, where familial intimacy is both liberated (or "liberalized") and "shattered" by the corridor. The privacy that allots only one door per room finds its complement in the circle of experts given access to that corridor to treat the inhabitants. I say "treat," because many of those who preceded the twentieth century's social workers and magistrates were doctors produced in the new research universities. These were both medical doctors and doctors of philosophy, who transformed categories like race and gender into instruments with which to govern: physicians, psychiatrists, educators, social reformers. Beside them were architects, as well as domestic reformers. In the middle of it all was the family, which, in the transition from aristocratic to bourgeois rule, had gone from the governor to the governed. As Donzelot puts it: "From being the plexus of a complex web of relations of dependence and allegiance, the family became the nexus of nerve endings of machinery that was exterior to it."[22] In other words, "What was at issue, then, was the transition from a government of families to a government through the family."[23]

It was exactly in this milieu that Friedrich Engels wrote "The Housing Question," first as a series of articles in *Der Volksstaat* in 1872, in Leipzig, and then, in revised form, as a pamphlet in 1887.[24] The immediate context was a series of anonymous articles that had previously appeared in *Der Volksstaat*, the author of which was later revealed to be a certain A. Mülberger, M.D., of Württemberg. *Der Volksstaat* was an organ of the German Social Democratic Party, and Dr. Mülberger's articles had advocated solutions to the urban housing shortage in Germany that Engels readily identified with the French anarchist (Engels calls him a petit-bourgeois socialist) Pierre-Joseph Proudhon. Point by point, Engels attacks Proudhon's position, via Mülberger, and no more so than when Mülberger insists that the housing shortages generated by rural-to-urban migration (with, we can add, its "floating population") are to be alleviated by policies that enable subsistence farmers or rural piece-workers to gain ownership of their land and houses, and hence of their collective destiny. Engels quotes the German doctor's lament that "The real nodal point of moral and family existence, hearth and home, is being swept away by the social whirlpool."[25] In response to which Engels puts Mülberger through his paces, pointing out that:

> It is precisely modern large-scale industry, which has turned the worker, formerly chained to the land, into a completely propertyless proletarian, liberated from all traditional fetters and *free as a bird* [*vogelfreien*]; it is precisely this economic revolution which has created the sole conditions under which the exploitation of the working class in its final form, in the capitalist mode of production, can be overthrown. And now comes this tearful Proudhonist and bewails the driving of the workers from hearth and home as though it were a great retrogression instead of being the very first condition of their intellectual emancipation.[26]

Most histories, including that rehearsed by Foucault, locate the beginnings of this uprooting with Europe's first large factories, and factory towns, in the early nineteenth century. This larger context, and this longer duration, causes Engels to begin his response by rejecting the very premise of a housing crisis. Yes, he says, there are periodic housing shortages, particularly in big cities, but these are nothing new, nor are the appalling conditions under which workers often live, conditions that he had documented so vividly in his youthful work, *The Condition of the Working Class in England*, of 1845.[27] Such conditions are merely those suffered by oppressed classes everywhere, all the time. But the reason that, in the 1870s, the urban housing shortage drew so much commentary from so many quarters was that it affected the lives of the petty bourgeoisie as well as the proletariat. Engels's diagnosis was therefore quite straightforward:

> The housing shortage from which workers and part of the petty bourgeoisie suffer in our modern big cities is one of numerous *smaller*, secondary evils which result from the present-day capitalist mode of production. This exploitation is the basic evil which the social revolution strives to abolish by abolishing the capitalist mode of production.[28]

In short, there is no housing crisis, at least not in any structural sense; instead, the "housing question" always reduces down to the extraction of surplus value from labor power, a process that centers on the factory and extends out into the house or apartment building to the extent that the latter is defined by the laws of commodity production and circulation. All claims to the contrary are mere ideology. In response to Mülberger's claim that the rent-paying tenant is to the landlord what the worker is to the capitalist, and that homeownership is a means by which to break free from the grip of the rentier, Engels argues that rent, even when it includes what today's language would call the "option to buy" and even when credit for such is provided, is a "simple commodity sale."[29] And the housing question, if it is a question at all, is determined by the typical, rather than exceptional, character of housing as an instance of the commodity form.

Now, Engels is being a little disingenuous here, since it is unclear exactly what kind of commodity housing is. In the manuscript for *Capital*, Volume 2, on circulation, Marx differentiates between two main forms, or "departments," of social production. The first of these, Department 1, includes the means of production proper—things like raw materials, machinery, and factory buildings. The second department, labeled "articles of consumption," includes everything else: commodities consumed individually by both capitalists and the working class.[30] To the extent that it helps maintain the well-being of laboring bodies that keep the factories going, while also being exchangeable by individuals, housing arguably has one foot in each department. This ambiguity appears in the second section of Engels's polemic, titled "How the Bourgeoisie Solves the Housing Question," where we return to the scene we have already encountered with Foucault and Donzelot: medical science enters the working-class quarters to combat diseases—cholera, typhus, typhoid fever, smallpox—that also affect, as Engels puts it, "the more airy and healthy parts of the town inhabited by the capitalists." Sarcastically, he explains that

> Capitalist rule cannot allow itself the pleasure of creating epidemic diseases among the working classes with impunity; the consequences fall back on it and the angel of death rages in its ranks as ruthlessly as in the ranks of the workers.[31]

So, in come the philanthropic societies, the government commissions, and the doctors, to gather data for their reports and their books. Of the latter, Engels singles out a relatively obscure title, *Die Wohnungszustände der arbeitenden Klassen und ihre Reform* [The Housing Conditions of the Working Classes and their Reform], written by a certain Dr. Emil Sax and published in Vienna in 1869, as representative of the bourgeois line.[32] Sax, an economist, was a contemporary and colleague of Carl Menger, and was a somewhat alienated member of the Austrian School of liberal economists from which such figures as Ludwig von Mises and Friedrich August von Hayek, grandfathers to today's neoliberals, descended in the mid-twentieth century.[33] So if Sax is obscure, he is not unimportant. And in the passages from Sax that Engels cites, Donzelot's (and Foucault's) "moralization" of the worker is in full bloom. For

> by improving the housing of the working classes it would be possible successfully to remedy the material and spiritual misery which has been described, and thereby—by a radical improvement of the housing conditions *alone*—to raise the greater part of these classes out of the morass of their often hardly human conditions of existence to the pure heights of material and spiritual well-being.[34]

According to Engels, such "moral sermons" as these prevent a "good bourgeois" like Dr. Sax from recognizing the true source of the workers' misery in the inexorable tendency of capitalist production to produce the "large reserve army of unemployed workers" in the first place, drive them to the cities, and require the landlord to maximize profits.[35] What Engels does not acknowledge is the instrumentality of these sermons in restructuring the social relations of industrial capitalism through the family, and, hence, in restructuring the means of production, or Department 1.

Like the anarchist Proudhon, the bourgeois Dr. Sax proposes homeownership as a solution to the nonexistent housing question, though this time by more frankly acknowledging that, as Engels says, "the worker *'becomes a capitalist'* by acquiring his own little house."[36] His ideal is the English cottage system; but when achieving it proves untenable in the big cities, Engels mocks Sax's proposed compromise: dwellings containing four-to-six units rather than the more common "barracks," or multiunit dwellings, as a travesty of the town versus country antagonism. In lieu of pie-in-the-sky solutions like those proposed by Charles Fourier or Robert Owen, Engels finds Sax advocating the working-class colonies that some industrialists had set up at the periphery of the big cities, such as the proto-garden city of Akroydon, built by the Halifax millowner Edward Ackroyd, and designed in the Gothic Revival style by George Gilbert Scott, beginning in 1859.[37]

Scott is a fascinating case: a prolific architect of workhouses, asylums, prisons, and schools, as well as cathedrals, churches, and public monuments to urban industrialization, including St. Pancras Station in London.

In Akroydon, as in his asylums, schools, and prisons, Scott's Gothic Revival architecture sacralizes the disciplinary institution with an accretion of small details, thereby securing, on the aesthetic register, the moralization to which we have been alluding in social, spatial, and political terms. As early as 1857, speaking of domestic architecture, Scott observes of the Gothic that "no style is equally capable of adapting itself to varied requirements, or of enlisting in its service the inventions, materials, and ideas which are introduced by the advance of social improvement."[38]

Among the other bourgeois reformers Engels finds behind Sax is Victor Aimé Huber, a conservative professor of romance philology in Berlin writing in 1843. Huber had traveled to the factory towns of England and France to see the living conditions firsthand. There he found charity and alms insufficient, and concluded that the propertied classes and possibly the state must assist the working class in forming "latent associations," or building societies, savings societies, and cooperative housing colonies, that strengthened community and family ties while still embodying the conservative ideal of "self-help."[39]

Just prior, in 1841, C. W. Hoffmann, *Landbaumeister* to the Prussian court, had begun a series of initiatives directed at architects in Berlin to develop plans for worker housing. Informed by Huber's advocacy of "inner colonization," or the establishment or housing colonies that promoted homeownership, in 1847 Hoffman established the *Berliner gemeinnützige Baugesellschaft* (BgB, Berlin non-profit Construction Company). By 1851 the BgB was responsible for housing 700 persons in thirty-two new buildings in Berlin. Set up as a joint stock company to raise capital, the BgB also included a residents' cooperative oriented toward selectively providing housing to working-class families sorted for respectability, with a bias toward artisans over factory workers.[40]

Mercilessly, Engels mocks Sax for fixating on that "great showpiece of the continental bourgeois" that we have already encountered, Mülhausen, or Mulhouse, in the French region of Alsace, describing the housing colony as a product of "the open association between the Second French Empire and the capitalists of Alsace."[41] By 1867, Mulhouse, which was founded in 1853 by the industrialist and millowner Jean Dollfus and designed by the architect Émile Muller, comprised 800 individual dwellings grouped in small clusters with gardens over twenty hectares, with communal facilities including swimming pools, baths, schools, shops, and "free medical consultations."[42] A report on the project by a certain Dr. Achille Penot states its purpose:

> The convenience and cleanliness of a dwelling have a greater influence than one might initially suppose on the morality and well-being of a family... if we give each man a small garden in which he can occupy himself happily and productively, and where, in anticipating his modest harvest, he will learn to appreciate the true value of that natural

instinct of property which Providence has sown in us, will we not have solved in a satisfactory manner one of the most pressing problems of social economy? Will we not have contributed to a tightening of the sacred bonds of the family? Will we not have rendered a true service to the class of our workers, so worthy of our concern, and to society itself?[43]

As Foucault noted, Mulhouse remained a model for housing reformers for the latter half of the nineteenth century, as a means of managing revolutionary upheaval by integrating workers into the entangled systems of property and family morality. By 1889, in a journal of public health, the problem could be stated architecturally:

> Between individual houses and collective blocks, whether one is considering them from the point of view of hygiene, or the point of view of morality, hesitation is not permitted, the choice should be in no doubt.[44]

This typological distinction, which would structure so much subsequent housing discourse, only came into full view *after* what Marx and Engels—and Foucault and Donzelot—described as a "floating population" was driven from country to city by the machinery of capital. According to Foucault, the apparatus of sexuality responded with techniques for governing the family, such as psychoanalysis, to which Donzelot adds the "tutelary complex" and the "invention of the social." The result was a strategic redistribution of power that produced the object of discourse known as "housing," and, with it, housing experts to pose the "housing question" in ways that Engels could dismiss as ideological. Housing therefore *underlies* the social relations that underlie industrial capitalism, even as it emerges from them. This is even more clear today, when, as Foucault observed, the neoliberal project increasingly depends on the social development and care of "human capital."[45]

Foucault made this observation in his 1979 lectures on biopolitics. Some years before, in 1971, just prior to the publication of *Discipline and Punish* and the further elaboration of the "apparatus" of sexuality, he and the sociologist Daniel Defert addressed directly those excluded by the emergent regime of "human capital" when they founded the Groupe d'Information sur les Prisons (Prison Information Group, or G.I.P.). The group, which included Foucault, Defert, Deleuze, the writer Hélène Cixous, the journalist Jean-Marie Domenach, and the classicist Pierre Vidal-Naquet, among others, focused on the brutal treatment of domestic political prisoners in France, and on the repressive conditions that prevailed in the French prisons generally. Its aim was less action or reform than the gathering of information from inmates, former prisoners, their families, their guards, and any other sources that could shed light on what its members regarded as systemic violence and oppression. The G.I.P. circulated questionnaires in prisons, published pamphlets, and staged rallies. It arose in a larger context that included the prison uprisings in the United States—Foucault visited Attica state prison while lecturing in Buffalo in 1972, calling it a "machine for elimination"—as well as the Soviet Gulag, the scope of which was revealed to Western readers by Alexandr Solzhenitsyn in 1973.

The irony that G.I.P. meetings were held in Foucault's apartment was not lost on his biographer, David Macey, who acknowledged that the "open-house policy that was adopted, with large numbers of prisoners' wives and ex-inmates coming and going, may have occasioned some surprise to Foucault's concierge and to the eminently bourgeois inhabitants of 285 rue de Vaugirard...."[46] The group's first pamphlet, written by Foucault, announced that "[its] investigations are not being made by a group of technicians working from the outside; the investigators are those who are being investigated."[47] Macey portrays one such investigator, Dr. Edith Rose, as an Oppenheimer-like specific intellectual who challenged the apparatus's regime of truth. Rose was the psychiatrist at the Centrale Ney prison in the small town of Toul, where, in 1971, 200 prisoners had staged a revolt to protest intolerable treatment. From her position within the prison system, Rose published an open letter describing the shocking conditions; Foucault publicly celebrated what he called the historic "discourse of Toul," produced by a woman "who, after all, and if only because of her knowledge, was 'part of power,' 'involved in power....'"[48]

With such endorsements, the G.I.P. claimed not to speak on behalf of oppressed prisoners, only to break through the ring of experts in order to enable prisoners to speak for themselves. Here is Deleuze speaking to Foucault, in a conversation from the following year, 1972: "In my opinion, you were the first—in your books and in the practical sphere—to teach us something absolutely fundamental: the indignity of speaking for others."[49] In a seminal essay published much later, in 1988, Gayatri Chakravorty Spivak took Foucault and Deleuze to task for their assumptions regarding the immediacies of subaltern speech, including speech on behalf of anti-colonial militants. In "Can the Subaltern Speak?" Spivak challenges the monolithic subjectivities presupposed, in this unguarded moment of "friendly exchange," by the philosopher of madness and the schizo-analyst.[50] She accuses Foucault and Deleuze of insinuating a "realism" whereby the intellectual, whose own subjectivity becomes transparent to the actualities of the "workers struggle" on the factory floor or inside the prison, merely reports on these activities and offers a space (we can think literally of Foucault's apartment) in which the oppressed may "speak for themselves." Spivak argues that this presumed transparency reproduces the international division of labor, wherein elite identification with the struggles of oppressed persons, reconstructed as relations of power and desire rather than of class interest or ideology, is unable to recognize the still more ferocious, and more directly economic, exploitation of subaltern groups, particularly women, and particularly in the third world, on which the entire edifice depends. In short, Spivak projects a "macrological" (today we would say "global") frame onto the micrologies of power that Foucault and his colleagues found in the French prisons, not to pit one world against another, but to challenge the transparencies and the unities presumed by the particular model of the intellectual they advocated and practiced.

Spivak overlays this frame with a critique of representation, which doubles up into a speaking-for-another (*vertreten*), as in a representative or proxy, and a re-presenting (*darstellen*), as in speaking-for-oneself, both mediated by class and, indeed, the family. On this, she cites Marx:

> In so far as millions of families live under economic conditions of existence that separate their mode of life... they form a class. In so far as... the identity of their interests fails to produce a feeling of community... they do not form a class.[51]

Marx is speaking about the conditions that prevent the "small-holding" French peasantry, whom industrial capitalism has formed into a socioeconomic class, to represent themselves politically as such. Spivak points out that the family tends to be identified with "instinct" that is superseded by self-representation as a class, and that Marx therefore tends to reproduce the patriarchy that subtends class belonging. Unless, that is—and she finds evidence of this in Marx himself—the family is denaturalized as a unit of social and economic production.

Recall that these "small-holding" peasants are the very same petty landowners, and homeowners, whom Engels finds idealized as bearers of "hearth and home" by anarchists like Proudhon and by bourgeois housing experts like Dr. Emil Sax. They also may well be the class to which belong (or formerly belonged) the four children—siblings? cousins?—shown in the photograph (Figure 1.1), with which the original version of Robin Evans's article, "Figures, Doors and Passages," concludes. In his caption, Evans quotes the United Nations document from which the photograph is drawn: "Forecasts are that scenes like this will become more common unless some of the problems of human settlements are solved immediately." To which he adds (this is 1978): "We may be approaching a time when the caption, not the picture, will appear obscene. At that point modern architecture will have truly disappeared."[52] This doubling-up of captions summarizes the dilemma we have been tracking. The experts on housing, human settlements, and "habitat" assembled to this day at the United Nations are direct descendants of those nineteenth century doctors and twentieth century social workers who reshaped the family into a unit of governance. Evans grasps the workings of their discourse, but in accusing these experts of repressing the carnal intimacy shown in the photograph, he fails to grasp the housing question. Not until we are able also to see in such a photograph the international division of labor, including that of the absent mother, the production of racial norms as well as racial apartheids, and the rural-to-urban

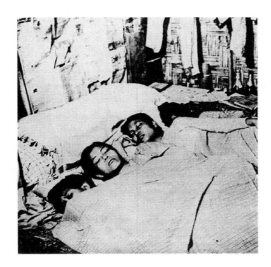

Figure 1.1 United Nations photograph. Source: Robin Evans, "Figures, Doors and Passages," *Architectural Design* 48, no. 4 (1978). In his original caption, Evans quotes the UN Photo: "Forecasts are that scenes like this will become more common unless some of the problems of human settlements are solved immediately." Evans adds, "We may be approaching a time when the caption, not the picture, will appear obscene. At that point modern architecture will have truly disappeared."

migration that attends all of this and the tutelage that addresses it, will we have lived up to the task of the specific intellectual: namely, to speak of the very things made unspeakable by our own discourse. In which case, the housing apparatus will have finally posed the housing question—to itself.

N.B.
Originally written in 2015, this chapter has been only lightly edited for publication in this volume. Since that time, the "housing question" was posed once again—in an affirmative fashion—by left-progressive activists, policy analysts, and politicians in the United States, in direct opposition to authoritarian, neoliberal austerity, and racial oppression. Among the most visible instances of this were the simultaneous proposals in November 2019 of a "Green New Deal for Public Housing Act" by US Representative Alexandria Ocasio-Cortez and US Senator Bernie Sanders, and of a "Homes for All Act" by US Representative Ilhan Omar. The Ocasio-Cortez/Sanders bill strategically connected decarbonization with democratization by funding the energy-efficient upgrade of existing public housing as a safeguard against further divestment, thus leveraging federal assets to enact the principles of a wider Green New Deal. With respect to the housing question, it is especially notable that Omar, a Somali refugee from Minnesota, recognized the demands of a growing housing justice movement when she proposed the construction of "9,500,000 publicly owned dwelling units over 10 years."[53]

Omar's proposal, which like the Ocasio-Cortez/Sanders bill languished in a Congress overwhelmingly dominated by neoliberal interests, was prefaced by language that established a "right to housing"—unheard of in neoliberal policy circles—while still characterizing the shortage of affordable housing as a market failure rather than a structural consequence of capitalist development.

Both proposals abandoned the language of public housing as social reform, treating such policy straightforwardly as economic stimulus and subsidy to offset racialized dispossession. To these legislative efforts was added a tenants' movement to "cancel rent" in the face of severe economic distress associated with the COVID-19 pandemic, as well as demands to "defund" or "abolish" the police deriving from the nationwide protests led by the Movement for Black Lives in the aftermath of the vicious police murder of George Floyd on May 25, 2020. While such demands have not yet extended to the "policing of families" associated with a diffuse housing apparatus, all remain signs of an expanding popular imagination. Perhaps "housing experts"—including architects, urbanists, and scholars—will catch up.

Notes

1 This text was delivered on March 12, 2015 as a keynote lecture in "The Housing Question: Nomad Seminar in Historiography," a conference at the University of San Diego organized by Can Bilsel and Juliana Maxim, in collaboration with Carmen Popescu. I am grateful to the organizers for raising the questions addressed by the conference. The text is published here for the first time in its original English form with added endnotes. A German translation, "Das Wohnungswesen in der Geschichte: der Fall des spezifischen Intellektuellen," was published in Friedrich Engels, *Zur Wohnungsfrage*, ed. Jesko Fezer et al. (Berlin: Haus der Kulturen der Welt, 2015).

2 See Timothy Mitchell, *The Rule of Experts: Egypt, Techno-Politics, Modernity* (Berkeley and Los Angeles: University of California Press, 2002).

3 Michel Foucault, interviewed by Alessandro Fontana and Pasquale Pasquino, "Truth and Power," in Foucault, *Power/Knowledge: Selected Interviews and Other Writings 1972–1977*, ed. Colin Gordon, trans. Colin Gordon, Leo Marshall, John Mepham, Kate Soper (Brighton, Sussex: The Harvester Press, 1980), 126.

4 Foucault, "Truth and Power," 132.

5 Foucault, "Truth and Power," 126.

6 Gwendolyn Wright, *Building the Dream: A Social History of Housing in America* (New York: Pantheon Books, 1981); Dolores Hayden, *The Grand Domestic Revolution: A History of Feminist Designs for American Homes, Neighborhoods, and Cities* (Cambridge, MA: MIT Press, 1981), and *Redesigning the American Dream: The Future of Housing, Work, and Family Life* (New York: W. W. Norton, 1984); and Dianne Harris, *Little White Houses: How the Postwar Home Constructed Race in America* (Minneapolis: University of Minnesota Press, 2013).

7 Robin Evans, "Figures, Doors and Passages," *Architectural Design* 48, no. 4 (1978), 267–278. See also Robin Evans, "Rookeries and Model Dwellings," in *Translation from Drawing to Building* (Cambridge, MA: MIT Press, 1997), 92–114.

8　Michel Foucault, *The History of Sexuality, Volume 1: An Introduction*, trans. Robert Hurley (New York: Vintage Books, 1990), 17.

9　Foucault, *The History of Sexuality, Vol. 1*, 103.

10　Michel Foucault, in conversation with Alain Grosrichard, Gerard Wajeman, Jacques-Alain Miller, Guy Le Gaufey, Dominique Celas, Gerard Miller, Catherine Millot, Jocelyne Livi, and Judith Miller, "The Confessions of the Flesh," in Foucault, *Power/Knowledge: Selected Interviews and Other Writings 1972–1977*, 194–195.

11　Foucault, "The Confessions of the Flesh," 202–203.

12　Foucault, "The Confessions of the Flesh," 203.

13　Foucault, "The Confessions of the Flesh," 204.

14　On the "reserve army of workers," Samuel Hollander, *Friedrich Engels and Marxian Political Economy* (New York: Cambridge University Press, 2011), 54. On heterotopias, see Michel Foucault, "Of Other Spaces," trans. Jay Miskowiec, *Diacritics* 16, no. 1 (Spring 1986): 22–27.

15　Michel Foucault, "La politique de la santé au XVIIIe siècle," in Foucault, Blandine Barret-Kriegel, Anne Thalamy, François Béguin, and Bruno Fortier, *Les Machines à guérir: aux origines de l'hôpital moderne* (Brussels: Architecture + Archives / Pierre Mardaga, 1979), 7–17.

16　Jacques Donzelot, *The Policing of Families*, trans. Robert Hurley (New York: Pantheon, 1979), 48 [originally published as *La Police des familles* (Paris: Les Éditions de Minuit, 1977)]; on the family as the inner circle of a concentric "apparatus," 103.

17　On the "tutelary complex," see Donzelot, *The Policing of Families*, 96–168.

18　Donzelot, *The Policing of Families*, 113–115.

19　Donzelot, *The Policing of Families*, 103–104.

20　Donzelot, "Preface to the English Edition," *The Policing of Families*, xxii–xxiii.

21　Gilles Deleuze, "Foreword: The Rise of the Social," in Donzelot, *The Policing of Families*, ix–x.

22　Donzelot, *The Policing of Families*, 91.

23　Donzelot, *The Policing of Families*, 92.

24　Frederick [Friedrich] Engels, *The Housing Question*, ed. C. P. Dutt, Marxist Library vol. XXIII (New York: International Publishers, n.d.); first published as three articles in *Der Volksstaat*, Leipzig, 1872–1873; second revised German edition *Zur Wohnungsfrage* (Hottingen-Zürich: Volksbuchhandlung, 1887).

25　A. Mülberger, quoted in Engels, *The Housing Question*, 27.

26　Engels, *The Housing Question*, 28.

27　Friedrich Engels, *Die Lage der arbeitenden Klasse in England: nach eigner Anschauung und authentischen Quellen* (Leipzig: O. Wigand, 1845); *The Condition of Working Class in England in 1844 with Appendix Written in 1886*, trans. Florence Kelley (New York: John W. Lovell, 1887).

28　Engels, *The Housing Question*, 22.

29　Engels, *The Housing Question*, 19–20.

30　Karl Marx, *Capital, Volume 2: The Processes of Circulation of Capital*, ed. Frederick [Friedrich] Engels (New York: International Publishers, 1967), 395.

31　Engels, *The Housing Question*, 43.

32　Emil Sax, *Die Wohnungszustände der arbeitenden Klassen und ihre Reform* (Vienna: Pichler, 1869).

33　Eugen Maria Schulak and Herbert Unterköfler, *The Austrian School of Economics: A History of Its Ideas, Ambassadors, and Institutions*, trans. Arlene Oost-Zinner (Auburn: Ludwig von Mises Institute, 2011), 49–52.

34　Dr. Emil Sax, *Die Wohnungszustände der arbeitenden Classen und ihre Reform* (Vienna: A. Pichler and Son, 1869), quoted in Engels, *The Housing Question*, 46.

35 Engels, *The Housing Question*, 46–47.

36 Engels, *The Housing Question*, 51.

37 Engels, *The Housing Question*, 58–59. See also John Burnett, *A Social History of Housing 1815–1970* (London: David & Charles, 1978), 176–177.

38 George Gilbert Scott, *Remarks on Secular and Domestic Architecture, Present & Future* (London: John Murray, 1857), 20.

39 Engels, *The Housing Question*, 44, 55; for Engels's critique of "self-help," 63. On Huber, see Nicholas Bullock and James Read, *The Movement for Housing Reform in Germany and France, 1840–1914* (New York: Cambridge University Press, 1985), 25–28.

40 Bullock and Read, *The Movement for Housing Reform in Germany and France, 1840–1914*, 31–35.

41 Engels, *The Housing Question*, 51, 61.

42 Bullock and Read, *The Movement for Housing Reform in Germany and France, 1840–1914*, 318.

43 Dr. Achille Penot, "Projet d'habitations pour les classes ouvrières; rapport presenté au nom du comité d'économie sociale," *BSIM*, XXIV (1852): 140–141, quoted in Bullock and Read, *The Movement for Housing Reform in Germany and France, 1840–1914*, 321.

44 E. Muller and Dr. O. du Mesnil, "Des habitations à bon marché au point de vue de construction et de la salubrité," *Annales d'Hygiène Publique et de Médecine Légale*, 3rd series, XXII (1899): 152, quoted in Bullock and Read, *The Movement for Housing Reform in Germany and France, 1840–1914*, 324.

45 Michel Foucault, *The Birth of Biopolitics: Lectures at the Collège de France, 1978–1979*, trans. Graham Burchell (New York: Palgrave Macmillan, 2008), 224ff.

46 David Macey, *The Lives of Michel Foucault* (New York: Vintage Books, 1995), 268.

47 Macey, *The Lives of Michel Foucault*, 269.

48 Macey, *The Lives of Michel Foucault*, 277.

49 Gilles Deleuze and Michel Foucault, "Intellectuals and Power," in Foucault, *Language, Counter-Memory, Practice: Selected Essays and Interviews by Michel Foucault*, ed. Donald F. Bouchard (Ithaca, NY: Cornell University Press, 1977), 209.

50 Gayatri Chakravorty Spivak, "Can the Subaltern Speak?" in Cary Nelson and Lawrence Grossberg, eds., *Marxism and the Interpretation of Culture* (Urbana and Chicago: University of Illinois Press, 1988), 271–313.

51 Karl Marx, *The Eighteenth Brumaire of Louis Bonaparte* (New York: International Publishers, 1963), 124, as quoted in Spivak, "Can the Subaltern Speak?" 277.

52 Caption 28, in Robin Evans, "Figures, Doors and Passages," 278.

53 Sen. Bernard Sanders, S. 2876 "Green New Deal for Public Housing Act," November 14, 2019, available at https://www.congress.gov/bill/116th-congress/senate-bill/2876/text; Rep. Alexandria Ocasio-Cortez, H.R. 5185 "Green New Deal for Public Housing Act," November 19, 2019, available at https://www.congress.gov/bill/116th-congress/house-bill/5185/text; and Rep. Ilhan Omar, H.R. 5244, "Homes for All Act," November 21, 2019, available at https://www.congress.gov/bill/116th-congress/house-bill/5244/text?r=6&s=1. Quotations, "Homes for All Act," 2.

2 Humanitarian Homemaker, Emergency Subject

Questions of Shelter and Domesticity

Anooradha Iyer Siddiqi

The housing questions in this chapter, while couched in terms of shelter, center on domesticity. In particular, they consider forms of making and inhabiting shelter in a refugee camp. The following episode exposes the labor-intensive processes of invention, transaction, and caregiving behind humanitarian shelter, which constitute an insurgent practice of domesticity in emergency. The intersection of shelter and domesticity spans international and local spaces—both deterritorialized and situated—in the development of a settlement called Ifo, one of the camps in the large complex administered by the United Nations High Commissioner for Refugees (UNHCR) near Dadaab, Kenya.

To understand what domesticity might mean in this context, the chapter focuses on a project that represents the intersection of three vectors (Figure 2.1). The first is the global field of emergency response as represented in the international setting of Dadaab. The second is an architecturally and historically significant intervention by the Norwegian Refugee Council (the NRC, an international nongovernmental organization specializing in humanitarian shelter) and its aid workers in Dadaab, which include architects, engineers, builders, and community mobilizers. The third is the work of Shamso Abdullahi Farah, a refugee from Somalia trained by the NRC to implement a prototype in a large-scale shelter initiative to be used in these camps, which, at the time, carried the potential for applications worldwide. Together, the convergence of these three scales of emergency shelter activity resulted in unexpected forms of domesticity in Ifo.

The government of Kenya and the UNHCR together established Ifo camp, the first of several humanitarian settlements near the village of Dadaab, in order to provide food, water, and medical care, and also to contain a large number of people who suddenly fled southern Somalia after a breakdown in civil society, armed conflict, drought, and food and water insecurity, which displaced an estimated 1.7 million people in 1991. Refugees self-settled a plot of designated land that year and have lived there continuously, even as other settlements were established nearby (two the following year, and others decades later; Figure 2.2). By relying on a water supply from an aquifer, the little-developed region has been able to support the prolonged existence

DOI: 10.4324/9781351182966-4

Figure 2.1 Shop designed and built by Shamso Abdullahi Farah and NRC, Ifo
Camp, Dadaab, Kenya, 2007. Photo: Anooradha Iyer Siddiqi, 2011.

of camps intended to be temporary. These have grown from a settlement,
Ifo, established for 30,000 refugees, to a population of approximately a
half million official and unofficial forced migrants. Some people arrived
in Ifo to pause on the way to other destinations, but many have passed
decades in the settlement. It is home to the first secondary school for refugees in Dadaab, which has graduated classes of students for over ten years.
Such educational initiatives have not led to greater mobility. Indeed, people
living in Dadaab are restricted in multiple ways. They are not allowed to
move freely outside of the camp complex. They face a curfew within the
camps and police checkpoints between them. Their ability to work and pur-
sue higher education is restricted. Over the years, refugees in Dadaab have
become dependent upon aid and the subsidiary economies that stem from
the sale of rations and supplies. Nevertheless, in flight from wars and other
environmental insecurities, people have continued to move into the Dadaab
settlements, settling and unsettling even the most established camps. Most
of the residents of the Dadaab settlements have come from Somalia.

One of these residents, a woman named Shamso Abdullahi Farah, from
Bula Hawo, a town on Somalia's border with Kenya, arrived in Ifo with her

Figure 2.2 Aerial image of Ifo Camp, Dadaab, Kenya, 2009. Photo: UNHCR, 2009.

extended family in 2003 (Figure 2.3). The following narrative of her work on a shelter initiative draws from her own account in 2011, as well as those of other refugees, aid workers, officials, and professionals in Dadaab and elsewhere who could contextualize this work.[1] The interviews with Farah were limited in scope, and focused on her intellectual and physical labor in helping to seed an initiative with historically significant ties to discourses and practices of dweller controlled housing processes that have fueled political economic adjustments made by nations throughout the twentieth century. As remnants of those structural adjustments, these emergency practices express dissonant qualities, to be discussed below, tied up as they are at once with the geopolitics of nation-states and the political status of individuals. Nevertheless, such practices are rarely recounted through their materiality or the labor of real individuals.

Figure 2.3 Shamso Abdullahi Farah inside shop, Ifo Camp, Dadaab, Kenya, 2011. Photo: Anooradha Iyer Siddiqi, 2011.

This focus on an individual within a historical narrative is intended to demystify and render concrete processes of emergency sheltering and domesticity. Historiographically, such processes are often abstracted within the global initiatives or humanitarian expertise they constitute, due to the exclusive reliance on official archives and organized documentary collections, rather than situated in terms of the experiences of protagonists in these histories. Notwithstanding, interviews with Farah specifically avoided questions of a personal nature, especially those related to her flight or refuge. While these might have provided context for the events, they would have done so at the expense of her privacy. Centering forms of domesticity she was able to generate—through the exercise of her own faculties, agency, and valuation of her diverse resources—instead offered the potential to contextualize her work while respecting the boundaries of her privacy. This historiographical attentiveness is intended to highlight a form of fullness in her practice that other modes and metrics of documentation tend to miss.

In spite of the limited scope of the interviews with Farah, much could be surmised from interviews with her co-workers and those in related spheres, as well as via her social and environmental context in Dadaab. She did not come to this project with formal education or training in design or construction, and was not selected to participate due to any preexisting expertise. She was pregnant at the time of the interview, and, like many women in the camp, had a large family with many children. To have obtained refugee status, and to become visible to the NRC in order to take part in this initiative, she would have had to have had community support. Other questions—about her present circumstances, her position in the community or her clan, the status of her family, the social organization of the camp or the place from which she fled, any particular skills or knowledge she exhibited or gained vis-à-vis the NRC, or her personal growth and evolution—went unanswered as they would have been invasive without offering needed historical context.

As explained below, Farah played a critical and instrumental role in the NRC shelter initiative in Dadaab. Her work would anonymously cement the expertise and global reputation of the NRC in the financially speculative and existentially high-risk field of humanitarian relief. Her project inaugurated a large-scale emergency shelter initiative punctuating one strand in a history of modern design and building in regions identified as "the tropics": a history of construction led by dwellers, for ecological and social sustainability. Her central role in the project positions her as a meaningful protagonist in this global history. Her domesticity in emergency, in turn, offers a way to consider questions on housing.

Building a Shelter[2]

A milieu of acute emergency dominated Farah's first three years in Ifo, in which refugees needed shelter as urgently as food and water. However, refugees in Ifo mistrusted the motives and competence of the shelter aid programs that had been instituted in the camp.[3] CARE, the international relief and development organization that had been managing aid distribution and social services in the Dadaab camps since the year after their establishment, had constructed shelters that proved deadly after heavy winds blew the roofs off of several structures. To respond to this and produce an international response to such problems, the UNHCR initiated a program of shelter research and prototype development at its Geneva headquarters, and contracted the NRC for its expertise in shelter aid.[4] The NRC had integrated into its staff specialists in the spatialization of humanitarian operations. From 2006, when it started work in Kenya, it employed several project managers trained in architecture or construction, many holding degrees from European architecture schools. In the Dadaab settlements, it built 3,000 shelters in 2007 and 3,500 in 2009, each considered a high volume of production for shelter aid.[5] However, when the NRC arrived to Ifo camp, it had to respond to a complex humanitarian context, with several competing concerns.

The NRC relied upon architectural expertise, and its approaches to shelter valued the discipline's concerns. In the context of the global field of humanitarian shelter relief, it was understood that a dwelling unit held high value for the user and high cost for the aid provider. Nevertheless, the organization paid attention to design details, the craft of building, and a rational process of construction in the units it made. The NRC circumvented the rationale of the global market through the largesse of the Norwegian government. It produced a strange, carefully detailed, and well-made object, which inserted latent representations of the Norwegian state into Ifo's aesthetic, political, socioeconomic, and ideological fabric (Figure 2.4). Its shelter unit was at once part of the territory of the Kenyan state, the material culture of Somali and other pastoralist communities of the Kenyan Northeast, the political space of the international order, and the social world of refugees and the stateless.

According to one refugee who was trained and eventually employed as a team leader and community mobilizer by the NRC, its architectural design

Figure 2.4 Dwelling designed and built by Shamso Abdullahi Farah and NRC, Ifo Camp, Dadaab, Kenya, 2007. Photo: Anooradha Iyer Siddiqi, 2011.

and construction methods took into account Dadaab's extreme environmental factors.[6] Under a mud plaster protective exterior, the walls of its dwelling incorporated squared, wire-cut, kiln-fired, cement-stabilized soil blocks—a modern technology surpassing technical and aesthetic standards elsewhere in the refugee settlements and surrounding towns. This technology offered possibilities for prefabrication and mass fabrication. Humanitarian engineers designed the walls to be supported by foundations set ten bricks deep into the ground, within a one-meter foundation dug by a specially trained NRC team. These measures were intended for durability and longevity, to combat flooding, and to secure the vertical structure for roof support.

The process of making this object was central to the initiative conceived by NRC staff members. They oriented the organization's commitment to durable, well-crafted architecture to work doubly in refugee settings, mobilizing communities through training in the construction of shelters. According to the staff in Dadaab, they approached the craft, and subsequently the labor, for shelters with the intention of establishing a sense of ownership in refugee communities.[7] This work was intended to empower refugees by instituting livelihoods training, skills-building, and physical protection against natural and social elements as multiple derivatives of the shelter aid package.

Farah was among the first refugees who participated in the NRC's pilot shelter initiative in 2007, in which refugees were provided construction materials and required to perform all construction labor. Such "participatory" practices grew out of self-help development models, which in turn emerged from planning discourses in the 1960s and 1970s.[8] By the time that Farah began her work with the NRC, the "best practices" for such self-help had been thoroughly disseminated through international humanitarian networks. In Ifo camp, "participation" was negotiated within a space in which residents were not citizens, land users could not legally own property, and the state denied refugees the right to waged compensation for labor. Yet, this asymmetrical process was nevertheless transactional; in return for her participation, Farah was granted materials, and trained in design and construction.

Refugees in Ifo camp resisted this shelter initiative. It demanded work beyond that of other shelter programs, drained family resources, and exacted labor that might be applied more productively elsewhere. Refugees were forbidden from subcontracting the construction and discouraged from trading shelter materials that could provide higher value as commodities. The housing quality that they produced surpassed that in the camps and the region, exacerbating hostilities and misgivings felt by the host community, and aggravating tensions by expressing refugee permanence. Donors viewed the high unit costs as inappropriately luxurious, and chafed as potential beneficiaries in the refugee camps criticized the program's ideals as well as the shelters themselves for these excesses.

Nevertheless, Farah found a utility in the NRC's aid package. She requested additional materials to build a small shop, where she could trade goods acquired from selling portions of the family ration. She executed the project by working from specifications provided by the organization and directed a team of skilled and unskilled workers that included her spouse and children, perhaps confounding the gender expectations of aid workers. She leveraged the broader work of homemaking into a form of economic and sociopolitical actualization.

Domesticity

The claim of political actualization in this ambiguous situation turns to the question of how subjecthood is formed when the urgent domesticities of forced migration and emergency inscribe practices onto the land, but are not necessarily coterminous with the nation-state, and when the labor to create domesticity in emergency produces ambiguous ground. I argue that the domestic space of the shelter and the domestic space of the state intersect precisely in refugees' relationships to the land and to labor in Dadaab.

Within the setting of the camp, many forms of domesticity have been instantiated—at the level of individual households as shelters, at the level of the settlement as a residential structure, and at the level of the state whose domestic interior provides the territorial contour for refugee space. However, in contrast to the vernacular notion of dwellings being connected to the environments in relation to which they have been constructed, the architecture of the settlement is delinked from the land: legally, figuratively, symbolically, and—in some ways—practically. The camp is excluded from the space and territory with which it is contiguous. People may only traverse its boundaries by taking great pains. Nevertheless, the condition of Dadaab as a destination for forced migrants and a site of forced settlement must be understood as bracketed within a long history of migratory living. Many of the camps' inhabitants come from pastoralist or agro-pastoralist communities in East Africa, for which the connection to the land is intimate, and not demarcated according to conventional capitalistic principles. People have migrated across the region for trade, animal husbandry, and other forms of subsistence, documented and undocumented. Nomadism has framed ways of life for centuries. It has left behind many strong material iterations, in which provisional architectures have served as permanent architectures. Here, the tent has not signified emergency or destitution, but instead has contoured and symbolized a direct habitation of the land for generations. This has been so, even during the period marked by modernity. Indeed, ephemeral and migratory domestic architectures have offered a rejoinder to modernization, by not complying with its infrastructures, but by behaving as an immanently fugitive architecture, an architecture of displacement. Such connotations must be read into domesticity in Dadaab.

Two mobile architectures have made this complex condition legible, and they in turn correspond to two analytical problems. The first consists of installed imported structures, such as the UNHCR single-family shelter and

Figure 2.5 Dwellings in Ifo Camp, Dadaab, Kenya, designed in an initiative by the UNHCR and the International Federation of the Red Cross and Red Crescent Societies, and built as part of shelter distribution services in refugee camps administered by the UNHCR. The individuals in this photograph declined to be named. Photo: Anooradha Iyer Siddiqi, 2011.

the large World Food Programme food storage unit (Figures 2.5 and 2.6). Each is a tensile architecture with a fabric skin—flat-packed, warehoused, and deployable from storage sites in the global supply chain. These conform to the political economies of actual states, but not to the land the camp occupies. Analytically, they create a territorial problem. Architecture often takes form as it emerges in relationship to a state economy that adheres to geopolitical boundaries. The refugee camp and its architectures cannot. In other words, the camp settlements are in Kenya but not of Kenya; the shelter is of Norway but not in Norway. While planners defined the spatial implementation of humanitarian operations at Dadaab, the settlement complex grew not in response to planning but in response to multiple forces of domestic structuring. The domestic space of the state has defined, but not constituted, the domesticity of the refugee camp. The Dadaab planners may not be architects without a country, but the refugee settlements do not correspond to any single political entity. These paradoxes of domesticity ensue from the camp as well as the mobile architectures that make it material.

Figure 2.6 World Food Programme storage warehouses, Ifo Camp, Dadaab, Kenya, designed for and built as part of food distribution services in refugee camps administered by the UNHCR. Photo: Anooradha Iyer Siddiqi, 2011.

The second consists of a very different set of portable structures, the vernacular dwellings built from plant materials and recycled building elements, in which many refugees live for years (Figure 2.7). These do not map directly onto any national political economies but instead concretely onto the land, and the Commiphora (myrrh) bushes that grow in this region. Even if the land of the refugee camps was plotted by planners, these structures have been built from and are situated in compounds bordered by live fencing growing from the ground. Analytically, they present a problem of materiality. The structures correspond to the politics and uses of the land, and often the very soil and earth. In Dadaab, the risks ranging from hyena attacks to sexual violence for those transgressing the demarcated perimeter of the camps (for example, for women seeking food, water, or cooking fuel) demonstrate the hegemony of the horticultural border and its power to effect zoning. In an episode recounted by one aid worker, a group of mothers dug out the clay soil around the perimeter of the camps to make bricks for shelters. The large pits that remained filled

Figure 2.7 Dwellings in Ifo Camp, Dadaab, Kenya, designed and built by individuals and families living outside the perimeter of the refugee camp. The individual in this photograph declined to be named. Photo: Anooradha Iyer Siddiqi, 2011.

with water during the rainy season, and turned into mosquito breeding grounds. This stirred a public health crisis, which illustrates the coherence of disease over what has otherwise been a division of populations, within the domestic interior of the state. The affected populations included one of refugees cared for by foreign doctors, and another of citizens overseen by domestic health care workers. The brick production caused a battle over trade and contracts, which produced bizarre entanglements between domestic economic interests and international refugee law and policy. In such scenarios, the abstraction of a refugee camp cannot hold any more than that of the nation-state can. Both become concrete through forms of domesticity—at the scale of the shelter and of the state. In such a scenario, the architectural referent assumes paramount potency. Rather than architecture symbolizing or referring to power elsewhere, meaning and power are located directly within built forms of domesticity. The refugee camp may be disconnected from the territoriality of the land— that is, the camp may disallow land as a referent for architecture—but it cannot be disconnected from the materiality of the land. Land elements literally constitute forms of domesticity.

In addition to these considerations of land, the other central issue in the domesticity discussed here is that of labor. The issue of labor is central to a consideration of Farah's work. The architecture her work brought into being exceeded requirements for shelter that would meet the most basic needs for survival. Indeed, the constructed form represented the result of an involved, scientific process. It offered a technical, professionally engineered solution for mitigating the extreme environmental challenges of the region. Moreover, the design and implementation process produced evidence-based data that broadened the NRC's platform of technical expertise. This furthered the organization's social construction of expert status. These practices at Dadaab cemented the organization's empirical knowledge base, while also building its international profile, as professional staff members disseminated findings from this high-profile site of humanitarian operations in conferences and other circuits. This construction of institutional reputation drew from the physical and intellectual labor of refugees, including that of Shamso Abdullahi Farah. Labor's multiple valences in this process—intellectual or manual, performed by refugee, citizen, or other—constituted the potency and the stakes of Farah's work. This was a labor based in domesticity.

Predicated upon the labor induced by this process of creating domesticity in emergency, architecture produced various forms of legitimacy. It cohered relief with a legible aesthetic regime, even a roofline that recalled Norwegian design in Somali Kenya. It redirected material flows, from the soil and cement of the brick walls to a nongovernmental organization's laboring bodies. It signified actual states as well as the international refugee framework. It institutionalized Farah as an architect in charge of programming, design, construction, and use of a set of buildings and, indeed, of an expanded domestic space. While formally certified architects, refugees, and unregistered others have been jointly responsible for the mass construction and architectural grain of the Dadaab settlements, Farah's architectural work—her *homemaking*, writ large—rendered banal matters such as professional licensing, because of the emergency context in which she labored. She engaged deeply with humanitarians and institutions, in spite of an asymmetry between herself and the state. Farah, the NRC, and the UNHCR together ordered a sphere of sociality, politics, and differentiated aesthetic and cultural work. These interventions disrupted the normative order of the nation-state. Indeed, they interrupted Farah's liminal status as a refugee. Rather than the political sphere producing built form, architectural forms of domesticity effected Farah's political subjecthood. Moreover, they rendered her a subject of emergency as much as of any state or international order. The subjecthood set by these conditions of emergency, as well as her embodied practice of designing, building, and intersecting with a paternalistic and transnational political, economic, and social system, produced alternate forms of authority in the camp. For her, they enacted situated expertise, power, and mobility. Her homemaking, in the emergency context, was a form of worldmaking.

How might this world be understood, in which domesticity is rooted in emergency, and provisionality is expressed in bricks and mortar? Taking those paradoxes in hand, how is such a world to be brought into scholarly view, when conventions of the state break down, causing archives to do as well? A theory may be found in the violated landscapes, mill towns, and slums famously sketched by Engels in *The Condition of the Working Class in England*, long before the tumultuous events that propelled his writing *The Housing Question*, the basis of the present volume.[9] In short, Manchester, like Dadaab, presents the stakes of walking through historical space to see the panoply of vignettes it might offer.

Manchester in Dadaab

Engels' thick description of the built environments of Manchester suggests ways of knowing Dadaab. His was a rhetoric of direct contact, which demonstrated a commitment to an esthetic experience and an immersive embodied engagement in a sensorium. Together, these forged a politics for the resulting histories to be written. This is to say, the method carried with it a politics, arguably separate from those of the writer. Thus, while the many critiques and counter-critiques of Engels' own perspective must be heeded—a privileged, imperialist, Eurocentric, masculinist, and racist perspective, particularly notable in his comments on the Irish poor—nonetheless, this politics of historiography remains.

When Engels wrote the chapter "The Great Towns," in *The Condition of the Working Class in England*, ethnography had yet to find its footing in colonial thought, and it would be a hundred years before the democratizing practices of participatory action research, social history, and oral history would produce a body of sociospatial analyses as rich as those he constructed by walking his reader through the working-class neighborhoods of London, Dublin, Edinburgh, Glasgow—and, most graphically, Manchester, "as I had occasion to observe them personally during twenty months."[10] He wrote:

> ...350,000 working-people of Manchester and its environs live, almost all of them, in wretched, damp, filthy cottages... the streets which surround them are usually in the most miserable and filthy condition, laid out without the slightest reference to ventilation, with reference solely to the profit secured by the contractor... in the working-men's dwellings of Manchester, no cleanliness, no convenience, and consequently no comfortable family life is possible... in such dwellings only a physically degenerate race, robbed of all humanity... could feel comfortable and at home.[11]

Engels' lament for a humanity robbed by forms of spatial violence illuminates the abstracted modern subject upon whom his democratizing and socialist, if othering, gaze might descend. He limned the modern subject through a trenchant figuration of spaces that seemed to lie outside of history—ironically, through vigorous description of real, historical places. His narration of built environments speaks to the power of centering the parallel figure of the contemporary refugee, who is often abstracted in the context of contemporary forced displacement.

Just as this theoretical method wrote Manchester into the historical narrative, it might suggest an approach toward writing Dadaab. This proposition might be considered in juxtaposition with the ideas in *Speaking of Buildings: Oral History in Architectural Research*, in which Janina Gosseye polemically situates the reception of two projects. *Project Japan: Metabolism Talks*, by Dutch architect Rem Koolhaas and London Serpentine Galleries director Hans Ulrich Obrist, and "Indigenous Architecture Through Indigenous Knowledge: dim sagalts'apkw nisim´ [together we will build a village]," the PhD dissertation of Luugigyoo Patrick Robert Reid Stewart, each critically mobilized polyvocality and primary source complexity, demonstrating the democratizing potential of oral history in two non-Western projects.[12] The first sought to give flesh and substance to an understudied avant-garde. The second stepped away from canonical figures, objects, and events, and even outside of the conventional linguistic parameters of academic scholarship, to think about Indigenous ways of knowing. Gosseye writes that the comparison between the former and the latter (the first described by her as better received than the second) demonstrates the "hurdles to overcome for those interested in changing the map of architectural historiography."[13] While such a map may not be as fixed as she contends, nor does the oral historical method alone provide an antidote to the problems of historiography, the critical potential she identifies applies to the problem of writing the emergency environment; it may begin to restore absences and silences in the historical record, expand historical writing and enable new forms of it, reinstate difference and establish polyphonic narratives, and negotiate with the unspoken and the unspeakable.[14] Indeed, Indigenous and feminist thinkers have long been articulating decolonial approaches that locate knowledge formation and consciousness with multiplicities of "authorship" and narration.[15] Their emphasis on the value of plurality, communality, and collectivity are meaningful rejoinders to singular ways of knowing, speaking, and writing, with special implications for understanding contemporary contexts of emergency. Similarly, approaching housing, and housing questions, from the spatial and temporal rubric of emergency may offer a special and expanded polyphonic historiographical potential.

To the point, the vantage point of emergency allows histories of work done by designated bodies of international relief and the structural forms of governance that they enact to be visualized alongside histories of homemaking by individuals and families coping with catastrophe. This strategy reveals the act and architecture of domesticity in emergency. Within it lies a history of emergency subjecthood. Overview histories resist an expanded, polyphonic historiographical potential, not to mention a proper historical treatment, by normalizing a reproduction of crisis and its claims of urgency. In contrast, thinking through an episode from the recent past on the border of Somalia, in which an emergency intervention ushered in the social transformation of a woman, a relief aid organization, and the surrounding institutional and built environments, it is possible to see the transformation of a humanitarian home-maker into an emergency subject, and from that a wider historical frame.

If a politics of emergency demands a visual rhetoric of expediency and ephemerality from housing, its most common form, shelter, paradoxically produces architectures rooted in the land and people's labor. It also re-produces emergency subjects as architects. These empirical objects and subjects—the border camp setting, the humanitarian aid organization, the shelter construction, the refugee architect—are the counterpoint to Engels' poor, or rather his practice of seeing, documenting, and writing them. Farah's labor and the domesticity it undergirded suggest that a migratory and emergency environment, with attendant interruptions of spatiality, tempo-rality, and historicity, works against essentializing definitions of normativ-ity and precariousness. Instead, such an environment enables narrations that depend upon new architectural referents, protagonists, and narrators.

Methodologically, just as Manchester did for Engels, Ifo refugee camp at Dadaab here revealed the political implications and limitations of architec-ture.[16] Farah's work as a builder destabilized the meaning of the architect as a figure legitimated solely by the state, and instead suggested deeper forms of authority that architecture calls upon. Farah's work in building and inhabiting the minimum dwelling *par excellence* lives at the intersec-tion of histories of design, planning, political economy, humanitarian ide-ology, and contestations around land, labor, and the state.

Shelter and the Housing Question

In conclusion, and to further test the limits of the problematics posed in this volume, it may help to understand the story of Shamso Abdullahi Farah's work within the stream of thinking that Friedrich Engels initiated in his 1872–1873 *Zur Wohnungsfrage* articles, and in doing so, it is important to differentiate the humanitarian project from the social one. The separation may not register within modern liberal architectural discourse, in which the ideologies of sympathy for the suffering of others (at the root of which is a conception of humanity) and democratic burden sharing across classes (at the root of which is a conception of society) are together immanent in the notional and material iterations of shelter. The recent history of hu-manitarian shelter further complicates this understanding, in that it maps almost directly, if anachronistically, onto the critiques that Engels posed in those articles.

His first criticism was of the utopian socialist straw man of the rent-to-ownership scheme. He took issue with its disregard of economic reality (following Proudhon, "who never bothered himself about the real and actual conditions under which any economic phenomenon occurs") and any retreat into abstractions of law and justice, which he felt could never come into being without economic grounds.[17] For Engels, housing only placated class difference that needed no longer persist after the Industrial Revolution. As he wrote,

> …it is precisely this industrial revolution which has raised the productive power of human labour to such a high level that – for the first time in the history of humanity – the possibility exists, given a rational division of labour among all, to produce not only enough for the plentiful consumption of all members of society and for an abundant reserve fund, but also to leave each individual sufficient leisure so that what is really worth preserving in historically inherited culture – science, art, human relations is not only preserved, but converted from a monopoly of the ruling class into the common property of the whole of society, and further developed.[18]

His second criticism targeted the misguided and self-preserving efforts of the bourgeoisie in disregarding the economics of the housing shortage, as "a necessary product of the bourgeois social order; that it cannot fail to be present in a society in which the great masses of the workers are exclusively dependent upon wages."[19] For Engels, just as Proudhon responded to the housing shortage by taking refuge in law, the bourgeoisie responded with morality: foreclosing the possibility of revolution in favor of charitable philanthropy. In so doing, they moved in lockstep with the goal of segregating publics via the built environment, qua discourses of hygiene and material sanitization, as causal rather than symptomatic.

This aim of separation via the built environment is one for which the refugee camp has served distinctly as an instrument. Engels' critiques of the positions of utopian socialists and the bourgeoisie alike, and the segregation of populations they sanctioned, apply to the context in Dadaab in which Farah labored to develop a shelter initiative in conjunction with the nongovernmental but state-funded NRC. In that context, the categories of the state (for example, property ownership or rent) have been insufficient, and more fundamental forces have been exerted.

In a sociopolitical milieu in which refugees were denied the rights to work and education through law and to freedom of mobility through aggressive policing, and thus were rendered structurally dependent upon humanitarian aid, the UNHCR administered multiple contracts with international organizations to provide their shelter and care. These organizations engaged in two practices in managing displacement that do not depart far from the very arguments laid out by Engels, and thus merit consideration here. First, they took a certain refuge from politics provided in the letter of international law, to justify creating camps and their constituent architectures—that too, with recruitment of refugee labor—even as the socioeconomic and material conditions in a location such as Dadaab suggest the rather different possibility, to make people's lives. Second, organizations such as the NRC, standing in for Engels' bourgeoisie, and operating within a realm of emergency that is in turn predicated upon a subtext of urgency, co-constructed a structural framework of the moral. This framework sees little of history or politics, and in turn produces residual interests, effects, and affect, which efface or supplant possibility for political change.[20]

In emergencies, these two practices—retreating from the political and fashioning the moral—condition the subjecthood of refugees. While the social project carved the chamber within which to hear Engels' clarion call, and contoured his 1872 adjudication with regard to these two practices, the humanitarian project in recent history behaves differently: precisely as pertains to the making of singular emergency subjects. As Miriam Ticktin argues, humanitarianism

> is characterized by a tension between a focus on the exceptional individual and a collective humanity. Humanity is accessed and treated through individual, suffering bodies, even as it is also figured or imagined en masse, particularly in the Global South. Humanitarianism is practiced on humanity conceived of as a set of singular individuals facing exceptional circumstances.[21]

Further to that thinking, as Liisa Malkki has written, refugees are figured as a "blur of humanity," particularly those from Africa.[22] Those with black bodies have been particularly susceptible to this figuration. They have been rendered as a body of individuals, rather than a social body—a body of political sovereigns, rather than a body politic. This distinction matters, especially when one of the individuals takes sovereign action, makes an intervention, or begins to make a world.

Farah's homemaking in an emergency context offers ways to think about shelter as an element in a historical stream, which runs parallel to and yet is distinct from that of housing. Farah's domesticity—building a shelter, housing her family, becoming a technical expert and social organizer through her home—poses questions of whether shelter is inalienable from the nation-state, and how it exerts state and nongovernmental dynamics. A history of her work suggests that the limit-concept for the refugee camp was not necessarily the nation-state, its territory, and its borders, but more materially her labor and the land, and the use, negotiations, and transgressions of each. Within these propositions lies another, on looking to one woman's shelter to see history unfold.

The paradox of a shelter that can be provided only on the condition of ephemerality illustrates Engels' point that solutions do not reside in architecture as a form of improvement. Yet, Engels framed his argument upon the clear and essential position of wage workers within a domestic political economy. The work of a refugee such as Shamso Abdullahi Farah overturns his case for a dialectic between the status quo and political revolution, and instead lays bare the continuum of ground between the two. Farah is not a wage worker whose labor is fixed within the political economy of a nation, and yet, she is a modern subject. The modern subject need not necessarily be a subject of the state, or a subject in training. Farah's work shows that the modern subject may be sovereign in ways that lie outside the nation-state construct. Her sovereignty might be tied to the land, instead of to its extraction, or to her own labor, instead of to its quantification. That is to say, this modern subject lived on the land, rather than off it. Her work created domesticity, instead of a domesticity framing her work. These small steps can be the building blocks for histories.

This chapter owes a debt to attentive care and meaningful insights provided by Juliana Maxim, Can Bilsel, and an anonymous reviewer, as well as from the following concurrent collaborations: Architecture and the Housing Question (including editors and authors in this volume and symposium participants), Insurgent Domesticities (Columbia University Center for the Study of Social Difference), Feminist Architectural Histories of Migration (Rachel Lee and authors in the collections), The Art and Architecture of Partition and Confederation (Maristella Casciato, Zirwat Chowdhury, Farhan Karim, for the Getty Research Institute, and symposium participants), and Settlement (Hollyamber Kennedy and other contributors).

Notes

1 This article distills several years of research in state, academic, cultural, and humanitarian archives, individual and group interviews with approximately 500 refugees, aid workers, officials, and architects in camps and other contexts, and observation of built environments in refugee contexts in East Africa and South Asia. Many of the interviews were conducted by the author on behalf of the Women's Refugee Commission (a US-based international research and advocacy organization founded by members of the board of the International Rescue Committee), and are held in the Duke University Libraries, some of which informed the report *Preventing Gender-based Violence, Building Livelihoods: Guidance and Tools for Improved Programming*, https://www.womensrefugeecommission.org/resources/document/798-preventing-gender-based-violence-building-livelihoods-guidance-and-tools-for-improved-programming, last accessed June 8, 2020. This article draws primarily from an interview with Shamso Abdullahi Farah, by the author and Bethany Young, with translation and interpretation by NRC staff member Hashim Keinan. During a day spent together in March 2011, Keinan provided real-time translation from Somali to English as we examined Farah's plot and the buildings she and her family members built. I directed my questions to Farah, she responded directly to me, and Keinan translated and interpreted. He occasionally intervened and responded directly to my questions, sometimes referring to Farah in

the third person. My interpretation of the discussion makes analytical allowances for his.

2 For another examination of the central episode in this article, see Anooradha Iyer Siddiqi, "Writing With: Togethering, Difference, and Feminist Architectural Histories of Migration," in *e-flux Architecture* (July 28, 2018), "Structural Instability," eds. Daniel Barber, Eduardo Rega, and e-flux Architecture, last accessed June 27, 2021.

3 Anonymous, interview by author, 2011.

4 Multiple interviews confirmed that shelter and settlements is one of the NRC's recognized areas of expertise. It is a stated core competence of the NRC; see https://www.nrc.no/what-we-do/activities-in-the-field/shelter/, last accessed June 8, 2020.

5 NRC Shelter Adviser, interview by author, 2012.

6 Former NRC incentive worker, multiple interviews by author, 2012–2014.

7 NRC staff members in Dadaab and elsewhere, multiple interviews by author, 2011–2014.

8 Interviews with Farah, other refugees, and aid workers who worked with NRC attested to this. Anooradha Iyer Siddiqi, "Architecture Culture, Humanitarian Expertise: From the Tropics to Shelter, 1953–1993," *Journal of the Society of Architectural Historians* 76, no. 3 (September 2017): 367–384. See also Farhan Karim, ed., *The Routledge Companion to Architecture and Social Engagement* (New York: Routledge, 2018); Helen Gyger, *Improvised Cities: Architecture, Urbanization, and Innovation in Peru* (Pittsburgh: University of Pittsburgh Press, forthcoming 2018); M. Ijlal Muzaffar, "The Periphery Within: Modern Architecture and the Making of the Third World," Ph.D. diss., Massachusetts Institute of Technology, 2007.

9 I am grateful to Clive Dilnot for this insightful prompt.

10 Friedrich Engels, "The Great Towns," *The Condition of the Working Class in England in 1844 with Appendix Written in 1886*, trans. Florence Kelley (New York: John W. Lovell, 1887).

11 Engels, "The Great Towns."

12 Janina Gosseye, "A Short History of Silence: The Epistemological Politics of Architectural Historiography," in *Speaking of Buildings: Oral History in Architectural Research*, eds. Janina Gosseye, Naomi Stead, and Deborah van der Plaat, 16–19. Rem Koolhaas and Hans Ulrich Obrist, *Project Japan: Metabolism Talks* (Köln: Taschen, 2011). Luugigyoo Patrick Robert Reid Stewart, "Indigenous Architecture Through Indigenous Knowledge: dim sagalts'apkw nisim´ [together we will build a village]," PhD diss., University of British Columbia, 2015.

13 Gosseye, "A Short History of Silence," 19.

14 Gosseye, "A Short History of Silence," 20.

15 In addition to the work already cited, this is an important and continuously growing body of work, and I reference only a few thinkers here. Linda Tuhiwai Smith, *Decolonizing Methodologies: Research and Indigenous Peoples*, 3rd ed. (London: Zed Books, 2021); Sylvia Tamale, *Decolonization and Afro-Feminism* (Ottawa: Daraja Press, 2020); Silvia Rivera Cusicanqui, *Ch'ixinakax utxiwa: una reflexión sobre practices y discursos descolonizadores* (Buenos Aires: Tinta Limón, 2010), and "Ch'ixinakax utxiwa: A Reflection on the Practices and Discourses of Decolonization," *The South Atlantic Quarterly* 111, no. 1 (2012): 95–109. See also Kiddle, Rebecca, Luugigyoo Patrick Stewart, and Kevin O'Brien, *Our Voices: Indigeneity and Architecture* (Novato, CA: ORO Editions, 2018).

16 I am grateful to Juliana Maxim for this insightful prompt.

17 Friedrich Engels, "How Proudhon Solves the Housing Question," *The Housing Question*, ed. C. P. Dutt, Marxist Library vol. XXIII (New York: International Publishers, n.d.).

18 Engels, "How Proudhon Solves the Housing Question."

19 Friedrich Engels, "How the Bourgeoisie Solves the Housing Question," *The Housing Question*.

20 For more on the "humanitarian paradox" or the "humanitarian alibi"—the criticism that humanitarian intervention derails political intervention—see David Rieff, "The Humanitarian Paradox," in *A Bed for the Night: Humanitarianism in Crisis* (New York: Simon & Schuster, 2002), 31–56; Fiona Terry, *Condemned to Repeat? The Paradox of Humanitarian Action* (Ithaca, NY; London: Cornell University Press, 2002); Adi Ophir, "The Sovereign, the Humanitarian, and the Terrorist," in *Nongovernmental Politics*, eds. Michel Feher et al. (New York: Zone Books, 2007), 169.

21 Miriam Ticktin, "Humanitarianism's History of the Singular," in Daniel Bertrand Monk et al., "A Discussion on the Global and the Universal," *Grey Room* 61 (Fall 2015): 83.

22 Liisa Malkki, "Speechless Emissaries: Refugees, Humanitarianism, and Dehistoricization," *Cultural Anthropology* 11, no. 3 (1996): 387.

3 "Oh, but This Isn't Architecture!"

The Paradoxical Heritage of French Public Housing

Sandra Parvu and Alice Sotgia

In France housing, architecture, and urban affairs have rarely been under the supervision of the same government ministry. During the 1960s the Direction of Architecture, supervised by the Ministry of Culture, had little involvement in the politics of construction when major urban transformations took place in France and in the debate over housing construction, which was then, as now, supervised by the Ministry of Equipment and Transports.[1] An example might help put into context the quotation in the title of this chapter. These words were said by the Minister of Equipment in 2003 to Christine Piquéras, Director of Architecture at the Ministry of Culture. For him, the question of public housing and its demolition, which was soon to be massively funded, was not her problem since housing "isn't architecture."[2] At the time Piquéras was attempting to get seats on the board of directors of the newly created National Agency of Urban Renovation (ANRU) in order to be able to object to the debasement or, worse, the irremediable demolition of housing complexes designed by French modernist architects.[3] Significantly, on a board composed of thirty-six members, including public figures and local politicians involved in housing policies, the state filled its sixteen seats with eight delegates from the Ministry of Social Affairs, under whose supervision the Department of Urban Affairs was placed. The latter rapidly established operational and financial cooperation with the Ministries of Equipment and of Economy. In spite of its efforts to become involved in the debate over the renovation of the postwar housing stock, the Ministry of Culture remained fairly marginal, with only one delegate on the ANRU board.

The ANRU is the last to date of many plans of action initiated in France since the 1980s with the declared ambition of reducing social inequities through spatial interventions. These urban policies are part of a wider debate on the causal effect of space on society, to which French sociologists have contributed since the 1950s, as shown by Susanna Magri.[4] There is a continuous stream of studies coming out of the fields of geography and political science, which also underscores the fact that the history of urban and housing policies in France is deeply entrenched in resolving the social question.[5] In this posture, also shared by government officials, "the social"

DOI: 10.4324/9781351182966-5

is viewed through an economic lens. To remediate social inequality is to disentangle residents' lives from stigmatized neighborhoods where they have little access to the job markets and where the concentration of problems that grow out of unemployment forecloses horizons of opportunity for the younger population. As central as "the social" may appear in the debate on public housing, however, this approach has actually reduced the administrative conception of the social realm from a multifold understanding of how people live and inhabit a place to an economic problem.

In a book relying on more than twenty years of fieldwork research conducted in neighborhoods undergoing urban renovation, the sociologists Barbara Allen and Michel Bonetti criticize the way residents are considered and the role of dwelling and inhabitation, or the lack of it, in the history of urban policies in France.[6] Their introductory chapter reflects on the ways in which dwelling and living conditions have been addressed in social studies over the past sixty years. In their view, postwar studies of housing have been strongly influenced by Marxist thought. Going back to the major references of that period—including works by Manuel Castells, Henri Lefebvre, and Francis Godard—housing appears to be massively apprehended as the expression of the conditions of production and reproduction of the capitalist system and the domination of one class by another. Space is above all a means of inscribing stakes of power.[7] During the 1980s a discursive shift occurred: if the Marxist-inspired authors failed to address the relationship that residents develop to their living environment on a more individual basis, during the 1980s the spatial question disappeared altogether. The emphasis put on segregation and exclusion in the administrative lingo portrays residents as economically fragile and marginalized from the production system. Habitat and the relation to habitat disappear, as if, being excluded from the realm of production, inhabitants were incapable of building other meaningful relationships.[8] According to Allen and Bonetti, the continuous erasure of the relationship and interactions that residents establish with the places where they live over the past sixty years within both administrative and academic discourse supports the historical and still relevant opposition at the heart of the housing question between the spatial and social dimensions. Indeed this dichotomy is performed today in the new program developed by the ANRU: the programs, time schedules, and budgets of the public interest group in charge of social support and the bureau in charge of urban renovation are entirely distinct.

The social question in relation to housing is thus often addressed by way of political and economic considerations from which the spatial and therefore architectural dimensions are almost absent. This was already the case in the writings of Friedrich Engels, who famously stated that

> it is not the solution of the housing question which simultaneously solves the social question, but only by the solution of the social question, that is, by the abolition of the capitalist mode of production, is the solution of the housing question made possible.[9]

The history of housing policies in France, with its ever-changing divisions of power as well as its administrative implementation, embodies the potentially dual dimension of housing as a social and political project, on the one hand, and as an architectural program, on the other, with the Ministry of Social Affairs (today the Ministry of Territorial Cohesion) on one side and the Ministry of Culture and the body of architectural practitioners on the other.

In this chapter we contest the historical tendency to marginalize the architectural implications of housing in favor of the "social question" by examining various contemporary architectural practices that apprehend the social through an understanding of what dwelling means. The introduction of this notion to the debate puts the "social" in a new light. Instead of allowing individuals to disappear behind their class or economic status, dwelling reveals a more granular representation of the social: one centered on the tension between the individual appropriation of space and the need to share it and live collectively. Therefore, going beyond the acknowledgment that spatial realities make visible social problems, [10] we propose to examine how this tension inherent in the notion of dwelling is negotiated by government officials and the architectural profession. Indeed the spatial question that appears so difficult to put forward in the public policies discussed by Allen and Bonetti is one that architects are well equipped to address. Although they are called upon primarily for their synthetic know-how regarding building structures, construction processes, and environmental performance, architects have found, thanks to this technical entrée into the debate, a way of developing various positions regarding the question of heritage, more specifically the heritage of modernism.

In order to illuminate how certain architectural practices articulate connections between the social and the spatial, we have conducted a series of nondirective interviews with civil servants who had worked or were still working on the preservation of postwar public housing in the Direction of Architecture at the Ministry of Culture, as well as with architects who designed renovation projects of collective housing. The choice of interviewing only one side of the players involved in the debate over the future of public housing came precisely from our desire to determine whether and how the social dimension had become instrumental in catalyzing architectural discourse and practices. As previously developed in an article retracing the genealogy and implications of a sound art piece in the fight against the demolition of a housing project in East Los Angeles, this method has proved to be a useful means of exploring the various layers and contradictions inherent in this kind of debate.[11] With this in mind, we will first discuss the issues raised by the preservation discourse that proceeded from the creation of the ANRU. In the face of a massive demolition to come, architects, officials in charge of architectural preservation, and social scientists initiated a debate over the disappearance of a collective housing type that had become part of urban history.[12] Public housing forced defenders of a fairly straightforward approach to preservation to reproduce the socio-spatial divide: What was to be preserved? The form of the buildings? Their history? Did their history include that of the residents? Which residents?

In the second part of the chapter we will examine how architects take into account the dwelling dimension. Their approach extends the long-established tradition of French ethnography centered on dwelling as an object of study and a daily activity capable of qualifying space.[13] It is also informed by the inclusion of social sciences and their methods in the syllabus of French schools of architecture since 1968. This second part will be structured around the alternative proposed by *Plus: Les grands ensembles de logements, Territoire d'exception*, a manifesto on housing renovation written by the architects Frédéric Druot, Anne Lacaton, and Jean-Philippe Vassal in 2004, which introduced a new point of view to the debate over the demolition of public housing and, in the process, questioned the Ministry of Culture's position on preservation. We will assess the consequences of the manifesto by discussing the projects and building-site experiences shared during their interviews by three architects: Anne Lacaton of Lacaton & Vassal, Arnaud Bical of bmc2, and Laurent Lehmann of Eliet & Lehmann. With the exception of their geographic locations, these projects are quite similar in all respects, including size and regimes of ownership. All were composed entirely of rental units and managed by government-run local offices, and their renovation budgets consisted of state-funded aid combined with regional and local funds. The awards and publications as well as the international attention that these projects have drawn make them, for different reasons, national icons of French housing renovation.[14] Beyond considering their merits, we will conclude the chapter with a discussion of how they have raised new issues, displaced the debate regarding the heritage of modern architecture, and expanded the spectrum of professional practices at large.

The Paradoxes of Public Housing

Until the beginning of the year 2000, public housing was considered as an architecture without qualities. The growing threat of systematic demolition, as well as its actual implementation in 2003 with the creation of the ANRU, created a turning point in the way of considering this type of housing.[15] Roundtables in architecture schools and articles began discussing in ideological rather than concrete terms the possibility of seeing these structures not as failed experiments in modernist construction but as architectural and social heritage.[16] This rethinking of social housing introduces paradoxes to a field already thick with paradoxes. On the one hand, the architect and urbanist Philippe Genestier points out the paradox according to which these dwellings born from French state interventionism at its best are today frowned upon by the same public authorities as if the result of a makeshift solution by disorganized individuals. He sees the possibility of overcoming this paradox by attributing to the state a positive, and therefore more coherent, approach to this type of housing. This is close to the paradox identified by François Tomas, in which the *grand ensemble*, or large-scale housing project, is regarded by public authorities as both the solution to a housing crisis and a symptom of suburban unrest.[17]

On the other hand, some paradoxes also emerge in the aftermath of housing becoming architecture. Benoît Pouvreau introduced his defense of making *grands ensembles* heritage by acknowledging that already too many historic monuments are not properly maintained for lack of sufficient public funding.[18] In a slightly different realm but still in the same vein, the French sociologist Emmanuel Amougou writes that in terms of architectural heritage, at least in France, heritage building values usually reflect the position and social recognition of their architects, residents, or owners. When it comes to public housing, the absence of heritage value is determined by the social depreciation of the people who inhabit them.[19] In other words, to preserve a building, one must value not only the work of the architects who have conceived it but also the lives of those who live in it. Christine Piquéras has acknowledged this issue, which distinguishes public housing from more traditional monuments:

> For a very long time, heritage meant unique objects, small objects and, in general, uninhabited objects.... *Grands ensembles* pose lots of problems. They are primarily a recent heritage. They are also inhabited, so it means that they are used, and this use gives them a humanity, a life that cannot be neglected in a process of restoration that was originally designed for empty objects.[20]

Another paradox emerges therefore from the relation between the building and its residents. More precisely, in the inconsistency between the narratives told by architects or architectural historians about a building and the narratives told by the many people who have lived in it. To go further into this paradox, let us look at Eliet & Lehmann's project in Fontainebleau, completed in 2011. It involved the renovation of 280 housing units originally built by Marcel Lods, an important architectural figure in the French postwar landscape. Close to Le Corbusier, he was famous for his intense collaborations with engineers in developing innovative steel structures, experimental prefabricated elements, and generally taking advantage of the construction industry development. Out of the six buildings that made up the project, only one was inhabited at the time renovation started. People living in Fontainebleau, which is a fairly affluent town south of Paris, hated the buildings, which had been badly maintained but also debased by renovations during the 1980s. At the same time they also had memories of the complex's initial residents and called it the "American neighborhood" because American officers had been housed there with their families, bringing in a comfortable lifestyle, including cars, cigarettes, and the like.

In 2010, the complex was bought by a social landlord who agreed to im-plement the architectural project as defined by the French architectural firm Eliet & Lehmann. This mid-sized firm of roughly ten architects, expert in the construction and renovation of collective housing, was created in 2002 by Denis Eliet and Laurent Lehmann. Their practice maintains a continuity with the Modern Movement heritage. Lehmann explains that part of the project consisted in convincing the client to tell this story again and make the lives of those early residents more vivid in the collective imaginary.[21] They exhibited, for instance, archival photographs from this period during the annual heritage days. This resonated with Eliet & Lehmann's own ar-chitectural approach. A significant part of the time allocated to the project consisted in looking at drawings and photographs from the Marcel Lods archives in order to understand the original constructive and spatial inten-tions, testing the structure with new bearing norms in order to prove that it should be preserved, restoring the existing facade by internally insulating it, and so on (Figures 3.1 and 3.2).

That the apartments had been vacated for quite a few years made it easy in this case to achieve the concordance between the architectural history of the buildings and the narrative relating to their inhabitants. The positive

Figure 3.1 Marcel Lods, Facade before renovation, La Faisanderie, Fontainebleau. Photo: Pierre-Yves Brunaud, 2017. Courtesy of Eliet & Lehmann.

Figure 3.2 Eliet & Lehmann, Renovated apartment with thickened facade by interior insulation, La Faisanderie, Fontainebleau. Photo: Laurent Lehmann, 2017. Courtesy of Eliet &
Lehmann.

narratives told by some preservation processes can also raise questions,
however: just as in Fontainebleau, the memory of residents often becomes
part of the building's heritage, and its multiple layers are erased in favor
of the creation of an official narrative mostly taking into account the stories of its original residents. A recent study in Saint-Etienne shows that if
authorities preserve a building by erasing memories in the same way that
they might remove layers of insulation in order to return it when possible
to its initial design, from the residents' point of view this approach is more
questionable.[22] It nevertheless seems widely accepted in the administrative
sphere, since Christine Piquéras said that

> often residents are not the ones who were the first to inhabit these
> apartments, and that the people who actually live in these estates don't
> know anything about them, whereas the ones who came first are still
> part of history, they know the story of how they settled in their town,
> how it has evolved.[23]

There is thus a tension between the rich and often contradictory narratives of a building's occupants and the need to promote only one compelling story in order to justify its preservation.

Plus: The Manifesto in Context

What the paradoxes identified by various researchers in the previous part of this chapter have in common is the conflictual relation that remains along the abovementioned socio-spatial boundary. Genestier and Tomas's paradox is underlined by the fact that the authorities shifted over time from seeing the *grands ensembles* as a construction feat to regarding them as a rising social problem. Significantly, the position endorsed by traditional approaches to preservation, such as that of Amougou and Piquéras, does not supersede this paradox and only reverts to the same historical divide previously reached by housing activists, policy makers, and partisans of demolition alike. Instead of marginalizing architecture and putting the social question at the core of the debate, traditional preservationists place architectural quality in the center and disregard the life that takes place in it. While this relation between housing and its occupants creates a paradox for most, the process of renovating public housing proposed by Lacaton & Vassal associated with the architect Frédéric Druot seizes this relation as a valuable asset to rethink the heritage of these buildings. In 2003 the three architects conducted a one-year research project financed by the French Ministry of Culture. The ministry's objective was to recognize the heritage value of some public housing estates. The results of this research came out one year later in *Plus: Les grands ensembles de logements, Territoire d'exception*.

The report is divided into three parts. A discussion between the three authors introduces their outlook on architecture and the modern heritage, their position on history and housing, the evolution of norms, the qualities of French public housing, and the notions of reuse and recycling at the core of their understanding of preservation. The choice of themes and their considerations gradually expose the theoretical basis and motivations underpinning the architectural solution they propose in the second part of the report. The latter appears mainly through visual diagrams of simple actions that together make up their renovation toolbox: open the facade wall, add a picture window, add a continuous balcony or winter garden, replace the partition wall with a moving partition, and so on. The last section applies these actions to the specific geometries, floor plans, facades, and orientation of four *grands ensembles* situated on the outskirts of Paris, Le Havre, Nantes, and Saint-Nazaire. The detailed presentation of this research and results was made available to an English-speaking audience in 2007 by the renowned architectural publisher Gustavo Gili, under the title *Plus: Large-Scale Housing Developments; An Exceptional Case*. Following this publication in an expanded, larger-format multilingual edition, the architects were invited to discuss their research, point of view, and proposals regarding the transformation and future of public housing in many different countries and forums. Lacaton & Vassal's practice thus gradually gained international attention through their advocacy against demolition, as well as projects such as the renovation of Palais de Tokyo, Paris's Museum of Contemporary Art, to culminate in being the laureates of the 2021 Pritzker Architecture Prize. The Tour Bois-le-Prêtre, their first public commission for the renovation of a collective housing tower, has thus become a flagship on the international stage for a debate on the preservation of public housing.[24] What has been less highlighted is the discussion that the report prompted at the French Ministry of Culture, which had originally commissioned it. This contextualization is relevant in this chapter as it enables us to understand how Druot and Lacaton & Vassal's position fits into the wider debate on public housing and heritage in France. Beyond that, it also reveals that the gap between the Ministry of Culture's point of view and that of the architects is constituted mainly by the discrepant role they each give to the social dimension, as will be discussed in the next part of this chapter.

Plus was published shortly after the creation of the National Agency of Urban Renovation, whose task was to select a significant number of public housing projects across France for demolition or renovation. According to Piquéras, then director of the office that commissioned the report,

> the research had one purpose: to allow the Ministry of Culture to have a seat on the agency's board of directors in order to negotiate the protection of worthy modernist housing complexes. In other words, the task of the ministry's delegate was to educate administrators to see these buildings not only in terms of social issues and dilapidated housing but also as architecture.[25]

From the Ministry of Culture's point of view, *Plus* failed in its initial purpose for various reasons. First and foremost, *Plus* unsettled the ministerial take on preservation by asking whether buildings should be preserved not because of their architectural quality and design but because of their capacity to be transformed. As Druot asserts in an interview:

> Any area of built floor is potentially capable of being reused. To what degree can we consider its capacity in order to make the most of it? It seems vital to us to examine heritage in relation to its use value above all. The notion of preservation is contextual and evolving.[26]

Vassal further completes Druot's point of view:

> The Ministry mustn't restrict its contribution only to regarding the preservation of buildings by famous architects such as Jean Renaudie, Fernand Pouillon or Jean Dubuisson. What's in play is political as well

as cultural, and this concerns both the Ministry and the architectural profession the Ministry represents.[27]

Instead of recognizing the work of an author and its unique dimension, the report extends the notion of preservation to recognize the actual use value of a building and its capacity to continue to be used through a process of transformation. Although this view has become somewhat widely accepted in academic circles, especially those focused on preservation in the age of sustainability,[28] this view was and still is in some respects irreconcilable with that of the ministry. The clash most significantly materialized in the latter asking Druot and Lacaton & Vassal to mention in the report the names of the architects who had originally built their case studies. They refused to do so. Understandably, to do so may have implied that some buildings may not be worthy of preservation because of their historical insignificance to the field of architecture. *Plus* also doesn't identify the original types of building structural systems and the construction techniques through which they were built.

As noted in the methodological handbook issued and updated by the Ministry of Culture, an important step in the process that leads to the listing of a historic monument is the identification of material qualities: the physical, archaeological, and historical description of the object. This is still valid for less formal preservation, such as inscriptions and labeling also provided by the Ministry of Culture. From the latter point of view, the material description enables one to distinguish an architectural object against the backdrop of numerous others and eventually set aside financial means to protect it. This process of identifying housing units worthy of interest was implemented in monographs published by the ministry after the report, including *Les grands ensembles: Une architecture du XXe siècle*, a large-format book in which 108 housing estates are presented as index cards recording the name of the architect, the history and modes of construction, their unique dimension if relevant, and so on. The diverging viewpoints of the Ministry of Culture and the authors of *Plus* regarding what preservation should encompass are anchored in the fact that the ministry extended the understanding of preservation focused on architectural and historical value to public housing, while *Plus* broke with this tradition in order to envision a form of preservation oriented toward the future uses of a given site rather than its glorious past.

Plus: The Manifesto in Action

The published version of *Plus*, in contrast to the initial report, includes a new section in which the architects present two completed residential projects that offer an alternative to demolition.[29] The main difference between the four theoretical cases studied in the original report and these two actual projects consists in the attention the architects gave to the residents and their varied contributions to space. To examine the potential use value of a building means not only considering the soundness of its construction system or revealing its contextual qualities but also taking into account the attachment of the families to the building in which they live and their personal use of space.[30] The addition of real residents to the manifesto introduces the question of how to integrate into the equation their present and future needs.

Let us look at an image of the Grand Parc, their last renovation project completed in 2016: the 530 housing-unit estate was built in the 1960s on the outskirts of Bordeaux. The image functions as a collage consisting of a background in which one can see the remnants of a domestic interior with paintings and a clock still hanging on the walls, a table with flowers and various objects lying on it. The chairs, upright mattress, and covered television set reveal that a turn of events has upset the day-to-day activities while the foreground introduces the contrasting image of ongoing construction: unfinished concrete surfaces, metalwork without glass. The floor, protected and covered in dust, functions as a transition between the two parts of the photograph. Similarly to the temporal copresence construed by Goethe in his description of the *Laocoön*,[31] the image articulates three mutually exclusive time frames: the past domestic everyday, the present building site, and (off-camera) the promise of the future project (Figure 3.3).

Figure 3.3 Lacaton & Vassal with Frédéric Druot and Christophe Hutin, Newly opened facade with existing owners' belongings, Grand Parc, Bordeaux. Photo: @ Philippe Ruault, 2014

One distinctive characteristic of the housing renovation projects of the architects Druot, Lacaton, and Vassal is that they are conducted with the residents living on-site. Obvious logistical and financial advantages convince landlords of this solution. Nevertheless, the architects' decision to have residents present for a process that involves a maximal intensity of disturbance in terms of dust and noise, let alone living out of a suitcase for months, reveals an agenda that exceeds the merely practical.[32] The tenants' uninterrupted and persistent residence on the site puts into perspective the three temporal frames inherent in the notion of dwelling: the capacity to reside in the thickness of the past, the confidence in the future to come, and the ability to feel situated in time and space in the present. Putting the manifesto into action displaces the "social question" from the theoretical realm to a series of individuals with whom the architects interact and have to invent a specific form of dialogue:

> We do not ask people what they need…. There is no point in asking them one day what they want, then the next day, and then after it's over. It's not a matter of hearing what people want but rather about decoding what they have to say, understanding how they organize themselves. If someone says, "We want three bathrooms," well, we cannot handle this kind of direct answer. It is more relevant to relate the capacities of a building and see what can be added to it. In the regulatory framework, there are budgets; there is technology. This approach is then confronted with what the people can say about their lives. That's why when we meet the residents we go with a thorough knowledge of the building.[33]

Notwithstanding the surveys that took place across various French public housing estates during the 1970s, the "social needs" of the residents are not the starting point of the project. Architects consider the building and its capacity to be transformed as the point of departure, and it is on the basis of this architectural and technical knowledge that they hear what the residents have to say. The building and its structure thus continue to be the backbone of the project. But instead of finding reasons to preserve it by looking back at the archives and the original architectural intentions that guided its construction, Druot and Lacaton & Vassal look forward to its transformation using the multiple ways in which people live inside it as a springboard for their project. Listening to the residents as a means to preserve the building runs up against not only the Ministry of Culture's approach to heritage but also the mechanics of any form of state management that would by the nature of its structure rather encourage a repetitive and generally applicable series of actions. For instance, for a project in Rouen, completed in 2012, that included 290 housing units, Arnaud Bical proposed meeting with each family in order to pragmatically decide on a case-by-case basis what needed to be changed. He described the fight he had to put up against the flattening administrative machine wanting to entirely refurbish each apartment:

> We struggled a little at some point on a kind of very trivial subtlety which consisted in taking a look at the state of each bathtub because overall to remove it, put a new one back in, redo the tiles and so on, that costs say 500 to 1000€ per bath. We were in a financial crisis. So we were defending this extremely fine work and the renovation machine is rather a little more systematic. It does surveys and then decides it's just as easy to remove everything.... But the most interesting moment happened before the fight with the administration, when we came into contact with the inhabitants, it was right at the beginning when we started doing surveys, we started to understand exactly, we started to classify each problem.... It's always quite surprising, because we came across lives, with surprises ... here ... there are people here![34]

bmc2, an architectural office established in 2001 by Arnaud Bical and Laurent Courcier, successfully working on a variety of programs, including cultural facilities, office blocks, and the creation and renovation of collective housing, is a Paris-based office with links to Lacaton & Vassal. Their case-by-case approach, in order to economically juggle with the available budget, is therefore close to that envisioned by Druot and Lacaton & Vassal at the Tour Bois-le-Prêtre and in their project in Bordeaux for which they partnered up with the Bordeaux-based architect Christophe Hutin. The latter asked the photographer Philippe Ruault to document the interior of each apartment (Figure 3.4). The photographs were generally taken from the same place in the room: with his back to the entrance door, Ruault took a shot of the entire room with the facade window in the background. The contrast between the various decorations and ways in which people inhabit their space brings forth visually the multiple threads of narratives and lifestyles. Photographing with the camera facing the light source is not traditionally recommended, but it allows the architects to show the impact of their proposal on the existing space. Using a collage technique, they open the facade wall and add a picture window and a winter garden in the background of the photograph while keeping the existing dwelling and its varied modes of inhabitation undisturbed. A second series of photographs is produced once the construction is completed and the residents are again comfortably installed in their apartments. The decorations and living environments are still wide-ranging, but minute changes show that the architects have integrated specific residents' requests. Allen and Bonetti suggest that lack of attention to dwelling is the source of the historic socio-spatial boundary that has plagued French urban policies since their inception. The two photographic series foreground dwelling and its manifestations, and in some way perform the erasure of this historic socio-spatial divide, thus testing Allen and Bonetti's hypothesis (Figures 3.5 and 3.6).

Figure 3.4 Jean Royer, Interior before renovation, Grand Parc, Bordeaux. Photo: @ Philippe Ruault, 2013.

Figure 3.5 bmc2, Renovated facade with corner of the tower opening on the existing landscape, Grand Mare, Rouen. Photo: Stéphane Chalmeau, 2012. Courtesy of bmc2 Arnaud Bical and Laurent Courcier architectes.

The attention given to the existing internal organization of the space emphasized by the photographs and also present in Lacaton & Vassal's discourse calls into question the transformation of building facades: "The project of transformation starts from the interior of the dwellings" is a sentence they often repeat. This is at the center of the debate, since during the 1980s and 1990s a specific fund dedicated to housing renovation encouraged a process in which external insulation provided opportunities to change the monotonous existing facades with decorative motifs, balconies, and large-scale openings called "urban windows." While most recent housing policies predominantly support demolition, changing the facades was in those days the accepted approach to making these buildings more acceptable for their residents and in the eyes of the public. It also provided

Figure 3.6 bmc2, Facade highlighting the co-presence of existing and new windows for stragetic budget management, Grand Mare, Rouen. Photo: Arnaud Bical, 2012. Courtesy of bmc2 Arnaud Bical and Laurent Courcier architectes.

a solution to the need to add thermal insulation to buildings in accordance with new regulations. Insulating facades has been a constant goal in the history of renovating public housing in France. More often than not, these interventions debased the existing building facades. To rethink the building from the inside or the outside, to hide or preserve the facade while continuing to keep housing up to date with new environmental norms is thus a heavily loaded question. In Fontainebleau, Eliet & Lehmann insulated the building internally. In Rouen, bmc2 adopted what the architects describe as a pragmatic approach. The addition of insulation depended on each situation, sometimes internal, sometimes external. In Bordeaux, Lacaton & Vassal added on top of the existing facade winter gardens that act as a thermal buffer zone and that could be considered external insulation. These three cases reproduce the more generally applicable rule: the closer to a historical preservation, the more attention was given to keeping the facade intact. Lacaton & Vassal's detachment from a historical approach produces the freedom to give the building a new facade.

While Lacaton & Vassal's interventions avoid reaffirming the socio-spatial divide, they nevertheless raise other problems. *Plus* recommended entirely redefining facades, and the implementation of this at the Tour Bois-le-Prêtre and also in Bordeaux and Saint-Nazaire, though aimed at encouraging innovation, actually produced a result that could be seen as dogmatic and repetitive.[35] For instance, the competition for an entirely new residential and office building in Geneva, won in 2014 by Lacaton & Vassal, entails outside perspectives of the building that strongly resemble those of the Tour Bois-le-Prêtre, thus questioning the specificity of their approach to renovation.

Furthermore, while sharing the general position against demolition supported by Anne Lacaton and Jean-Philippe Vassal, Laurent Lehmann recognizes within the string of urban policies adding layers of painting, insulation, or balconies to facades, the difficulty French officials and architects have in constructively building a dialogue with modern architecture. Indeed, although Lacaton & Vassal's approach proceeds as we have seen from an interior understanding of the dwellings, its result may, however, read as the extension of such policies. Lehmann argues that adding a new layer to the original facade literally supports the process of making this architectural period invisible and implicitly provides in the long term backing for its demolition. The renovation of the Tour Bois-le-Prêtre was very much praised by architects, critics, and academics but was also attacked by some who considered the work of Raymond Lopez, its original designer, to have architectural value in the first place. Critics argued that the facades of his tower should therefore have been restored to their original design instead of being hidden behind a new layer of winter gardens. Thus a new paradox emerges: if Druot and Lacaton & Vassal's project has made Bois-le-Prêtre part of the contemporary architectural discourse, it has also defaced a building that is part of modern heritage.

* * *

In this chapter we have seen that the relation between public housing, its buildings, and its residents was seen in France to be at the root of a certain number of paradoxes underlying the divide between the urban and social questions. Instead of choosing a side—the side of the urban, of the building and its history, or the side of the social, of the residents, their memories, and their problems—Druot and Lacaton & Vassal use this apparently dysfunctional relation as a foundation stone to bring public housing into the realm of the contemporary architectural debate. They anchor their housing projects in surveys that take into account the lives of residents and the modes in which they inhabit the spaces they are called on to transform. Dwelling becomes a pivot in the articulation of the socio-urban divide. As such, they consider the social not as a community of "public neighbors" but as a series of individuals living in a specific place, with specific ties.[36] More than public housing renovation, their projects could be considered as a series of successive transformations of people's homes. The problem that springs from this process that seeks to supersede the historic boundary ingrained in French urban and housing policies is that the building is treated not as modern heritage but as opening up a field of future possibilities. Thus a new paradox emerges. For the Ministry of Culture and other advocates of a traditional approach to preservation, public housing becomes architecture once its heritage value is recognized. For Anne Lacaton, Jean-Philippe Vassal, Arnaud Bical, and other architects and critics, public housing becomes architecture by becoming the site of a transformative project. This implies the acknowledgment of a new architectural practice and position in the context of designing public and collective housing. It is in this respect that the national and international awards won by the architects we interviewed are relevant.

Beyond the tensions and paradoxes that divide architects and the members of involved ministries over the different ways in which to preserve public housing, however, there is another theme that emerged from the different interviews. In the process of carefully looking at this type of housing—whether in terms of construction details, material design, history of a neighborhood, or actual ways in which residents live in it today—architects become aware of a different practice and understanding of the architectural project. Arnaud Bical stated, "This is not scholarly architecture, in discourse and writing, it is a kind of social practice like that of a country doctor; we have to struggle a little against ourselves, because we as architects do not have this culture."[37] And Laurent Lehmann explained,

> In Fontainebleau, we made a housing prototype in order to develop all the technical details, which for us are very simple details. We work with plasterboard. In our architectural approach we must be economical; there is no demonstrative side in our architecture. We have no technological approach to problems, neither high-tech nor low-tech. What we like is the 'standard-tech,' something that comes out of the construction industry.[38]

Besides producing a pioneering manifesto against demolition in the form of *Plus*, the effort to preserve public housing has made more visible an architectural practice in which finding solutions for a lived-in building site, managing thermal and acoustic insulation within standardized preexisting volumes, and generally operating with sparse economic means has become more exciting than signature buildings and exuberant formal feats. If only to foster this new trend in architectural practice, liable to expand to other periods of architecture and building uses, the debate over the preservation of public housing is worth having.

Notes

1 For a detailed history of France's administration of architecture, see Eric Leng-ereau Eric, "L'architecture entre culture et équipment (1965–1995)," *Vingtième Siècle, revue d'histoire* 53 (1997): 112–123.

2 Christine Piquéras, interview by Sandra Parvu in her office at the *Musée national de l'histoire de l'immigration* on January 11, 2017.

3 From 1958 till 1973, roughly 4 million public housing units were built. The size and quantity of building operations was seized as an opportunity by many postwar renowned architects to try out their architectural research and experiment with new modes of construction.

4 Susanna Magri, "Le pavillon stigmatisé. Grands ensembles et maisons individuelles dans la sociologie des années 1950 à 1970," *L'Année sociologique* 58, no. 1 (2008): 171–202.

5 See, for instance, Daniel Béhar, "L'intégration à la française, entre rigueur et pragmatisme : le cas des politiques de l'habitat," *Hommes & Migrations* 1229 (2001): 77–85; Philippe Estèbe, "Solidarités urbaines: la responsabilisation comme instrument de gouvernement," *Lien social et politiques* 46 (2001): 2–14; Gérard Baudin and Philippe Genestier, eds., *Banlieues à problèmes. La construction d'un problème social et d'un thème d'action publique* (Paris: La Documentation française, 2002); Thomas Kirszbaum, *Articuler l'urbain et le social. Enquête sur onze sites "historiques" en rénovation urbaine* (Paris: Comité d'évaluation et de suivi de l'ANRU, 2010); Jacques Donzelot, *La France des cités. Le chantier de la citoyenneté urbaine* (Paris: Fayard, 2013).

6 Barbara Allen and Michel Bonetti, *L'Habiter, un impensé de la politique de la ville. Pour un renouvellement du sens de l'action* (La Tour d'Aigues: L'Aube, 2018).

7 Ibid., 22.

8 Ibid., 28.

9 Frederick Engels, *The Housing Question* (English translation of the second German edition of 1887), eds. C. P. Dutt, Marxist Library volume XXIII (New York: International Publishers / Co-operative Publishing Society of Foreign Workers in the USSR, n.d. [1935]).

10 Michel Lussault, *De la lutte des classes à la lutte des places* (Paris: Bernard Grasset, 2009), 209.

11 Sandra Parvu and Alice Sotgia, "Building by Ear: Ultra-red and Union de vecinos in Boyle Heights, Los Angeles," in *Speaking of Buildings: Oral History in Architectural Research*, eds. Naomi Stead, Janina Gosseye, and Deborah Van der Plaat (New York: Princeton Architectural Press, 2019): 135–153.

12 During its first decade the agency demolished 150,000 units, rebuilt 130,000, and renovated 310,000 for a total cost of 47 billion euros; in 2014 a second ten-year plan has allowed the agency to continue the renovation and demolition of another set of housing units.

13 See, for instance, Nicole Haumont, *Les pavillonnaires. Étude psychosociologique d'un mode d'habitat* (Paris: Institut de Sociologie Urbaine, Centre de Recherche d'Urbanisme, 1966); Henri Lefebvre, *Le droit à la ville* (Paris, Éditions Anthropos, 1968); Colette Pétonnet, *Espaces habités, Ethnologie des banlieues* (Paris: Éditions Galilée, 1982); Gérard Althabe et al., *Urbanisation et enjeux quotidiens. Terrains ethnologiques dans la France actuelle* (Paris: Anthropos, 1983); Michel de Certeau, *The Practice of Everyday Life*, trans. Steven Rendall (Berkeley: University of California Press, 1984); Michel de Certeau et al., *The Practice of Everyday Life II: Living and Cooking* (Minneapolis: Univ. of Minnesota Press, 1998); Marion Segaud, *Anthropologie de l'espace: Habiter, fonder, distribuer, transformer* (Paris: Armand Colin, 2007).

14   Among other forms of national and international recognition, Druot, Lacaton, and Vassal's transformation of the Tour Bois-le-Prêtre won the Équerre d'Argent prize for architecture in 2011, the London Design Museum's Designs of the Year award for architecture in 2013, and the transformation of the Grand Parc in Bordeaux won the Mies van der Rohe Award, an EU Prize for Contemporary Architecture in 2019. Eliet and Lehmann's project in Fontainebleau was nominated for the Équerre d'Argent in 2015 and was selected as a case study for energy and climate management in modern buildings by the Getty Conservation Institute in 2016; and bmc2's project in Rouen was one of six narratives presented at the French Pavilion at the Venice Architecture Biennale in 2016.

15   Vincent Veschambre, *Traces et mémoires urbaines. Enjeux sociaux de la patrimonialisation et de la démolition* (Rennes: Presses Universitaires de Rennes, 2008).

16   The first critiques to publish on this shifting point of view were Bruno Vayssière, "Pour une patrimonialisation délibérée," *Urbanisme* 322 (2002): 77–79; Philippe Genestier, "Les paradoxes du grand ensemble," in *Banlieues à problèmes. La construction d'un problème social et d'un thème d'action publique*, eds. Gérard Baudin and Philippe Genestier (Paris: La Documentation française, 2002): 175–206; Cyria Emelianoff, "Reconstruire la légitimité des grands ensembles," *Annales de la Recherche Urbaine* 97 (2004): 27–33. Within a decade, the explosion of special issues of journals, academic conferences, and scientific articles produced a more consistent ground on which to open up the definition of preservation and more specifically discuss the possibility of preserving this long-neglected type of housing. For further references, see bibliography, and more specifically articles published in the journals *Urbanisme*, *Echogéo*, and *Métropolitiques*.

17   François Tomas, Jean-Noël Blanc, and Mario Bonilia, *Les grands ensembles: une histoire qui continue* (Saint-Etienne: Université de Saint-Etienne, 2003), 9.

18   Benoît Pouvreau, "Faut-il 'patrimonialiser' les grands ensembles?" *Métropolitiques*, March 28, 2011, http://www.metropolitiques.eu/Faut-il-patrimonialiser-les-grands.html.

19   Emmanuel Amougou, *Les grands ensembles. Un patrimoine paradoxal* (Paris: L'Harmattan, 2006), 16–17.

20   Piquéras, interview by Sandra Parvu.

21   Laurent Lehmann, interview by Sandra Parvu, Eliet & Lehman, architects' offices in Paris, on March 2, 2017.

22   Rachid Kaddour, "Prise en compte de la pluralité des mémoires d'habitants dans la 'patrimonialisation' des grands ensembles," *EchoGéo* 33 (2015), http://journals.openedition.org/echogeo/14337.

23   Piquéras, interview with Sandra Parvu.

24   Craig Buckley, "Never Demolish: Bois-le-Prêtre Regrows in Paris," *Log* 24 (2012): 43–50; David Huber, "Lacaton and Vassal Have Pioneered a Strategy for Saving France's Social Housing," *Metropolis. Architecture and Design at all Scales* (January 2016): 80–87.

25   Piquéras, interview with Sandra Parvu.

26   Frédéric Druot in "Eco-culture," Frédéric Druot, Anne Lacaton, and Jean-Philippe Vassal, *Plus. Large-Scale Housing Developments. An Exceptional Case* (Barcelona: Gustavo Gili, 2007), 66.

27   Jean-Philippe Vassal, Ibid., 67.

28   See, for instance, Maria Gravari-Barbas, ed., *Habiter le patrimoine: Enjeux, approches, vécu* (Rennes: Presses Universitaires de Rennes, 2005); Nathalie

Heinich, *La fabrique du patrimoine. De la cathédrale à la petite cuillère* (Paris: Maison des Sciences de l'Homme, 2009); Max Page, *Why Preservation Matters* (New Haven, CT: Yale University Press, 2016).

29 The two projects are an unbuilt competition in Saint-Nazaire (2004, 55 units) and the Tour Bois-le-Prêtre in Paris (2011, 97 units). More recently the renovation of a tower in Saint-Nazaire (2014–2016, 80 units) and the transformation of the Grand Parc ensemble in Bordeaux (2016, 530 units) have also implemented the alternative proposed by the research.

30 Druot et al., *Plus*, 193.

31 Johann Wolgang von Goethe, *Goethe on Art*, trans. John Cage (Berkeley and Los Angeles: University of California Press, 1980).

32 For a poignant portrait of the experience of living through the building site of the Tour Bois-le-Prêtre, and its disturbances, see the film of Guillaume Meigneux, *Habitations Légèrement Modifiées - Tour Bois-le-prêtre, chronique d'une métamorphose* (Rouen: Cellulo Prod, 2013).

33 Anne Lacaton, interview by Sandra Parvu, Lacaton and Vassal, architects' offices in Paris, December 29, 2017.

34 Arnaud Bical, interview by Sandra Parvu, bmc2, architects' offices in Paris, February 23, 2017.

35 This approach to transforming facades has also been applied by other architects, such as LAN, whose renovation of a housing project in Lormont completed in 2015 was the only French project selected by Alejandro Aravena for the Venice Architecture Biennale in 2016.

36 Lawrence J. Vale, *From the Puritans to the Projects: Public Housing and Public Neighbors* (Cambridge, MA: Harvard University Press, 2000).

37 Bical, interview by Sandra Parvu.

38 Lehmann, interview by Sandra Parvu.

Part II
Housing and the State

4 Inventing Socialist Modern

Housing Research and Experimental Design in the Soviet Union

Daria Bocharnikova

Finding the ultimate solution to the housing question was one of the central concerns of the Russian Revolution. First steps were taken immediately after the Bolsheviks took power in October 1917. The Decree on Land, issued the day after the revolution concluded, abolished private ownership of land. In 1918, amid violent civil war, private ownership of real estate in cities was eliminated. These radical reforms aimed to uproot inequality in living conditions and create mechanisms for the redistribution of wealth. The abolition of privately owned land and real estate gave Soviet politicians, architects, and urban planners unprecedented opportunities for social and spatial experimentation. It was not until the 1950s, however, that the Soviet government succeeded in consolidating enough resources to launch a comprehensive mass construction campaign that eventually diminished the housing shortage drastically. After decades of state violence and state mobilization for the cause of rapid industrialization and warfare, in the second half of the twentieth century housing in the Soviet Union became the territory for a peaceful renegotiation of the contours of socialism between the state and the society. In other words, contrary to Engels's teleological reading of proletarian revolution as capable of resolving the housing question at once, Russian revolutionaries, and architects in particular, struggled for at least four decades to work out a feasible solution. Finally, in December 1954 Nikita Khrushchev, the first secretary of the Soviet Communist Party, addressed the Second All-Union Convention of Construction Workers and Architects to denounce the current state of affairs in the building industry and architectural practice and to call for extensive industrialization of construction and standardization of design. This political intervention ushered in a new approach to construction that prioritized standard design and prefabrication technologies, which in turn made it possible to envision a resolution to the housing crisis in the Soviet Union in approximately thirty years.[1]

This paradigmatic shift in the Soviet approach to housing is associated with four major innovations: (1) the introduction of prefabrication technology, (2) the principle of type designs (*tipovoe proektirovanie*), (3) the policy of distributing one apartment per family, and (4) the adoption of the

DOI: 10.4324/9781351182966-7

mikroraion, or microdistrict, as an urban-planning scheme. This episode in the history of Soviet architecture is rather well studied, and as recent scholarship has shown, all four were not exactly innovations of the Khrushchev era. It was during his rule, however, that the technology of prefabrication and *tipovoe proektirovanie*, together with the new distribution policy and the *mikroraion* planning solution, became the backbone of the approach to housing in the Soviet Union as well as in the broader Soviet bloc.[2]

The first and most celebrated example of this novel approach to housing was ninth block of Novye Cheremushki, a new *mikroraion* in southwestern Moscow, built in 1956–1958.[3] This project allowed Soviet architects to showcase and test different systems of prefabrication and several designs for small apartments, as well as to present the advantages of the *mikroraion* scheme, as opposed to the perimeter block (*kvartal*), which was the most common urban-planning solution in the previous decades. Beginning in the late 1950s the Cheremushki model became dominant in Soviet building practice. Rather quickly *cheremushki* became the common noun for the new neighborhoods of prefabricated housing springing up across the Soviet Union, later also referred to as *khrushchevki*. This new type of housing was infamous for tiny apartments and poor-quality construction. Yet it also provided Soviet citizens with major modern amenities—such as running water, sewer systems, and central heating—as well as easy access to various public facilities, including schools, kindergartens, shops, cinemas, and public transport (Figure 4.1).

Figure 4.1 A splash pool in Novye Cheremushki, 1964. Source: John Reps Papers, #15-2-1101. Division of Rare and Manuscript Collections, Cornell University Library.

This approach to housing has been seen as the major outcome of the forty-year-long quest to solve the housing question under socialism. It could be even claimed that the combination of the four innovations made socialist housing into a success story on a global scale. Between 1954 and 1991 housing construction throughout the Soviet bloc uplifted millions of citizens from poor living conditions. Although the housing campaigns did not transform the Soviet Union into a fully egalitarian society or produce egalitarian cities, they did create a massive urban infrastructure intended to improve the everyday lives of Soviet citizens.[4] The design and policy framework that produced them had been developed by a relatively small group of architects, urban planners, and policy makers in the preceding decades.

Conflicting notions of home, family, citizenship, and individual versus collective identity were forged by the residents of these new neighborhoods, but instead of focusing on the lived experience of the residents and the many meanings this type of housing acquired for both state and society, this chapter will look closely at how this particular solution to the housing crisis was invented and at the role of architects in developing it.[5] More precisely, I will argue that what was special about the Soviet solution to the housing question was not necessarily the particular technology, the design process, the urban-planning scheme, or the distribution policy but rather how this solution was worked out through fundamental research at the Academy of Architecture and through state-sanctioned experimental work at design offices aimed at reorganizing the construction industry. In other words, I will argue that in order to understand the Soviet approach to the housing question, we need to better understand the notions of housing that reigned in the circles of the architects who developed Novye Cheremushki and that were embraced by the state after 1954.

Research on Housing at the Academy of Architecture

Novye Cheremushki is widely recognized as an emblematic project of the so-called Khrushchev modern.[6] Yet it is often forgotten that the theory that informed this experimental construction was developed at the Academy of Architecture well before Khrushchev's intervention. It is not uncommon for scholars to depict the academy as "a bastion of reigning stylistic orthodoxy" of the Stalin era.[7] Looking at the history of the Academy of Architecture through the eyes of the reformers of the Khrushchev era only reinforces this image of the institution. Nikita Khrushchev and the architect Georgii Gradov attacked the academy for promoting aestheticism and archaism in Soviet architecture and for ignoring the issues of construction costs.[8] Gradov underlined in a speech in 1954 that only "several out of 120 members of the Academy of Architecture of the USSR have dealt with mass construction."[9] One of the immediate victims of this public campaign was the Academy's president, Arkadii Mordvinov, dismissed from his position. This post-1954 reputation of the academy, however, significantly obscures the diversity of research institutions and fields that it encompassed, let alone the diverging ideological orientations of the research conducted within its walls.[10] One such striking example of the academy's activities is the gigantic project of translation of almost all Renaissance architectural treatises into the Russian language carried out before World War II by Aleksandr Gabrichevskii and Vassilii Zubov.[11] How does the fact that such figures as Gabrichevskii and Zubov carried on with their scholarly work at the academy in the turbulent decade of the 1930s change our understanding of the history of this institution? The little-known detail that the Communist Party sanctioned the translation of "classics of architectural thought"—including Leon Battista Alberti, Andrea Palladio, and Giacomo Barozzi da Vignola— challenges our understanding of Stalinist isolationism and the role of fundamental research in it. The Academy of Architecture in this context emerges as another site of Soviet cosmopolitanism and transnationalism where Soviet intellectuals could carry out fundamental research on world culture in order to forge socialism and to participate in global debates.[12]

First, the All-Union Academy of Architecture was the most prestigious graduate school of architecture in the Soviet Union at the time. It was established in 1933 as a major research center and training program for the most talented young architects.[13] The first group of graduate students was admitted in 1934. One of the immediate goals of the academy was to reeducate Soviet architects who graduated in the 1920s, when avant-garde movements were still dominant at many architectural institutions. More broadly the academy's graduate program was aimed at bringing up a new generation of highly qualified architects who would develop a profound knowledge of world architectural history. The professors at the academy succeeded in part in fulfilling this goal. The academy's alumni appraised it "as a wonderful school of craftsmanship," and many of them indeed formed a new generation of talented Soviet architects.[14]

Second, in the 1930s and 1940s it became the de facto research powerhouse, uniting the most prominent architects of the time, including Boris Blokhin, Ivan Fomin, Vladimir Gel'freikh, Moisei Ginzburg, Ivan Golosov, Boris Iofan, Lev Rudnev, Vladimir Shchuko, Aleksei Shchusev, Aleksandr Vesnin, Viktor Vesnin, and Ivan Zholtovskiy and their junior colleagues Viktor Baburov, Andrei Burov, Georgii Gol'ts, Sergei Kozhin, Ivan Nikolaev, Mikhail Parusnikov, Ivan Sobolev, and others. The scope of the research topics explored at the academy was truly impressive, and it included, inter alia, the work of the *zhilishchniki*, a group of Soviet architects working on housing design.[15] Likewise, the debate on the neighborhood unit that emerged in the Soviet Union after World War II took place at the academy. This was the first professional discussion on the planning principles for socialist neighborhoods after the war.[16]

In 1946–1947 Aleksei Galaktionov, Evgenii Iokheles, and Natan Osterman wrote their doctoral dissertations on the theory of the neighborhood unit at the academy. Galaktionov became known as one of the key authors of *mikroraion* theory, while Osterman and Iokheles were the first to implement *mikroraion* theory with their work at Novye Cheremushki. I would argue that the views of the pioneers of the Khrushchev construction campaign were to a great degree shaped by the professional culture of the academy, which supported fundamental research, boosted the feeling of belonging to the elite of the profession, and allowed for modest dissent from the mainstream.

Natan Osterman entered the Academy of Architecture in 1940, immediately after graduating from the Moscow Institute of Architecture (MARKhI).[17] According to Osterman's biographers, from at the very beginning of his studies at the academy he took an interest in housing design and started working under the supervision of Andrei Burov. A former constructivist, Burov was actively engaged in research on large-block prefabrication methods and designed and built the first apartment buildings from prefabricated elements together with Boris Blokhin, a specialist in engineering systems.[18] Thus Osterman found himself at the epicenter of the experimental work on Soviet housing. Until the very end of his career he continued working on experimental designs, probing different approaches to mass construction.

Evgenii Iokheles was eight years older than Osterman. Before joining the academy for requalification courses in 1935, Iokheles already had significant practical experience in urban theory and construction. In 1926 he joined the architectural department of Vkhutemas-Vkhutein, the Soviet art and technical school, where he worked under the supervision of Konstantin Melnikov and Nikolai Ladovskii, the leaders of the architectural avant-garde. Iokheles worked with them on the "green city" project.[19] After finishing his studies in 1930, Iokheles began to work at the Giprogor, one of the major Soviet urban-planning institutes, in the sector of civil construction.[20]

The attitudes of Burov elucidate what was possible within the academy. A brilliant student of Aleksandr Vesnin and Ivan Zholtovskii, Burov developed his own approach to architecture quite early in his career by merging the insights of the two strongest schools of Soviet architecture, constructivism and neo-Renaissance.[21] He rated highly the works of Pavel Blokhin and Aleksei Zaltsman, who were his colleagues at the academy and the engineering and design geniuses of standardization and industrialization of housing construction.[22] Burov's students and colleagues remembered that he was always very straightforward in his judgments.[23] For instance, already in the 1930s and 1940s he was openly criticizing the excesses of architecture.[24] Burov's guidelines for designing simple, human-scale, and well-organized mass housing proved to be rather influential among his students.[25] It is worth mentioning, however, that he was not the only one voicing a critique of contemporary building practice. After the war the immense task of reconstructing cities across the Soviet Union brought the shortcomings of Soviet urbanism even more sharply into focus. And even the president of the academy, Arkadii Mordvinov, acknowledged the urgent need for change.[26]

Although few state resources were devoted to housing construction in the 1930s and 1940s, research on housing was not only an important topic at the academy but was also intertwined with a critique of the approach to urban development that was mainstream at the time. This should help us reconsider the image of the academy as a stronghold of Stalinist orthodoxy and picture it also as a site of critical thinking. This should in turn call into question our understanding of Stalinism and the organization of the architectural profession in those years. The dissertations written by Galaktionov, Iokheles, and Osterman at the academy are examples of such critique and a certain degree of intellectual sovereignty in developing planning priorities. In his introductory chapter Iokheles wrote:

> The significance of this work is not restricted to narrow, exclusively practical objectives. Its major goal is the exposition and theoretical explanation of the new tendencies in the field of design of residential quarters in newly constructed and reconstructed cities of the Soviet homeland. For a long time there has been no experimental work of that kind, which allows us to summarize the experience acquired in everyday practical work and to outline and formulate clearly the new visions and proposals with regard to the entire set of issues of settlement and urbanism.[27]

Galaktionov, Iokheles, and Osterman pursued similarly wide-ranging research goals of analyzing and synthesizing urban-planning theory and practice in the Soviet Union, Great Britain, and the United States in the previous twenty years. This fact demonstrates the perceived vacuum of knowledge and the lack of theoretical discussions in the previous decade. The authors agreed that there was a need to develop a comprehensive approach to Soviet urban planning and that Soviet architects had not paid enough attention to the issue of methods in previous years.[28]

Remembering the experimental works of the 1920s and early 1930s, Iokheles, writing in the 1940s, qualified the major problem with the urban-planning paradigm of the previous decade as conservatism. According to Iokheles, in the 1930s and in the postwar reconstruction plans, prerevolutionary multistory perimeter-block development became the reigning model after more than a decade of post-1917 experiments.[29] He demonstrated that this return to a prerevolutionary typology of buildings and understanding of the city as a set of streets led to an unfortunate split of the urban-planning process into two separate tasks: drawing plans, *planirovka*, and the "three-dimensional design," *ob'emnoe proektirovanie*, of the separate buildings. Hence the process of urban construction was interpreted as the assemblage of different buildings designed by architects along the red lines indicating streets on the plan, which were initially carefully drawn by the planners.[30] This, according to Iokheles, led to another problem, the excessive use of decoration:

> Oversaturation of every new building facade with decorative elements, popular in post-war Moscow practice, is not able to resolve the problem of unification of the separate parts of the city and creating its 'big

form' at all.... The future of big Soviet architecture should not be in decoration of separate buildings and not in their formal assemblage.[31]

The frustration with "oversaturation" and decoration is a common thread in all three dissertations. Osterman called for a relative simplification, *laconizatsia*, of the facades of mass housing.[32] He suggested that there was no need for either the excessive decoration of individual buildings or the "excessively pompous and grand" design of the quarters' interiors. He argued that harmonious and often symmetrical compositions that would look beautiful in a drawing often resulted in an environment characterized by "coldness and severity" in practice.[33] Similarly, Galaktionov, who was also clearly against "false magnificence," lamented this misguided understanding of the internal areas of the quarters. He underlined that the decoration of outdoor areas could not replace their major function. He criticized the architects who designed pompous gardens with fountains and forgot to plan a children's playground, leaving kids to play in the streets.[34]

All these calls for simple design and less pompous architectural composition are tightly linked to another recurring theme: the intimate character of mass housing neighborhoods. The major aim of the urban planners, according to the authors, was to create a comfortable environment for urban dwellers. They insisted that housing should not be grandiose. Its architecture should be different from the architecture of the central squares and streets. It was "comfort and coziness" that the architects should think of when designing residential quarters (Figure 4.2).[35] The idea of lyricism in

Figure 4.2 Illustrations of the ninth block. Source: *Arkhitektura SSSR*, **no.** 7 (1956).

housing entered into professional discussions in the wake of World War II. In that respect it was not a uniquely Soviet theme but a pan-European post-war phenomenon of the increased value of home life and domesticity.[36]

Research Exchange as Politics: Translating Neighborhood Unit into Socialist Modern

Galaktionov, Osterman, and Iokheles rightfully acknowledged in their research in the 1940s that the neighborhood unit principle had become dominant in English and American urban development during the previous two decades. It had been widely applied in both the renovation of old cities and the construction of new ones. The concept of the neighborhood unit first appeared in the United States in the 1920s.[37] The authorship of the neighborhood unit model is conventionally ascribed to Clarence Perry. It was he who first attempted to clarify the idea, which was present in an uncrystallized form in professional discussions starting around 1900, and to develop a general design of the neighborhood unit. The scheme by Perry was published in 1929 as a contribution to the Russell Sage Foundation's *Regional Survey of New York and Its Environs*.[38] Soon the idea crossed the Atlantic Ocean and gained popularity among British architects, including Patrick Abercrombie. The neighborhood unit principle was developed and widely applied in the construction of British new towns after World War II.[39]

In general, the development of neighborhood unit theory must be read as a critique of the capitalist city. According to Lewis Mumford, a harsh critic of capitalist metropolises and a vigorous supporter of decentralization, the neighborhood unit was one of the few alternatives to uncontrolled city growth in the first half of the twentieth century. In his article written in defense of the neighborhood unit principle in 1954, he stated: "Neighbourhood unit organisation seems the only practical answer to the giantism and inefficiency of the over-centralised metropolis."[40] Soviet architects at the academy were also interested in counteracting the "giantism" of mainstream urban schemes of the Stalin era and initially turned to neighborhood unit theory for alternative planning solutions for postwar reconstruction and construction of new cities in the Soviet Union. They turned out to be extremely critical of the political program of this urban-planning paradigm, however, and rejected most of the political content of the conception.

Among the three researchers, Natan Osterman was particularly harsh in his criticism of the political aspirations of neighborhood unit theory. One reason for this is rather obvious. He submitted his dissertation in 1947, after the launching of the anticosmopolitan campaign in the Soviet Union, which accused mostly Jewish intellectuals, artists, and scientists of lack of patriotism and of "kneeling before the West." It was also after Winston Churchill's speech at Fulton, Missouri, in 1946, in which the British prime minister stated that "an iron curtain has descended across the Continent." The onset of the Cold War made the lives of Soviet intellectuals interested in world culture and Western expertise more difficult. Having a Jewish surname and voicing support for Western theories was becoming a dangerous combination at the time. In the opening pages of his dissertation Osterman made sure his attitude on those matters could not be misunderstood:

> Starting with the atom bomb and finishing with Hollywood blockbusters, scientists and writers, artists and poets subordinate their work for dollars and pounds to an odious and egoistic aim of reestablishing social injustice. Architects are no exception to this rule.[41]

It has to be noted that Iokheles, who finished his dissertation in 1946 and was less militant in his rhetoric with regard to Western theories, did not defend his dissertation. It is likely that in the context of unfolding attacks against pro-Western sentiments, such ritual dissociation from Western influences became vital for those working with foreign materials in order to secure their positions and prove loyalty. Yet can we see behind this ritualized critique the political position of the authors? The question of whether this critique was pragmatic or reflected the actual political stances of the researchers begs for closer investigation, especially given that at the same time they dared to voice some criticism of the dominant paradigm in Soviet urban planning. One would also be remiss simply to dismiss all the critiques as an obligatory smoke screen.

The major accusation leveled against Western proponents of the neighborhood unit was that they tried to solve socioeconomic problems through architectural and planning means, a critique that echoes Engels's stance. Likewise, for Osterman and Iokheles, mere social reformism was unacceptable. Iokheles, who was quite supportive of neighborhood unit idea in general, devoted an emotional passage to this critique:

> In the first place, we have to absolutely reject all the suggestions that assign to the principle of *mikroraion* the role of the decisive factor in the socioeconomic transformation of society. The authors of these theories prove with a serious look on their faces that the *mikroraion* can serve as a panacea against all vices and ills of contemporary society. If we listen to them, the unification of aristocratic quarters with proletarian ones should put an end to class antagonism.... The absurdity, unreality, and demagogic character of these socio-reformist theories are obvious and barely call for any proof.[42]

In very similar words the neighborhood theory was criticized by Nikolay Bylinkin in an article that efficiently brought the discussions on the neighborhood unit to a close. This further confirms that such critiques could not be qualified only as ceremonial accusations. Iokheles demonstrated his outrage at the fact that the architectural projects were considered a "panacea," a cure for all the problems of society. Bylinkin denounced neighborhood unit theory as an instance of "decrepit municipal 'socialism.'"[43] The term *municipal socialism* was widely used in the 1930s to denounce garden city and suburban movements in the Soviet Union. Soviet ideologists following Engels insisted that it was only revolution that could resolve the class conflicts and that no reforms could alleviate the position of the workers within the exploitative capitalist system. Osterman, who stated that the major goal of his dissertation was to "unmask the reactionary nature of the neighborhood unit concept," also addressed the social reformism of the theory as a major ideological drawback.[44] He underlined that the neighborhood unit principle was developed as a way to save or improve capitalism. But there could be no "social peace" in a capitalist society always torn apart by class antagonism: "The architect-urban-planner, slipping on the toga of the social reformer, tries to proclaim and establish 'social peace' by architectural means, doing this without undermining, but on the contrary, in affirming the fundamentals of capitalism."[45] Clearly, such a raison d'être of neighborhood unit theory could only be rejected by the Soviet architects. What is more interesting to determine is what critique was directed to strictly professional solutions to the neighborhood unit and what political vision could be identified within them.

One of the main theoretical concerns about the neighborhood unit principle was the disintegration of the city as a unified entity. The inability to introduce central planning under capitalism, paired with the boom in personal motor transport, according to Iokheles, led to the cutting up of the city into isolated islands separated by major motorways. He wrote:

> The characteristic trait of modern Anglo-American theories, different from our views, is the isolation of the *mikroraion*'s design and organization, which leads to disintegration of the city as a whole organism. The main reasons are: (a) the inability to regulate urban growth factors, typical of the capitalist economy, which influences the distribution of the population and its mobility [and] (b) hyper development of individual motor transport, which transforms city streets from the means of uniting the life of the city into zones of undivided dominance of the car, dividing the city into disconnected parts.[46]

Moreover, the neighborhood unit principle essentialized this division even further. In Soviet urban planning after the second urban-planning discussion of 1928–1931, urbanism—as opposed to disurbanism and decentralization—became a dominant principle. The architects underlined the unity of the socialist city and aimed to create its "big form." Thus application of the neighborhood unit principle posed a challenge to such a vision of the city. At the all-union meeting on low-rise construction in Tallinn in August 1946, the architects concluded that in Soviet urban planning a *mikroraion* should be considered "an integral part of the city organism."[47] The attempt of Western colleagues to "organize a *mikroraion* as a self-enclosed social, domestic, and territorial organism," according to Soviet planners, led to "isolation of the residents of the *mikroraion* from mass political and social life, from the common life of the city."[48] To ensure the connection of the *mikroraion* with the city, the Soviet architects suggested organizing a developed center in each *mikroraion* and linking it to the arterial streets connecting it to other parts of the city. In other words, in the Soviet version, the neighborhood unit, being an overall independent part, had to be thought through as an integral part of the whole.

The idea of bringing to the neighborhood all necessary domestic and social services—such as schools, kindergartens, grocery stores, a medical clinic, and other facilities that could serve the residents—was recognized as the most valuable contribution of neighborhood unit theory. It was also immediately claimed as originally Soviet. Indeed, the concept of large (укрупненные) blocks with the network of cultural and domestic services (сеть культурно-бытового обслуживания), propagated by the Soviet urbanists in the 1920s and developed in the early 1930s by Aleksei Galaktionov and Dmitrii Sobolev, became one of the core principles of socialist cities.[49] It was not widely applied in the 1930s and 1940s, however, due to the general lack of resources allocated for urban construction. In the 1940s supporters of *mikroraion* theory rejuvenated this idea and called for reintroducing it in urban-planning practice. In the context of the unfolding anti-Western campaign, the argument in favor of the *mikroraion* principle as originally Soviet also proved to be very useful. In his dissertation Iokheles argued that Western architects were guided in their work by the "progressive" methods developed in the Soviet Union: "It is significant that many prominent English and American architects rely on the methods developed by Soviet planners, which they consider to be the progressive basis for construction of the entire fabric of urban residential areas."[50] In particular, he supported this argument with the fact that in one of his articles Patrick Abercrombie used a scheme that was developed by Galaktionov and Sobolev and published the year before in the Soviet Union, which he called "Progressive unit planning."[51] In concluding remarks, Osterman also underlined that many of the principles discussed in the dissertation "are 'new' for domestic science only to a very relative degree."[52] Iokheles also stressed that his current work on *mikroraion* theory was a continuation of the earlier work of Soviet architects,

> who already in the beginning of the 1930s formulated the principles of designing residential quarters, which provide a comprehensive solution for the everyday needs of the residents, and who always underlined the priority of the city as a whole over the local interests of the quarters.[53]

Yet not everything good about neighborhood unit theory was of Soviet origin. All three researchers mentioned numerous practical solutions that they regarded as positive. They appraised the principle of mixed construction and simplification of fire-safety regulations. Osterman was particularly in favor of organizing the neighborhood unit interior as green space. They all embraced the provision of playgrounds and gardens within the neighborhood and the routing of heavy traffic away from the residential area as the key to success. All three agreed that decentralizing some public institutions—like libraries, clubs, and cinemas—by bringing them to each neighborhood was a positive idea that could reinforce the principle of the socialist city by providing a network of social and cultural services that had been neglected in the previous decade.

The research of Osterman, Iokheles, and Galaktionov demonstrates that at the beginning of the Cold War era Soviet architects were actively involved in the international exchange of professional knowledge. Moreover, the transfer of ideas went both ways, allowing Soviet architects to claim the role of leaders in progressive urban planning. Their critique of the neighborhood unit should thus not be dismissed as a cover-up of misplaced loyalty and must be read as part of a professional conversation across the Iron, or rather Nylon, Curtain.[54] Soviet architects had an ideal of urbanization in mind that was different from that of their Western colleagues, which sought to blend the neighborhood unit idea into the vision of a socialist modernity. The Soviet *mikroraion* theory developed by Galaktionov, Iokheles, and Osterman at the academy was not a sneaky appropriation of the Western principles dressed in anticapitalist critique but rather a result of critical engagement with international professional discourse on urban development. The *mikroraion* was imagined as a basic unit of the socialist city. Instead of being a tool of decentralization, it was conceived of by Soviet architects as a tool for controlling urban growth and ensuring the integration of the city as a unified whole. This research within the walls of the academy allowed them to articulate a new politics of urban development that was an alternative to both Stalin-era orthodoxy and capitalist modes of urban space production.

SAKB: A Municipal Lab for Experimentation and a Factory of Standard Designs

While the theory that informed Novye Cheremushki was developed at the Academy of Architecture, its design was created at the SAKB (Специальное Архитектурно-Конструкторское Бюро, or Special Architectural Design Bureau), established in July 1951 for the purpose of advancing standardization of mass construction.[55] Six weeks earlier, in June 1951, the Soviet Council of Ministers passed a decree that demanded the restructuring of planning organizations that so far had failed to supply builders with projects of high quality, had slowed down ongoing construction, and had not succeeded in decreasing the cost or improving the technology of mass construction. It also emphasized that Moscow planning organizations had failed to deliver designs of good quality. To address these problems, Mossovet (Moscow

Soviet of People's Deputies) decided, as part of a larger reorganization, to set up SAKB to

> develop standard designs for the construction of housing, schools, and hospitals, with the use of prefabricated elements, sections, and details, as well as to develop models and a catalog of building structures and building materials, details, and elements of building equipment.[56]

The ruling on the SAKB from 1951 also suggested the creation of a network of experimental laboratories for testing different materials and technological innovations. The mission of the SAKB was envisioned as speeding up the shift to standard design and prefabrication in mass construction. From the very beginning it enjoyed the status of a leading design bureau. In particular, the ruling on the SAKB recommended placing its employees on a payment grid on a par with other "leading planning organizations of the first (I) group."[57] In other words, the SAKB was established as the flagship of the modernization of mass construction and enjoyed a great deal of political support for its activities before the official turn to mass construction in 1954.

During its first years of activity, however, the Moscow press, including the newspaper *Moskovskii Stroitel'*, frequently reproached the SAKB for not fulfilling its purpose.[58] The journalists accused the leaders of the bureau, as well as authorities responsible for coordinating its activities, of failing to fulfill its plan and attempting to conceal the fact from the public. "The real picture of the bureau's progress—reported an article—is extremely unattractive and arouses legitimate alarm about the cause of standard design."[59] In September 1954 the leaders of the bureau, Rusiaev and Dorokhov, received a reprimand (*vygovor*) for their failure to organize efficient work at the SAKB.[60] In the first couple of years after its creation, the SAKB's main problem was indeed the lack of qualified specialists. In 1953, the positions of the director, chief architect, and chief engineer were still vacant.[61] At that time the SAKB employed sixty-five architects, including twenty-one women. One third of the architects were under thirty years old.[62] That was a rather modest size for an organization whose mission was to reorganize mass construction, even if only in Moscow. Consequently, the SAKB authorities made an effort to attract more specialists. In October 1953 Evgenii Iokheles was hired to head the SAKB studio and then promoted to the position of chief architect.[63] In March 1954 Natan Osterman was invited to head the studio of standard designs for low-rise housing and dachas.[64] Later that year, in October 1954, two months before the Convention of Construction Workers, another prominent specialist on housing, Mikhail Barshch, joined the ranks.[65] By mid-1950s the SAKB united under its roof a diverse group of enthusiasts for modern methods of mass construction, including Iokheles, Osterman, Mikhail Barshch, Sergei Liashchenko,[66] Georgii Pavlov, and many other young architects.[67] It was around this time and thanks to these new cadres that the SAKB finally became the "factory of standardized designs (*tipovoy proekt*)" that it was meant to be.[68]

The SAKB, however, continued to encounter difficulties promoting and experimenting with modern methods of mass construction even after 1954. Arguably, after Khrushchev's intervention at the Convention of Construction Workers in December 1954, its work should have been significantly facilitated. Created as a locomotive of mass construction for Moscow, the SAKB should have been the first beneficiary of the official turn to standardization and industrialization of mass construction. Indeed, already in February 1955 its key figures—including Iokheles, Osterman, and Liashchenko—promoted their approach to urban development in the press as the most effective method of creating comfortable living conditions and at the same time drastically reducing the costs of mass construction.[69] Yet one year after the reform the SAKB architects still reported obstacles:

> It seems that all the favorable conditions have been created for the execution of a rather worthwhile experiment. But no, nothing of the sort: up until now the APU (Архитектурно-планировочное управление, Architecture and Planning Department) has not solved the question of the exact site for construction, and the SAKB has not been able to get approval for the project from the head of the Mosproekt studio number ten comrade Mordvinov for a long time. He has refused to review the project and delays its implementation under various pretexts and meanwhile tries to promote without knowledge of the Council on Architecture and Construction, his own designs.... Despite the resolution of the Central Committee of KPSS and USSR Council of Ministers as of November 4, 1955, on adoption of standardized designs, Mordvinov designs individual projects for the construction of the quarter.[70]

Interestingly, it was the same Arkadii Mordvinov, the president of the Academy of Architecture, fiercely criticized by Khrushchev in the speech, who was still putting the obstacles on the way of the SAKB architects during 1955.[71] Officially Mordvinov remained in charge of construction in this area. Nevertheless, it was the SAKB architects who provided the designs for it.

On February 15, 1956, Moscow Gorispolkom, city executive committee, passed a directive that sanctioned construction of several living quarters in the former village Novye Cheremushki—in the South-Western margins of Moscow. It assigned the SAKB to develop the designs for the twelfth block and the ninth block by March 1, 1956, and March 20, 1956, respectively.[72] On February 29, 1956, the Council on Architecture and Construction of the APU approved the SAKB project for both blocks.[73] The council also noted that "the collective of authors at SAKB have accomplished important work of designing experimental housing with small-size apartments in a short period and of high quality."[74] They also acknowledged the contribution of the institute of housing of the Academy of Architecture in designing small apartments. In this way the council recognized research work carried out at the academy as one of the key contributions to quickly evolving mass construction under Khrushchev. A decree of April 20, 1956, by MGK KPSS, Moscow city committee of the Communist Party, further specified the goals of the construction in Cheremushki. It declared the ninth block as an experimental site for testing "new economical designs for housing, choosing more efficacious types of apartments and new types of materials."[75] The decree suggested that all the work should be accomplished by June 1957.[76] These regulations demonstrate that Novye Cheremushki and the ninth block in particular were assigned to be the testing ground for a new approach to Soviet mass construction. Just as the SAKB was envisioned as the flagship of modernization of mass construction, so the ninth block was imagined by architects and bureaucrats as the laboratory for a new approach to housing. The architects in charge of this experiment were those who undertook research on this topic at the Academy of Architecture. It is noteworthy that the state not only supported fundamental research on housing but also encouraged experimentation as a necessary element of architectural work on resolving the housing question.

The Ninth Block: The State Embraces Research and Experimentation

The "firstborn of Novye Cheremushki" designed at SAKB was the residential twelfth block.[77] It was completed as scheduled in 1957. It consisted of large-block apartment buildings, a school, and a kindergarten. The report on the activities of the SAKB written in 1961 described the achievement of the twelfth block: "In contrast to the Leningrad city experience, in which the architecture of large-block buildings completely replicated traditional classical forms, the construction of this block allowed for the testing of new architectural forms."[78] Nevertheless, the apartments were still designed for so-called *pokomnatnoe zaselenie* (one family per room distribution), which would become history in a year's time, when the ninth block would be built. The twelve-hectare experimental ninth block was fully finished in 1958–1959. According to the report,

> Here, free layout and construction according to the principles of *mikroraion* were tested for the first time; different types of single-family apartments were tried; construction of stand-alone stores was tried; on top of that, testing was initiated of different methods of construction, materials, and engineering equipment that were progressive for the time.[79]

To sum up, in blocks nine and twelve the architects of SAKB introduced a new style of architecture and new approaches to urban planning and interior design, tested new standard designs and building techniques, and prepared for a new distribution policy.

The design of the experimental ninth block initially provided for fourteen residential buildings of different types, mostly four-story. In 1958 three eight-story buildings were added to the plan (though earlier schemes specified only one). The layout of the block also included a school, a kindergarten, a day-care center, two food shops, a general store, a cafeteria, a telephone exchange, and a consumer services building, including a "red corner," a room or part of it set with communist attributes, and the building management office, or *domoupravlenie*. A parking garage was eventually replaced by a cinema.[80] Special attention was paid in the plan to the organization of children's playgrounds, gardens, and the interior of the neighborhood in general. The beautification of the neighborhood (the arrangement of green spaces and small architectural forms such as benches, a pond, entrance equipment, summerhouses, and planters) was an integral part of the design. Instead of conventional perimeter-block composition, the architects used a free layout (Figure 4.3).

For the housing of the ninth block the architects of SAKB sorted out fourteen plans from more than 200 standard designs developed in the 1940s at the academy, the studios of Mossovet, and the architecture studios in the Soviet republics. All apartments were small single-family apartments but differed in numerous technical aspects, including the height of the ceilings and window parameters, the location of the bathroom, and the room layouts. Most of them provided modern bathroom and kitchen equipment. Some were stocked with compact modular furniture.

The design of Novye Cheremushki, as well as the numerous articles explaining its main achievements that were authored by Cheremushki architects and other specialists and journalists, shows that the experimental ninth block encapsulated research carried out at the academy in the 1940s. The publications by the authors of the project demonstrate that they sharpened some of their positions from the earlier period.[81] This became possible due to the official turn in architecture in 1954 and a general warming of the political climate. For instance, it became fully legitimate to criticize decoration in architecture. Reliance in their work on the Western experience turned out to be an advantage. The authors, as well as reporters, readily mentioned that this project grew out of an examination of Western construction. There was nothing anti-Soviet after 1954 in the image of the architecture bureau where "drawing boards were piled high with mountains of domestic and foreign architecture journals."[82] This, apparently, was what the working space of modern architects engaged in experimental construction should look like.

Most of the articles, especially those written by the authors, began by opposing the free layout of the experimental ninth block to perimeter-block construction. The relief of the construction site was preserved, whereas perimeter-block construction along the red line often required the leveling of the relief. The buildings facing the arterial street were set back from the street with an eight-meter line of greenery. Thus, they were separated from the noise of street traffic, and the green zone diversified the streetscape. This image of the street was contrasted with the monotonous streetscape of

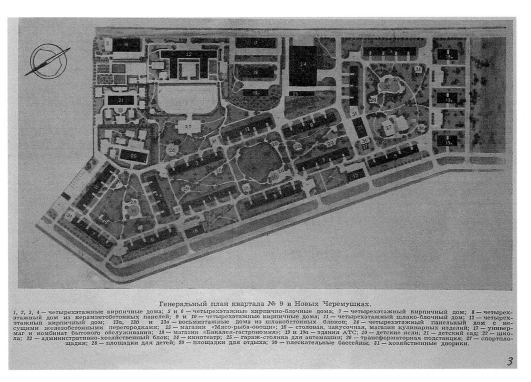

Генеральный план квартала № 9 в Новых Черемушках.

1, 2, 3, 4 — четырехэтажные кирпичные дома; *5 и 6* — четырехэтажные кирпично-блочные дома; *7* — четырехэтажный кирпичный дом; *8* — четырехэтажный дом из керамзитобетонных панелей; *9 и 10* — четырехэтажные кирпичные дома; *11* — четырехэтажный шлако-блочный дом; *12* — четырехэтажный кирпичный дом; *13a, 13б* и *13в* — восьмиэтажные дома из шлакобетонных блоков; *14* — четырехэтажный панельный дом с несущими железобетонными перегородками; *15* — магазин «Мясо-рыба-овощи»; *16* — столовая, закусочная, магазин кулинарных изделий; *17* — универмаг и комбинат бытового обслуживания; *18* — магазин «Бакалея-гастрономия»; *19 и 19a* — здания АТС; *20* — детские ясли; *21* — детский сад; *22* — школа; *23* — административно-хозяйственный блок; *24* — кинотеатр; *25* — гараж-стоянка для автомашин; *26* — трансформаторная подстанция; *27* — спортплощадки; *28* — площадки для детей; *29* — площадки для отдыха; *30* — плескательные бассейны; *31* — хозяйственные дворики.

Figure 4.3 The general plan of the ninth block. Source: *Arkhitektura*, **no.** 10-12 (1957). 1, 2, 3, 4: four-story brick apartment buildings; 5 and 6: four-story brick and block apartment buildings; 7: four-story brick apartment building; 8: four-story apartment building from lightweight clay-concrete panels; 9 and 10: four-story brick apartment buildings; 11: four-story cinder-block apartment building; 12: four-story brick apartment building; 13a, 13b, 13c: eight-story cinder-block apartment buildings; 14: four-story panel house with load-bearing reinforced concrete partitions; 15: shop for meat, fish, and vegetables; 16: canteen, snackbar, delicatessen; 17: department store and factory of household services; 18: grocery shop; 19 and 19a: automatic telephone station building; 20: crèche; 21: kindergarten, 22: school; 23: administrative block; 24: cinema; 25: parking garage; 26: transformer station; 27: sports field; 28: playgrounds for children; 29: rest area; 30: splash pools; 31: household yards.

lined-up buildings in perimeter-block construction. The neighborhood was zoned into public and residential areas. The public sector included a school, a kindergarten, and two stores, whereas the buildings of the residential zone were organized around three spacious green yards. This composition allowed architects to combine the "picturesqueness" of the free layout with the elements of a regular plan.

One of the new arguments in favor of free layout used by the architects was that it alleviated adoption of the standardized designs and reduced the number of different designs needed for the construction of the block. For instance, there was no need for the corner sections that had to be designed for each perimeter block:

> Using economical buildings of simple configuration without corner sections in no way impoverished the composition. It appeared that in the case of ensemble design of the block, relative simplicity of standardized buildings is compensated for a hundredfold by amplification of the construction plasticity in general. The architecture of a freestanding building ceases being self-contained, becomes an organic part of the ensemble.[83]

In line with this argument the authors repeated their old belief that residential architecture should not be grandiose. And there was no need for the ornate decoration of the facades that architects used in perimeter-block construction. It was not the surface of the facade that defined the look of the street or a quarter but the play of the volumes in the space of the entire neighborhood:

> Construction of blocks relying on two to three rectangular buildings and their combination will not lead to the lowering of the artistic quality of the ensemble; on the contrary, it will make us use volume-space composition, which is known to be the simplest and the most effective means of architectural expressiveness.[84]

According to the authors of the project, carefully designed details could provide distinctive features. For instance, they proposed to pay special attention to the entrances. Osterman also stressed that balconies cannot be used exclusively as a "compositional patch," as a decorative element of the housing facade, but must serve their function. In the ninth block all apartments starting from the second floor were designed with balconies. Each balcony was equipped with flower boxes, and colorful paint was applied to the railings. These little details were supposed to give a "stylish" look to the facades (Figure 4.4).

The neighborhood layout was designed in accordance with the major principles of mikroraion theory. Heavy traffic was routed away from the block, and the arterial streets served as a border to the quarter.[85] Within the neighborhood several children's playgrounds, athletic fields, and gardens were planned. The ninth block had a developed network of domestic and cultural services, all provided within easy reach of home.[86] The shops were designed as separate structures, as opposed to the construction of stores on the ground floor of perimeter-block buildings.

Special attention in the ninth block was paid to the organization and landscaping of the neighborhood. Osterman's earlier admiration for

Жилой четырехэтажный дом со стенами из крупных кирпичных блоков и шлакобетонными перемычками.

Figure 4.4 A four-story apartment building with enlarged brick blocks and clay-concrete connectors. Source: *Arkhitektura*, no. 10–12 (1957).

landscape gardening in neighborhood unit design, described in his dissertation, proved to be crucial for the Cheremushki design. In his article he stressed that earlier architects had not paid enough attention to this "fifth facade," whereas a "beautiful and functionally apt" solution for the interior of the neighborhood can improve the appearance of the ensemble significantly. "In addition, the funds needed for this are not only much less than the funds required for fake decoration of the facades, but they also allow for improvement in living conditions" (Figures 4.5 and 4.6).[87]

The architects of Cheremushki argued that such an approach to mass housing construction and neighborhood design allowed Soviet architects to adopt standardized design widely, cut the costs of construction, and created a truly comfortable living environment for Soviet citizens. The post–World War II leitmotif of creating comfortable, unadorned housing that guided their research work at the Academy of Architecture in the 1940s resurfaced as the main driving force for their designs in the 1950s.

Finally, the Cheremushki experimental project was embraced by the state as a showcase for a new approach to mass housing construction. For

Figure 4.5 Landscaping between residential buildings. Novye Cheremushki. 1964. Source: John Reps Papers, #15-2-1101. Division of Rare and Manuscript Collections, Cornell University Library.

Figure 4.6 View of the ninth block. Source *Arkhitektura*, **no.** 10-12 (1957)

the next ten years numerous foreign delegations of specialists and nonspecialists were invited to visit the block.[88] Apart from wide coverage in the Soviet press, the project appeared on the pages of international publications.[89] The general public and the residents were summoned to discuss the advantages and disadvantages of the different apartment layouts. Even before the architects of Cheremushki wrote the report summarizing critiques and formulating proposals for future construction and preferred apartment designs, the design, planning, and construction solutions used in Cheremushki had been widely acclaimed as the model for construction across the Soviet Union.[90]

∗∗∗

In its simplest form, the story of developing Novye Cheremushki is the story of inventing a model for socialist housing in the Soviet Union, called here socialist modern.[91] It allows us to grasp the institutional and discursive practices that shaped the architecture profession's approach to housing, and the state-led project of modernization and building socialist society through the provision of housing and forging a new mode of life. The model devised for Novye Cheremushki might not have offered the ultimate solution to the housing question, nor was it unique in its technological, political, or architectural aspects, but the nexus of institutions and forms of knowledge that produced it deserve closer scrutiny today as we again seek to resolve a housing crisis.

Novye Cheremushki, as a model and a theory, was the result of sustained collective research and experimental work carried out over the course of at least two decades and aimed at reorganizing the totality of building-industry and urban-planning policies. This research was facilitated by the alignment of the strategic priorities of the professional and ideological forces and was aimed at redefining the spatial and social aspects of a new mode of life. The Academy of Architecture—as a state-funded research powerhouse—and SAKB—as a municipal lab for experimental design—were essential support structures for revolutionizing building practice. Remarkably, they supported fundamental research aimed at resolving the housing crisis even at a time when the state could not allocate resources for housing construction.

This research and experimental work was also impressively cosmopolitan in its outlook. Not only did Soviet architects actively partake in the international knowledge exchange despite Cold War isolationism, but they also aspired to contribute to its debates. They sought to formulate a progressive approach to urban planning that challenged the conventions of capitalist space production across the globe. The Cheremushki model and the *mikroraion* theory that informed it should therefore not be read simply as a solution worked out for the Soviet Union. It was a solution with global ambition that was successfully translated and adapted at least across the Second World. After the end of the Cold War era of competing universalisms, this model and the history of its invention were archived in the box of failed socialisms. By unpacking that box today, this chapter proposes to deprovincialize the institutional knowledge and urban theory of the Soviet Union and transform it into a resource for thinking about new institutional and theoretical frameworks for resolving the housing crisis.

Notes

1 According to official statistics, more than 140,900,000 individuals moved into newly built housing between 1959 and 1974. See the data presented in Steven E. Harris, *Communism on Tomorrow Street: Mass Housing and Everyday Life after Stalin* (Washington, DC; Baltimore, MD: Woodrow Wilson Center Press; The Johns Hopkins University Press, 2013), 5. According to the all-union population census conducted in January 1979, the population of the Soviet Union was 262,442,000. See http://soviethistory.msu.edu/1980-2/sixth-all-union-census/sixth-all-union-census-texts/on-preliminary-results-of-the-1979-census/. For an overview of the dynamics of the allocation of housing in the Soviet Union between 1953 and 1990, see Michael Gentile and Örjan Sjöberg, "Housing Allocation Under Socialism: The Soviet Case Revisited," *Post-Soviet Affairs* 29, no. 2 (2013): 173–195.

2 Mark Smith, *Property of Communists: The Urban Housing Program from Stalin to Khrushchev* (DeKalb: Northern Illinois University Press, 2010); Iu.L. Kosenkova, *Sovetskii Gorod 1940kh-Pervoy Poloviny 1950kh Godov: Ot Tvorcheskikh Poiskov K Praktike Stroitelstva*, 2nd ed. (Moskva: Librokom, 2009); Harris, *Communism on Tomorrow Street*.

3 Ninth block here is a translation of *deviatyi kvartal*, which could also be translated as ninth district or ninth residential quarter. In Soviet architectural discourse the term *kvartal* was the designation for the planning unit of a neighborhood. Planning solutions for such units evolved in the 1940s and 1950s from a more conventional *kvartal* of perimeter-block structures to the free layout of the *mikroraion*. Iulia Kosenkova dated the first mention of the word *mikroraion* to 1945, when the "Contest on experimental projects for a residential city *mikroraion*" was announced. Kosenkova, *Sovetskii gorod*, 46–47. Mark Smith dates the first published reference to *mikroraion* to 1957. Mark Smith, *Property of Communists: The Urban Housing Program from Stalin to Khrushchev*, 46. In the 1940s and 1950s these terms were often used interchangeably and coexisted in the discourse on the reconstruction of Soviet cities.

4 Michael Gentile and Örjan Sjöberg describe the outcomes of this mass construction campaign as the creation of landscapes of priority. Gentile and Sjöberg, "Intra-Urban Landscapes of Priority: The Soviet Legacy," 701–729.

5 On the discursive production of housing, see Varga-Harris, Christine. *Stories of House and Home Soviet Apartment Life during the Khrushchev Years* (Ithaca, N.Y: Cornell University Press, 2015). Susan Reid, "Communist Comfort: Socialist Modernism and the Making of Cosy Homes in the Khrushchev-Era Soviet Union," *Gender and History* 21, no. 3 (2009): 465–498. Susan Reid, "Makeshift Modernity: DIY, Craft and the Virtuous Homemaker in New Soviet Housing of the 1960s," *International Journal for History, Culture and Modernity* 2, no. 2 (2014): 87–124.

6 Susan Reid introduced this term in 2006.

> Considered from the perspective of ordinary people's everyday experience and material culture, the Khrushchev era represented a great but uneven leap forward in creating the basis for a modern way of everyday life and a radical stylistic reorientation in domestic spaces and the visual appearance of cities towards a new aesthetic of socialist modernism, called here Khrushchev Modern.

> See Reid, Susan E. "Khrushchev Modern: Agency and Modernization in the Soviet Home." *Cahiers du monde russe* 47, no. 1 (2006), 227–268. I will use throughout this paper the term *socialist modern*, which shifts attention from the role of Khrushchev in this stylistic reorientation toward professionals' and

citizens' engagement with the promise of socialism. For a comparable use of this term, see Betts, Paul, and Katherine Pence, ed. *Socialist Modern: East German Everyday Culture and Politics* (Ann Arbor: University of Michigan Press, 2007).

7 Andrew Day, "Building Socialism: The Politics of the Soviet Cityscape in the Stalin Era" (PhD Dissertation, Columbia University, 1998), 248.

8 Khrushchev, N.S. "O shirokom vnedrenii industrialnykh metodov, uluchshenii kachestva i snizhenii stoimosti stroitel'stva." *Moskovskii Stroitel'*, 28 décembre 1954.

9 "Rech' Tov. Gradova G.A. na Vsesousnom Soveshchanii Stroiteley," *Stroitel'naia Gazeta*, December 3, 1954. 152.

10 For a detailed description of the research fields and different research institutes that functioned within the academy, see Iu.L. Kosenkova, "Akademicheskie Nauka i Obrazovanie v Istorii Sovetskoy Arkhitektury (1922–1963)," in *Rossiiskaia Akademia Arkhitektury i Stroitelnykh Nauk, Albom Tvorcheskikh Rabot Chlenov Akademii i Sovetnikov 2001–2006 Gg., Posviashchenny 15-letiu RAASN* (Moskva, 2007).

11 Branko Mitrovic, "Studying Renaissance Architectural Theory in the Age of Stalinism," *I Tatti Studies in the Italian Renaissance* 12 (2009), 233–263.

12 Clark, Katerina. *Moscow, the Fourth Rome: Stalinism, Cosmopolitanism, and the Evolution of Soviet Culture, 1931–1941* (Cambridge, MA: Harvard University Press, 2011).

13 "V TsK VKP(b) Ob Arkhitekturnom Obrazovanii," *Pravda*, October 18, 1933. See more on its history in Kosenkova, "Akademicheskie Nauka i Obrazovanie v Istorii Sovetskoy Arkhitektury (1922–1963)."

14 See the recollections of Stepan Satunts in A. Burov, *Pisma. Dnevniki. Besedy s Aspirantami. Sujdenia Sovremennikov* (Moscow: Iskusstvo, 1980), 225 or the remarks of Gennadyi Movchan in Movchan, "O Sebe i Svoikh Rabotakh," 124.

15 Harris refers to this research initiative in his discussion of the Stalinist origins of *khrushchevka* design. Harris, *Communism on Tomorrow Street*, 85–93. See also, for instance, the proposal of the Academy of Architecture "on industrialization and the introduction of new engineering equipment in housing and civil construction for the five-year plan of 1951–1955," passed in 1952, which called for studying postwar construction experience in the USSR in order to develop improved designs and catalogs of standardized building elements. RGAE (Russian State Archive of the Economy), f.293, op. 1, d. 483.

16 The materials on the discussion about the *mikroraion* can be found in RGAE. f. 9432, op.1, d. 194. These materials are cited in: Kosenkova, *Sovetskii gorod*, 46–47. Smith, Property of Communists, 46–47.

17 For a short biographical sketch, see A. Petrushkova and Ia. Dikhter, "Romantik i Praktik Realnoy Arkhitektury," *Arkhitektura i Stroitelstvo Moskvy* no. 6 (1999): 8–12.

18 Not to be confused with Pavel Blokhin, who also worked on standardized designs in the 1930s and 1940s. Boris Blokhin was a student of the prominent Russian architect and engineer Aleksandr Kuznetsov. Later at the MARKhI he taught courses on building materials and other aspects of engineering in architecture. Blokhin B. Burov A., *Opyt Skorostnogo Krupnoblochnogo Stroitelstva Zhilykh Domov Mossoveta* (Moscow, 1939).

19 For a short biographical sketch, see M. Lipovetskaia, "Evgenii Lvovich Iokheles," *Arkhitektura i Stroitelstvo Moskvy* no. 2 (1998): 8–12. For more on the ARU (Union of Architects and Urbanists), one of the organizations of Soviet rationalists, and its projects, see Khan-Magomedov, *Arkhitektura Sovetskogo Avangarda: Sotsialnye problemy* (Moscow: Stroiizdat, 1996), Chapter

2, http://www.alyoshin.ru/Files/publika/khan_archi/khan_archi_2_053.html or in Selim Khan Magomedov, *Nikolai Ladovsky* (Moscow: Arkhitektura-C, 2007).

20 For more on the Giprogor and its work, see Kazus, *Sovetskaia Arkhitektura 1920-kh Godov*, 154.

21 If asked which school he belonged to, he answered that he belonged to his own school. But, he stated, "if it is necessary to belong to someone, then I am closer to Vesnin." Burov, *Pisma. Dnevniki. Besedy s Aspirantami. Sujdenia Sovremennikov*, 240.

22 P. Blokhin and A. Zaltsman, "O Tipovykh Proektakh Zhilykh Sektsii Dlia Massovogo Stroitelstva 1939 Goda," *Arkhitektura SSSR* no. 2 (1939): 29–41. P. Blokhin and A. Zaltsman, "Tipy Zhilykh Domov i Problema Malometrazhnoi Kvartiry," *Arkhitektura SSSR* no. 3 (1940): 4–6. P. Blokhin and A. Zaltsman, "Novoie v Typovom Proektirovanii Zhilia," *Arkhitektura SSSR* no. 4 (1941): 30–35. A. Zaltsman, *Zhilishnoe Striotelstvo v SSSR* (Moskva, 1962).

23 Sergei Barkhin, "O Zvezde, Geroie, Uchitele—Andree Konstantinoviche Burove," in *MARKHI XX Vek: Sbornik Vospominanyi v Piati Tomakh*, vol. 3 (Moscow: Moskovskyi arkhitekturnyi institut, Salon-press, 2001), 216.

24 Burov, *Pisma. Dnevniki. Besedy s Aspirantami. Sujdenia Sovremennikov*, 240.

25 Ibid., 229, 230, 248, 252.

26 RGALI (Russian State Archive of Literature and Arts), f. 674, op. 2, d. 109, cited in Kosenkova, *Sovetskii gorod*, 32.

27 RGAE, f.293, op. 3, d.104, l.4. His dissertation, titled "On Certain Questions of the Design of Residential Quarters of Soviet Cities," was completed in 1946 and was not defended.

28 RGAE, f. 293, op. 3, d. 104, l. 4; RGAE, f.293, op.3, d. 232, l. 13.

29 RGAE, f.293, op. 3, d.104, l.38.

30 On the myth of the plan in Soviet urbanism, see Elam Day "Building Socialism," 109–113.

31 RGAE, f.293, op. 3, d.104, l.52-55.

32 RGAE, f.293, op. 3, d.232 l.191.

33 RGAE, f.293, op. 3, d.232 l.218.

34 V. Baburov and A. Galaktionov, "Zastroika i Blagoustroistvo Zhilykh Raionov," *Arkhitektura SSSR* no. 3 (1954): 3. In RGAE, f.293, op.3, d. 55, l.111.

35 Ibid.

36 Paul Betts and Crowley, David, eds. "Special Issue: Domestic Dreamworlds: Notions of Home in Post-1945 Europe," *Journal of Contemporary History* 40, no. 2 (2005): 123.

37 Peter Geoffrey Hall, *Cities of Tomorrow: An Intellectual History of Urban Planning and Design in the Twentieth Century* (Oxford: Basil Blackwell, 1990). Lewis Mumford, "The Neighborhood and the Neighborhood Unit," *The Town Planning Review* 24, no. 4 (1954): 256–270.

38 David A. Johnson, *Planning the Great Metropolis: The 1929 Regional Plan of New York and Its Environs*, vol. 1st, Studies in History, Planning and the Environment 18 (London; New York: E & FN Spon, 1996).

39 Philip Opher, *Architecture and Urban Design in Six British New Towns* (Headington, Oxfordshire: Urban Design Oxford Polytechnic, 1981).

40 Mumford, "The Neighborhood and the Neighborhood Unit," 266.

41 RGAE, f.293, op. 3, d.232 l.6.

42 RGAE, f.293, op. 3, d.104, l. 28.

43 Bylinkin, "Gradostroitelnyie Utopii Zapadnykh Arkhitektorov," 14.

44 RGAE, f.293, op. 3, d.232 l.7.

45 RGAE, f.293, op. 3, d.232 l.31 l.31.

46 RGAE, f.293, op. 3, d.104, l.35.

47 RGALI, f. 674, op.2, d. 160.

48 Ibid. also cited in Kosenkova, *Sovetskii gorod*, 47.

49 See, for example, the decree of the Central Committee that approved the design of a developed network of services, which is also known for bringing the urbanist-disurbanist debate to a close. "Postanovlenie TsK VKP(b) o Rabote Po Perestroike Byta," *Pravda*, May 29, 1930.

50 RGAE, f.293, op. 3, d.104, l. 6.

51 Patrick Abercrombie, "Slum Clearance and Planning: The Re-modeling of Towns and Their External Growth," *The Town Planning Review* 16, no. 3 (1935), 207.

52 RGAE, f.293, op.3, d.232. l.291.

53 RGAE, f.293, op. 3, d.104, l. 63.

54 This metaphor was introduced to better grasp "the economic, cultural, and political inter-penetration between East and West during the Cold War," see György Péteri, *Nylon Curtain: Transnational and Transsystemic Tendencies in the Cultural Life of State-Socialist Russia and East-Central Europe* (Trondheim: Program on East European Cultures and Societies, 2006).

55 "Pokazatelnoe Stroitelstvo v Novykh Cheriomushkakh." The list of authors was described as following: design instructions for housing and the neighborhood scheme are developed by studio no. 6 and no. 8 (headed by N. Osterman and S. Liashchenko) with the participation of studio no. 1, no. 2, no. 5, no. 7 (headed by V. Sergeev, E. Iokheles, I. Kastel, M. Barshch). The authors include the architects G. Pavlov, V. Kalafatov, V. Svirskii, M. Fradkin, G. Kurshanova, V. Nudelman, O. Goriachev, O. Subotin, Ia. Dobkin, A. Shapiro, Iu. Bocharov, E. Demchenko, P. Chechaev, N. Kornilova, G. Karlsen, V. Chernolusskii, I. Gohblit, V. Kuzmin, A. Petrushkova, K Blomerius, S. Arnauskas, and others; the engineers V. Shapiro, L. Shilina, Iu. Buyanova, F. Itsigson, and others.

56 TsAGM (Central Archive of Moscow City), f. 321, op. 1, d. 1, l. 2.

57 TsAGM, f. 321, op. 1, d. 1, l. 4.

58 Lashin, "Pochemu Net Tipovykh Proektov? SAKB Rabotaet Plokho." Or see Nikiforov, "Kogda Zhe Poiaviatsia Kachestvennyie Tipovyie Proiekty?"

59 Lashin, "Pochemu Net Tipovykh Proektov? SAKB Rabotaet Plokho."

60 See "Directive issued on 10.09.1954 on the breach, undermining of the pace of standardization of design" in TsAGM, f. 321, op. 1, d. 25, l. 49.

61 TsAGM, f. 321, op. 1, d. 8, l. 1.

62 TsAGM, f. 321, op. 1, d. 8, l. 4.

63 TsAGM, f. 321, op. 1, d. 25, l. 30.

64 TsAGM, f. 321, op. 1, d. 25, l. 1.

65 TsAGM, f. 321, op. 1, d. 51 , l. 3.

66 Sergei Liashchenko was admitted to the academy as a graduate student in 1932 and in 1934 he worked with Aleksandr and Viktor Vesnin on the project of Narkomtiazhprom. Some of his biographical details hint at his interest in progressive urban planning and explain why he became an important member of the SAKB bureau. Further research on this architect is needed.

67 "Pokazatelnoe Stroitelstvo v Novykh Cheriomushkakh." Among other "enthusiasts of standardization of design" the article mentions the architects Suris, Kapustina, and Dorokhov as well as "aspiring architectural youth."

68 Lashin, "Pochemu Net Tipovykh Proektov? SAKB Rabotaet Plokho." The second big "factory of standardised designs" was TsNIIEP (Центральный Научно-Исследовательский Институт Экспериментального Проектирования жилища, Central Institute of Research and Experimental Design of housing), headed by Boris Rubanenko and tasked with developing type designs for the

Soviet Union. SAKB and TSNIIIEP worked together closely. See Petrushkova and Dikhter, "Romantik i Praktik Realnoy Arkhitektury."

69 E. Iokheles, S. Liashchenko, and N. Osterman, "Po-novomu Reshat Voprosy Gradostroitelstva," *Moskovskyi Stroitel'*, February 1, 1955.

70 "Buianov Iu., Itsigson F., Liashchenko S., Mazur M., Nudelman V., Osterman N., Raikhenberg S., Svirskyi V.—Arkhitektory i Inzhenery SAKB. Kvartal Iz Krupnoblochnykh Domov," *Moskovskyi Stroitel'*, January 17, 1956.

71 A. Mordvinov was in charge of the construction of some streets in the southwestern district starting in 1939, when he designed Bolshaia Koluzhskaia Street, one of the main streets of the district.

72 TsAGM, f. 321, op. 1, d. 56, l. 67.

73 TsAGM, f. 534, op. 1, d. 321, l.58.

74 TsAGM, f. 534, op. 1, d. 321, l.60.

75 TsAGM, f. 321, op. 1, d. 56 , l. 90.

76 TsAGM, f. 321, op. 1, d. 56 , l. 91.

77 Petrushkova and Dikhter, "Romantik i Praktik Realnoy Arkhitektury," 10.

78 TsAGM, f. 321, op. 1, d. 156 , l.1.

79 TsAGM, f. 321, op. 1, d. 156 , l.1-2.

80 On the role of Ekaterina Furtseva in that change, see Timothy J. Colton, *Moscow: Governing the Socialist Metropolis* (Cambridge: The Belknap Press of Harvard University Press, 1995), 428.

81 Iokheles, Liashchenko, and Osterman, "Po-novomu Reshat Voprosy Gradostroitelstva." G. Pavlov and V Svirskii, "Opytnaia Zastroika Zhilogo Kvartala v Iugo-zapadnom Raione Moskvy," *Arkhitektura SSSR* 7 (1956): 21–26. N. Osterman, "Ob Udobstve, Krasote i Ekonomichnosti," *Stroitel'naia Gazeta*, July 16, 1958.

82 Golodnyi, "Kvartal Eksperimentov."

83 Osterman, "Ob Udobstve, Krasote i Ekonomichnosti."

84 Iokheles, Liashchenko, and Osterman, "Po-novomu Reshat Voprosy Gradostroitelstva."

85 Pavlov and Svirskii, "Opytnaia Zastroika Zhilogo Kvartala v Iugo-zapadnom Raione Moskvy." "Pokazatelnoe Stroitelstvo v Novykh Cheriomushkakh."

86 Compare this with what Baburov and Galaktionov in the previous year propagated as the major principles of the construction of residential quarters (*kvartals*): "When analyzing housing in large cities close to highways with heavy traffic, the placement of the facilities servicing urban populations should be carefully considered. For instance, it is important to provide enough schools for residential areas in the territory bordered by highways and place them in such a manner that children are not obliged to cross highways. It is also important to situate gardens with athletic fields within the limits of quarters. A garden with a club or a cinema, a library, a department store, a grocery store, a restaurant, and a post office—this is the minimal variety of public use buildings that should make up local centers." Baburov and Galaktionov, "Zastroika i Blagoustroistvo Zhilykh Raionov," 3.

87 Osterman, "Ob Udobstve, Krasote i Ekonomichnosti." For a more detailed discussion of the relationship between architecture and landscaping in the socialist city, see Crawford, Christina E. "The Case to Save Socialist Space," in *Routledge Research Companion to Landscape Architecture*, eds. Ellen Braae and Henriette Steiner (London: Routledge, 2019), 260–273.

88 RGALI, f. 674, op. 3, d. 1664.

89 Among the periodicals that published materials on Cheremushki were such journals as *Architecture d'Aujourd'hui* (1958, IX, 79), *Architect's Journal* (1958, 10), *Architecture and Building* (1958, 10), *Tribuna Ruda* (1958, 222),

Architectura (Poland, 1958, 6), *Xchevao* (China, 1958, 9), *Deutsche Architectur* (GDR, 1958, 9).

90 "Pokazatelnoe Stroitelstvo v Novykh Cheriomushkakh." "Po Vsey Strane Sovetskoy Stroitelstvo Idet." L. Rozova, "Saratovskie Cheremushki," *Stroitel'naia Gazeta*, March 4, 1959. V. Ivanitskyi, "Zhilishchnoie Stroitelstvo v Polshe," *Stroitelnaia Gazeta*, October 31, 1958. D. Iageman, "Desiat' Chekhoslovatskikh Cheriomushek," *Stroitel'naia Gazeta*, December 7, 1962.

91 On the diversity of socialist modern, see Daria Bocharnikova and Andres Kurg, "Introduction: Urban Planning and Architecture of Late Socialism," *The Journal of Architecture* 24, no. 5 (2019): 593–603.

5 "Production First, Living Second"

Welfare Housing and Social Transition in China

Samuel Y. Liang

As they rebuilt China after the devastating Japanese invasion (1937–1945) and the civil war (1945–1949), the leaders of the Chinese Communist Party (CCP) considered modern architecture to be a manifestation of capitalist ideology. Urbanization and urban construction played a marginal role in their revolutionary agenda.

Although the new regime relied on a few architects (some of whom had been trained in Europe or North America) in carrying out a number of showcase urban reconstruction projects, the lack of reinvestment in urban infrastructure and housing caused slow urban growth, the deterioration of old neighborhoods, and appalling housing shortages during the socialist period of the Peoples' Republic (1949–1979).

The urban housing problem worsened in the major cities as the revolutionary regime (dominated by the Maoist faction of the CCP leadership) adopted a variety of urban policies that attempted to eliminate the established urban tradition, especially the urban rich and bourgeois consumerism. This government approach reflected what scholars call Maoist antiurban politics.[1] The CCP had led a revolutionary movement of military struggles based in rural China; most CCP leaders came from hinterland rural families and had conducted military campaigns in remote bases for years before their armies captured the nation's major urban centers around 1949. Moving into the cities, they were wary of the urban bourgeoisie and their "corruptive" culture and did not even trust the urban working class to be loyal to the new regime, probably because of their memory of the CCP's utter failure in organizing urban revolution two decades earlier.

The regime's housing policies reflected its distrust of the urban working class, which had emerged in industrial cities such as Shanghai before the revolution: On the one hand, the regime sought to showcase improved living conditions for the working class by constructing a limited number of model housing projects; on the other, centralized economic planning prioritized industrial investment and neglected reinvestment in urban housing. The latter policy was often promoted with the slogan "Production first, living second."

DOI: 10.4324/9781351182966-8

In order to advance the national agenda of industrialization, the regime recruited new workers from rural villages, and this caused the urban population to grow rapidly in the first decade of the socialist period. The CCP advocated the traditional frugal lifestyle of villagers and urged socialist workers (most of whom had just migrated to the cities) to sacrifice private family life for the sake of contributing to the nation's industrialization. The state-led industrialization program suppressed the workers' private lives and consumerism, and it should be regarded as having exploited workers in order to accumulate industrial wealth in the public sector.[2]

In fact, the notion of the urban home as a comfortable private retreat was believed to reflect bourgeois values. The regime instead promoted the idea of the collective home for socialist workers. This collective home was an ideological construct (i.e., the imagined national space), and its best physical manifestation was probably the work-unit compound in which the employees worked as well as dwelled. Socialist urbanization advanced through the construction of a great number of work units under centralized economic planning and financing; in the process local authorities provided the work units with free land (usually acquired from rural villages located next to established urban centers) for construction. The work units were then built as walled compounds and functioned as self-sufficient economic entities separated from the preexisting urban fabric; this fragmented urban geography demonstrated a dichotomy of "revolutionary space" and old urban space, and managing the former was the state's priority and reflected the Maoist antiurban politics mentioned above.

The work units consisted of government functionaries and state-owned enterprises (mostly factories); they provided their members not only with employment but also with free (or low-rent) housing and other essential services (such as medical care and childcare) as social benefits of employment. Some work units offered better benefits than others, while urban residents outside the work-unit system did not get any welfare benefits from the state. Work-unit housing was then called *gongfang* (public housing), to be differentiated from *sifang* (privately owned housing) outside the work-unit system. Later, in the early reform and postsocialist periods (1980–1992 and 1993–present, respectively), the urban housing reforms introduced *shangpingfang* (commodity housing), real estate markets were introduced to replace work-unit housing, and the old *gongfang* were then labeled *fulifang* (welfare housing). The *fulifang* would be privatized (i.e., sold to sitting tenants) under the reforms and became *shangpingfang*, to be resold in the burgeoning real estate market.

Under the policy guideline "Production first, living second," the work units prioritized fulfilling state quotas for production and had very limited budgets for housing construction. This caused severe housing shortages in the work units. The home of an individual worker's family was usually a simple room without any basic amenities in a subdivided house or apartment; the family had to share tap water and a toilet with other families and use public bathing facilities. This simple household space in fact more closely resembled a peasant family's simple rural dwelling than a modern urban housing unit.

The discussion that follows provides an overview of the Chinese state's approach to housing since the 1950s by examining different types of work unit or "welfare" housing. The temporary features of these housing types reflected the social transition that the occupants experienced: from rural villagers to urban work-unit employees in the socialist era and from work-unit employees to middle-class homeowners in the postsocialist era. The last transition was indeed ironic as temporary welfare housing was meant to facilitate a transition to a utopian communist society.

Low-Standard Work-Unit Housing

Established in the major cities soon after the revolutionary regime took power, the earliest work units were accommodated in hastily constructed buildings intended as temporary housing for employees. The most common type of such temporary housing was a series of single-story row houses known as a *pingfang*, or "ordinary house." A *pingfang* was crudely built without any planning permits or architectural designs; it contained a row of residential units with no basic amenities, and each unit looked like a makeshift shed or hut (Figure 5.1). The residents of a unit used communal tap water, canteens, and restrooms inside the work-unit compound. Simple *pingfang* continued to be built in hinterland cities throughout the socialist period and even in the early reform period.

During the Great Leap Forward (1958–1962) and the Cultural Revolution (1966–1976), the party promoted "massive, fast, good, and economical" modes of construction, and many work units built a great number of *pingfang* and other temporary structures to address the housing shortage. Another common building type then was the two- or three-story walk-up with rooms aligned on one or both sides of a corridor on each floor; a room accommodated a family, who cooked in the corridor and used shared tap water and public restrooms. Such simple buildings were called *tongzilou*, or "barrel buildings" (Figure 5.2). A *tongzilou* was like a multistory version of a *pingfang*.

The state promoted the simple and fast construction of *pingfang* and *tongzilou* not only as pragmatic measures to relieve the housing shortage but also as part of a political movement that reflected Maoist antiurban politics and antibourgeois ideology. During the Great Leap Forward, an article published in the nation's leading architectural journal collected the designs of *pingfang* and *tongzilou* from around the country (see Figures 5.1 and 5.2). The author opened the article with a political statement:

> In the great antisquandering and anticonservative campaigns, the architectural design departments of all provinces and cities criticized

平房及二层住宅

1. 简易平房住宅，单方造价14.47元/m² （图1）

設計单位: 四川省城市建筑設計院。

居室面積一般为 12.8m²，每戶設有厨房，面积为 3.8~5.2m²，但无厕所，室內淨高2.6m。

砖混凝土墩基础立木柱，內外单竹編墙粉柴泥白灰，居室內1:3灰煤渣地面，厨房、內廊均为素土地面，粘土瓦屋面，

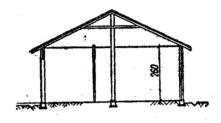

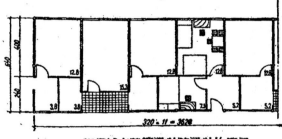

圖1 四川省城市建筑設計院設計的简易平房住宅平面及剖面

建筑面積226.56m²， 平面系數72.4%。

斑竹挂瓦条，天棚用竹席吊頂，居室有玻璃窗及木門，厨房采用竹花窗及竹栅門。

Figure 5.1 Plan and section of a "simple *pingfang* house." Source: Sichuan Urban Architecture Design Institute, *Jianzhu xuebao*, no. 6 (1958).

high standards and conservative ideas in architectural design. The designers' thinking had greatly improved, and they realized that economics and technology had to be combined with political thinking. During the Great Leap Forward of Socialist Production, the designers were full of enthusiasm and brainstormed proactively and creatively; following the party's policy guidelines of "building up our country thriftily" and "massive, fast, good, economical," the designers deepened their research, worked as a team, and produced a number of low-cost building designs that also met functional requirements.[3]

The architects' low-cost designs in fact reinvented the preindustrial tradition of building rural dwellings in the urban environment. The construction of *pingfang* and *tongzilou* relied on traditional craftsmanship and required little or no involvement of trained architects or engineers. Although these

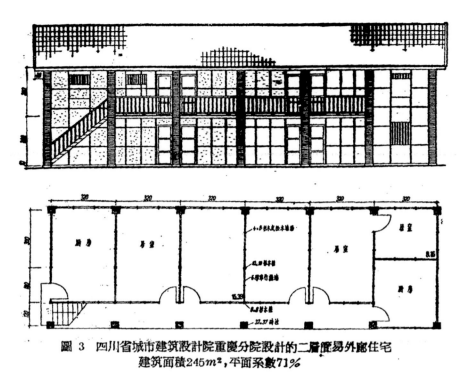

圖 3　四川省城市建筑設計院重慶分院設計的二層簡易外廊住宅
建筑面積245m²，平面系數71%

Figure 5.2 Plan and elevation of a two-story simple building with a corridor.
Source: Sichuan Urban Architecture Design Institute, *Jianzhu xuebao*,
no. 6 (1958).

structures were constructed using the fastest and cheapest measures in order to provide free temporary housing to work-unit employees (many of
whom had just migrated from rural areas), they remained occupied for
years or even decades because the work units lacked funds to reinvest in
housing projects.

As the *pingfang* and *tongzilou* continued to be occupied beyond their intended life spans, the residents' families grew larger and had to carry out
various self-help construction projects—such as adding a small kitchen or enclosing a small courtyard—in order to improve their living conditions. Over
the years these self-help additions, undertaken without any municipal or
neighborhood oversight or permitting, caused the densification and deterioration of the original complex and the work-unit neighborhood. The work units
and the local authorities allowed and even encouraged such self-help construction because they had no other resources to solve the housing problem.

By the beginning of the twenty-first century, the neighborhoods of *pingfang* and *tongzilou* that had survived the early reform period had been

labeled by local authorities as urban slums (*penghu qu*, or neighborhoods of hut homes) and slated for total demolition and redevelopment. The hasty construction of *pingfang* and *tongzilou* marked a rather unique form of socialist urbanization, a kind of informal urbanization. The dilapidated neighborhoods of these dwellings resembled the informal settlements of rural migrants or squatters found on the fringes of some third-world cities. Such neighborhoods (of partial self-help construction) provided affordable housing (and in the Chinese case, free housing provided by work units) for those who were making a transition from traditional rural living to modern urban living.

Socialist Transformation of Preexisting Urban Housing

In the socialist period the municipal bureaus of housing management in the major cities also managed a huge amount of low-rent housing. Work-unit employees could apply for a unit from the city with help from their employers. This type of "public housing" emerged after the socialist transformation of private property in the major cities. On taking over the cities in 1949, the revolutionary regime confiscated urban properties formerly owned by "counterrevolutionaries, war criminals, Japanese collaborators, and bureaucratic capitalists" and redistributed them as public assets to different work units. These upscale properties were then used as offices or subdivided into small residential units; the latter were then allocated to work-unit employees.

Small private landlords were allowed to keep their rental properties, but the regime set limits as to the rents they could charge tenants. The limits were so low that the landlords often preferred to hand over their rental properties to the government so as to avoid paying high maintenance costs. The socialist transformation of private businesses and industries in the mid- and late 1950s almost eliminated private landlords and greatly reduced the number of privately owned properties in large cities. During the Cultural Revolution rebels or those without adequate housing rushed to "occupy" private residences whose owners were either evicted or forced to hand over a great portion of their homes.

The socialist transformation of privately held properties entailed their "occupation" by a working class that consisted mainly of rural migrants. The workers' new homes were often simple rooms in a subdivided house or apartment. As urban populations continued to grow at a rapid pace, the housing shortage worsened, and poor maintenance and excessive subdivision caused the physical deterioration of old urban neighborhoods. Many residents carried out self-help construction projects and erected makeshift huts or shacks as extensions of their overcrowded homes. For example, the elegant old courtyard houses inherited from imperial Beijing were transformed into what local residents called "big mess yards" (*dazayuan*), cluttered with infill structures (Figure 5.3). Colonial-style

Figure 5.3 A courtyard house with later additions, Beijing, 2012. Photo: Samuel Y. Liang

garden villas in Shanghai were subdivided to accommodate multiple families: Garages became family homes; living rooms were divided into apartments and even remodeled into two stories. Because families did not want to share stoves and there were not enough stoves in the kitchen for each family, corridors and balconies were turned into additional cooking spaces. The lack of maintenance over time caused the houses to appear dilapidated: Plaster fell off, exposing bricks; wooden floors were deformed; ceilings were stained by water damage; and exposed wires were seen everywhere.[4]

The historic urban neighborhoods then came to resemble urban slums or informal squatter settlements. Such dilapidated neighborhoods continued to be occupied by low-income residents in the early reform and postsocialist periods, until they were demolished for redevelopment (Figure 5.4).

Self-Help Construction in Urban Slums

Housing conditions were even more deplorable in the neighborhoods that had been part of the urban slums (*penghu qu*) in the prerevolutionary cities. Zhabai, for example, an urban district located just north of Shanghai's former foreign concessions, was home to vast slum neighborhoods. The slums grew where war refugees and the urban poor (including the city's massive

Figure 5.4 A house with added self-help constructions, Shanghai. Photo: Samuel Y. Liang, 2017.

working class) erected temporary huts and shacks with straw, wooden planks, or bamboo mats.

After taking over Shanghai in May 1949, the new revolutionary regime began to clean up some slums. For example, the municipal government filled in the highly polluted Zhaojia Creek (which had become clogged during the Japanese occupation) and cleared the slum that had formed along the creek. The site was then rebuilt into Zhaojia Creek Road and a greenbelt, and the slum residents were relocated.[5]

The city, however, lacked resources and funds to rebuild the vast slum areas, most of which endured with extremely limited improvement throughout the socialist period. The regime nonetheless sought to improve the housing conditions of these areas. The first measure was to provide the slums with public amenities such as tap water, drainage pipes, fire lanes, and garbage collection. In the next stage the government encouraged and assisted the residents' self-help construction projects to rebuild wooden and straw huts into semipermanent structures of brick and tile. In 1952 the municipal construction committee issued "Temporary Regulations on Simple Houses" to direct the residents' self-help construction projects. The city and some work units provided material assistance to the residents. For example, the city provided free building materials for the residents displaced from the Zhaojia Creek slum to construct new homes in the Caojin area (where the city had acquired land from local villages). More commonly, the residents' work units provided materials for them to rebuild their hut homes. The program of "public-assisted private construction" (*gongzhu sijian*) legalized the squatter residences as private properties; it also eliminated wooden and straw huts as fire hazards in the city. According to official statistics, 2.2 million square meters of hut housing had been rebuilt by the end of 1960 to accommodate about 400,000 residents.[6] The new brick and tile structures built by the residents themselves lacked any coordinated planning or design, and the physical appearance of the slum areas did not improve. Most houses in the former slum neighborhoods were private properties built by their owners, and the neighborhoods endured with little change until the postsocialist period, when almost all of them were demolished and redeveloped into residential high-rise complexes (Figure 5.5).

The hasty and cheap construction of *pingfang* and *tongzilou* and the self-help reconstruction of huts and old houses were common practices that exemplified the informal urbanization of socialist China. This provided affordable housing to work-unit employees but extremely limited improvement in their living conditions. It was instrumentalized to support the accumulation of industrial wealth in the public sector while the workers' private lives suffered.

Modern Architecture in Socialist Housing

In order to improve the workers' housing conditions, municipal governments (especially those of major cities such as Shanghai) and some work units enlisted the services of architects and city planners in constructing large-scale housing projects. This approach in fact followed the established pattern of urbanization in the capitalist world. It embraced modern building technology and planning theories and stood in contrast to the antiurban policies of the CCP leadership.

For example, at the beginning of the Great Leap Forward, the Shanghai Planning Design Institute proposed a master plan to rebuild Zhabei, one of the city's former slum districts, where more than 70% of all buildings were simple huts or shacks that would last only fifteen years or less. The planners pointed out the urgent need to rebuild the neighborhoods of self-help structure:

> According to an incomplete survey by the district government, about 100,000 square meters of huts were rebuilt by their residents in 1957

Figure 5.5 A neighborhood with self-help constructions prior to demolition, Zhabei, Shanghai. Photo: Samuel Y. Liang, 2012.

alone. Self-help construction amounted to an investment of over 2 million yuan. These numbers show the residents' urgent need for better living conditions. But building densities in the slums are extremely high; there are usually only two or three meters between the huts. When these one-story huts are rebuilt into two-story brick structures, their environment and hygiene conditions further deteriorate.[7]

The master plan specified that the rebuilding of the Zhabei slums was to be carried out in multiple phases; the most dilapidated slums were to be rebuilt first into modern residential microdistricts, a planning concept modeled on the Soviet *mikroraion*. A detailed plan was soon produced to rebuild the slum area Fangua Lane, located next to a railway line in Zhabei. But the reconstruction of the slum did not start until 1963, when the nation recovered from the economic disaster that followed the Great Leap Forward. New Fangua Lane, a residential microdistrict, was completed in 1965, consisting of thirty-one five-story apartment buildings with a total floor area of about 69,000 square meters. Most units in the complex had only one or one and a half rooms, and the floor area of the average unit was eighteen square meters. The units exemplified the typical architectural designs of minimal-standard apartments in the socialist period.

Although the units of New Fangua Lane were extremely small, they introduced a new style of urban living with modern amenities (such as tap water and private toilets) to the former slum residents. When the residents moved into their new homes, they celebrated with a public ceremony of loud gongs and drums. The project served to showcase the achievement of the socialist regime; to display the radical change in the neighborhood to visitors, a few bamboo and straw huts were preserved in the north section of the compound.

The rebuilding of Fangua Lane was funded by the local government, and the completed project provided low-rent housing to the former slum residents. This socialist model of housing production could not be carried out on a larger scale because of the lack of municipal funds. Zhabei remained dominated by vast tracts of slums whose residents periodically rebuilt their homes into structures of varying heights and quality through the socialist and early reform periods. The total redevelopment of Zhabei was carried out after the privatization of land and housing was complete in the twenty-first century. Today the area looks no different from the rest of Shanghai, featuring an endless sprawl of high-rises in gated compounds (rather than socialist microdistricts).

New Fangua Lane was the best-known example of socialist urban renewal, but very few such projects were carried out in the socialist period. By comparison, a considerable number of modern-style apartment complexes were built on the peripheries of major cities, where the municipal government or work units acquired land from rural villages. All units in the completed projects were then distributed to work-unit employees as low-rent housing.

In 1952 Shanghai's municipal government announced that 20,000 units of workers' housing were to be built, thus initiating the large-scale construction of workers' housing. In the following years the city built a number of "workers' new villages" (*gongren xincun*) on the city's outskirts. These residential compounds were pilot projects to improve the housing conditions of work-unit employees. The workers' villages looked distinct from the old-style street blocks, as the architects (trained in the Republican period, 1912–1949) adopted the Western concept of the neighborhood unit to create quiet living environments that were closed to through traffic. Apartment units in the villages were allocated to selected model workers or those with "special needs." A unit usually contained just one room with shared kitchen and bathroom; the villages also provided shopping co-ops and communal gardens to the residents. Because the concept of the neighborhood unit was imported from capitalist countries, it was soon replaced by the residential microdistrict, which had similar planning features but was much larger in scale. Shanghai's new residential projects featured communal spaces and amenities that served as model displays of socialist communities but offered a limited number of housing units and little floor space. These projects did not solve the city's housing shortage.

In Beijing the municipal government built a number of residential micro-districts and allocated finished apartments to work units. Some work units constructed their own apartment complexes, forming the "great walled compounds" (*dayuan*) of educational, research, or military units in the city's west suburbs (i.e., the new built-up area west of Old Beijing). Apartments were then allocated to cadres and employees. Since the Cultural Revolution, smaller compounds or buildings were inserted into neighborhoods in Old Beijing without any spatial order or planning as the work units tried to acquire any buildable lots. By comparison, workers' new villages rather than work-unit compounds dominated socialist Shanghai, probably because the city's vast industrial working class predated the work-unit system.

Both the new villages (or microdistricts) and work-unit compounds consisted of apartment complexes based on standard architectural designs. Since the mid-1950s the nation's leading design institutes had produced standard designs for modern apartment complexes, usually three- to six-story walk-ups, and issued design codes for urban housing. The first set of standard apartment designs followed the Soviet model. These designs were soon abandoned because elongated rooms and small windows proved unpopular. Subsequent modified standard designs produced smaller units and more complex floor plans to meet the residents' demands for ventilation and natural light in all rooms, including kitchens and bathrooms. The standard residential unit was extremely small and varied from a studio to a two-bedroom apartment with a floor area between twenty and fifty square meters. Such small units, it was suggested, formed 70% of all housing units to be built in the socialist period.[8] Many designs included shared kitchens or toilets. These designs reflected the state's austere approach to solving the housing problem.[9]

Because only a very limited number of new housing units were produced in the socialist period, the per capita living space of major cities continued to decline. During the Great Leap Forward, an article published in the nation's leading architectural journal claimed that after "fully utilizing the potential of space," four or five people could live in a room of eight square meters and six or seven people could occupy a room of fifteen square meters (Figures 5.6 and 5.7).[10] In the following two decades, it was quite common that units based on "reasonable designs" (*heli sheji*, namely some of the above-mentioned standard designs) were "unreasonably used" (*bu heli shiyong*) in order to accommodate more residents.[11] For example, a small two-bedroom apartment designed for one family was shared by two families.

The modern-style apartments in microdistricts or work-unit compounds were also subject to informal spatial arrangements. Over time, socialist apartment complexes began to look dilapidated, similar to the neighborhoods of subdivided old houses or temporary structures. They too became targets of redevelopment in the postsocialist period.

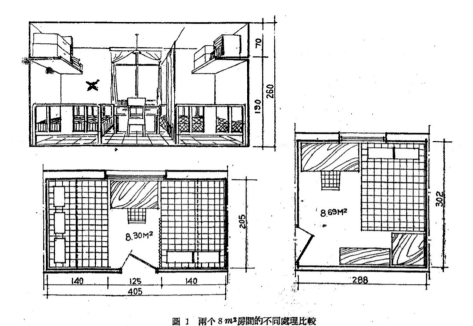

圖 1 兩个 8 m² 房間的不同處理比較

Figure 5.6 Ye Zugui and Ye Zhoudu, five beds in a room of eight square meters.
Source: *Jianzhu xuebao*, no. 2 (1958).

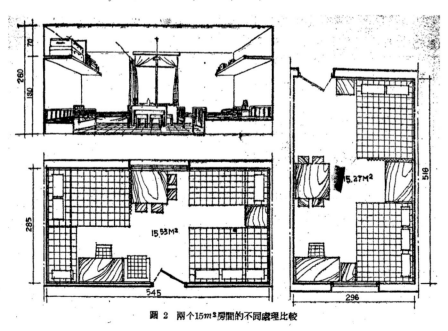

圖 2 兩个 15m² 房間的不同處理比較

Figure 5.7 Ye Zugui and Ye Zhoudu, seven beds in a room of fifteen square meters.
Source: *Jianzhu xuebao*, no. 2 (1958).

Housing Construction in the Early Reform and Postsocialist Periods

The mass production of housing units in socialist China in fact followed the trajectory of the modern architecture movement that had drastically transformed cityscapes worldwide in the second half of the twentieth century. Critics of the standard designs considered them to be following the same method that produced cheap housing in capitalist countries.[12] The radical Maoists of the CCP were too busy with their "permanent revolution" to be bothered with the housing problem. The Cultural Revolution was the Maoists' final and most fanatical attack on members of the urban elite who might have the slightest association with Western political and even technological ideas. New housing construction almost stopped during the decade-long political chaos. After the country recovered, the new CCP leadership purged the Maoists and sought to avoid similar "revolutions" by launching economic reforms. The reforms also initiated a rapid urbanization process and with it a massive boom in housing construction.

After neglecting reinvestment in housing for decades, the municipal governments and work units drastically increased urban housing production. For example, the annual production of new housing in Shanghai in the 1980s was about ten times that of the entire prior socialist period. The municipal governments acquired extensive tracts of rural land next to the urban cores to construct large-scale residential microdistricts, such as Quyang New Village in Shanghai and Jingsong Microdistrict in Beijing. In the meantime work units built new apartment complexes on any land parcels they managed to acquire in the old urban cores or new suburbs; the planning of such small-scale construction projects was less orderly.

Six-story walk-ups were the most common building type in the early reform period, while high-rises equipped with elevators first appeared in Shanghai and Beijing in the 1970s and became more common in the following decades. These walk-ups and high-rises were in the style of modernist or functionalist architecture; their drab, monotonous appearance, as well as the way they endlessly multiplied in the cities, led them to be characterized by the locals as stacked matchboxes.

At first, new apartment units were still limited to a few standard designs; the average floor area of a unit was forty to forty-five square meters and was soon expanded to sixty square meters.[13] As the nation's economic situation improved, the demand for better living conditions grew, and housing designs and neighborhood planning developed and diversified accordingly. In 1998 the city of Shanghai increased the minimum floor area of an apartment unit and removed the requirement that the average unit floor area be set for a housing development project. Following this policy change, an extremely rich variety of housing designs appeared in the booming real estate market in the next decades, including luxury apartment and villa designs that featured massive floor areas per unit.[14]

The initial objective of housing construction in the early reform period was to increase per capita floor area and provide each family with a self-contained apartment (i.e., a unit with a private kitchen and bathroom). The most common household space evolved from a simple room where living, sleeping, and dining functions were combined into a relatively comfortable unit with functional separations between living, sleeping, and dining areas.

In the meantime, work-unit housing and municipal housing became privatized. Old low-rent units were sold at subsidized prices to sitting tenants (i.e., work-unit employees). The housing reforms started in the 1980s with the introduction of "commodity housing" and were completed in 1998 with the termination of "welfare housing"—a label now applied to low-rent housing owned by the work units and municipal governments.

The privatization of housing coincided with the rapid growth of the real estate markets in the major cities, which drove up land values and transformed city-center areas into dense clusters of high-rises, many of which were apartment towers of twenty-seven stories or higher. As upscale housing, these high-rises looked distinct from the housing projects of the earlier socialist period; they featured sleek, minimalist designs or ornate architectural motifs, such as "European-style" arched windows, domes, and columns. Commercial developers made the transition from constructing simple walkups to erecting more luxurious high-rises in the 1990s and the 2000s. The high-rises are in fact a more decorated version of mass housing as modernist architecture; the luxury apartments are literally concrete boxes stacked one atop the other, as a more expensive version of the "matchbox" apartments.

This rapid urbanization testified to the success of modern architecture. Modernism in architecture proposed to solve social problems (i.e., inequities in the capitalist world) by introducing the technology of mass building programs, especially efficient and economical methods of constructing mass housing to be occupied by the urban working class. But in China today the mass housing projects that employ the language of modernist design have in fact become instrumental in the rise of a prosperous middle class in the major cities.

***

As China has been fully integrated into the global capitalist system, its mass housing projects has tapped into a burgeoning real estate market that has created a tremendous amount of wealth in the major cities. In the meantime the housing projects of socialist China have disappeared or declined into slum-like neighborhoods facing redevelopment and privatization. The brief history of China's socialist housing featured temporary hut-like dwellings, self-help structures, and low-standard apartments with shared amenities; these were all provisional measures to solve the housing problem under the policy guideline of "Production first, living second."

The socialist neighborhoods of work-unit employees epitomized a state-endorsed informal urbanization process that took place before professional urban planning controls and modern architectural designs were in place. This informal urbanization was envisioned as a transition to the utopia of communist society. But it in fact helped work-unit employees, most of whom had just migrated from rural villages into cities, make a transition to urban living. This transition continued to unfold in the postsocialist period, when most of the (former) work-unit employees became middle-class homeowners.

Work-unit housing met the workers' minimal demand for shelter because of the workers' resilience and frugal lifestyle. They sacrificed their private lives for the national agenda of industrialization, but they were still privileged workers compared to rural villagers and urban residents outside the work-unit system. Because socialist housing was not available to those outside the work-unit system and because huge disparities existed between housing projects constructed by different work units and local governments, the state's policy of prioritizing industrial production carried out by work units in fact created, rather than eliminated, social inequalities. The uneven geographies of socialist cities dominated by great work-unit compounds already anticipated the widening gap between the rich and the poor found in the property market of postsocialist China.

When the urban housing reforms initiated in the late 1980s gradually privatized socialist housing, work-unit employees became private homeowners and were one step ahead of others in entering the property market. Thus the low-rent housing units they once occupied functioned as stepping stones in their transition from rural villagers to work-unit employees in the socialist period and then to middle-class homeowners in the postsocialist period.

Both the state and the work-unit employees benefited from low-cost land acquisition, which had been key to socialist urbanization. Constructing welfare housing (and work-unit compounds) entailed taking land from rural villages, whose residents received meager compensation for what they had lost. The state's total control of land resources ensured its industrialization agenda while creating new social inequities. Welfare housing construction in fact anticipated rampant land grabbing in the real estate craze of postsocialist China.

The state's monopoly on land resources continues to play a pivotal role in rapid postsocialist urbanization, as local governments generate revenue by taking land from rural villages and then leasing it to commercial developers. Sometimes "affordable housing" or "relocation housing" is built in remote locations where the local government takes land from rural villages at low cost by using the same administrative method that the state used to take land from rural villages in the socialist period. This remnant of socialist housing has in fact become a key part of capitalist urbanization: It provides cheap housing units to accommodate those displaced from city-center areas where the local government has taken back the land of former socialist neighborhoods and leased it to commercial developers. The old neighborhoods then get demolished and redeveloped into upscale residential or commercial projects.

In sum, low-quality housing construction and informal urbanization were pragmatic measures adopted by the state in making a transition from a long-established agrarian tradition to socialist industrialization. The demise of socialist housing was also instrumental in the state-led transition to capitalist urbanization in the postsocialist period. China today has abandoned the Maoist ideology of continuing revolution and embraces architecture and urbanization as the means to national progress. Mass housing projects have not succeeded in creating a more just society, however, but have in fact widened the gap between rich and poor neighborhoods as they have become part of a stratified property market. If building mass housing projects helps to avoid political revolutions, it does so through the property market and by keeping urban residents moving from one apartment to another in search of their middle-class dream. This endless movement of urban residents, along with the movement of rural migrants to the cities, has made urban homes into transitional spaces and thus has prevented the concentration of the working class in one area for a long duration.

Notes

1 Rhoads Murphey, *The Fading of the Maoist Vision: City and Country in China's Development* (New York: Methuen, 1980).
2 This strategy in Chinese industrialization was heavily influenced by the Soviet model. See Thomas P. Bernstein and Hua-Yu Li (eds.), *China Learns from the Soviet Union, 1949–Present* (Lanham, MD: Lexington Books, 2010).
3 Jianzhu gongchen bu shejizongju difang sheji chu (Office of Regional Designs, General Bureau of Design, the Department of Building Engineering), "Residential Architectural Designs during the Great Leap Forward," *Jianzhu xue bao* (*Journal or Architecture*), 1958, no. 6, p. 1. Translation mine.
4 Wang Anyi, *Xunzhao Shanghai* (Searching for Shanghai) (Shanghai: Xuelin chubanshe, 2001), pp. 155–156.
5 Cui Guanglu et al., *Shanghai zhuzhai jianshe zhi* (History of Shanghai housing construction) (Shanghai: Shanghai shehui kexue yuan chubanshe, 1998).
6 Cui Guanglu et al., *Shanghai zhuzhai jianshe zhi.*
7 Gu Zhongtao and Wang Chenqing, "Shanghai shi Zhabei qu gaijian guihua" (The reconstruction plan of Shanghai Zhabei District), *Jianzhu xuebao* (*Architectural Journal*), 1958, no. 8, p. 36. Translation mine.
8 Ye Zugui and Ye Zhoudu, "Guanyu xiao mianji zhuzhai sheji de jinyibu tantao" (Further discussion on the architectural design of small-size residential units), *Jianzhu xuebao* (*Journal of Architecture*), 1958, no. 2, p. 30.
9 Hua Lanhong, *Chongjian zhongguo* (Reconstructing China) (Beijing: Zhongguo jianzhu gongye chubanshe, 2009), pp. 141–150.
10 Ye Zugui and Ye Zhoudu, "Guanyu xiao mianji zhuzhai sheji de jinyibu tantao."
11 Hua Lanhong. *Chongjian zhongguo*, p. 141.
12 Hua Lanhong. *Chongjian zhongguo*, p. 141.
13 Cui Guanglu et al., *Shanghai zhuzhai jianshe zhi.*
14 Yu Qi, *Zhuanxingqi Shanghai chengshi juzhu kongjian de shengchan ji xingtai yanjin* (The production and morphological change of urban residential space in Shanghai in the era of transition) (Nanjing: Dongnan daxue chubanshe, 2011), pp. 175–176.

6 "Pillars" of the Welfare State

Postwar Mass Housing in Belgium and the Netherlands

Miles Glendinning

This chapter focuses on the postwar social housing programs of two of the most elaborate "corporatist" welfare-state regimes in Europe: the "pillarized" societies of Belgium and the Netherlands. It demonstrates that even among western welfare-state societies with close cultural ties, the course of social housing policy and architecture could flow in sharply different directions, not just in the simple opposition of political left and right, or architectural modernism and traditionalism, but in more unexpected aspects, such as the role of the Roman Catholic Church in the framing of postwar social policy.

The Welfare State and *"Verzuiling"*

To reflect the diversity of the postwar European welfare state, social policy academics, most famously Gøsta Esping-Anderson in 1990, have proposed a variety of definitions of the welfare state, one being "corporatism": the political and cultural arrangement in many continental countries, under which social peace was maintained by consensual systems of proportional state intervention and provision between different interest groups, whether political, social (class) or religious, and by special efforts to protect the income of the individual worker, via social insurance systems – a strong contrast, in particular, to systems emphasizing strong unitary authority, such as Fifth Republic France or Great Britain.[1]

Of these "corporatist" systems, two of the most elaborate were those of Belgium and the Netherlands, where the legacy of previous generations of religious and political struggle was etched into the governmental apparatus through the system most widely known as "verzuiling" or "pillarization." Here, social services were organized into separate, parallel systems serving the main groupings. In Belgium, these comprised the anti-clerical socialists and liberals, and the traditionalist Catholics, while in the Netherlands, there was a more complex pattern of socialists, liberals, Protestants and Catholics.[2]

But in an emphatic demonstration of the incorrigible diversity of the European welfare state, the contrasts between the two countries were as

DOI: 10.4324/9781351182966-9

prominent as the commonalities, with the socio-religious and architectural conservatism and economic laissez-faire systems of Belgium opposed to the highly planned, self-consciously modern and progressive policies of their neighbors to the north – as we will see in this chapter, which first traces the more straightforward pillarization regime and restricted social housing system of Belgium before exploring in more detail the highly complex political-organizational and architectural-planning mosaic of the Netherlands.

That contrast was just as extreme in the built environment as in social politics. Even in the prewar years, Belgian house building – including the vast reconstruction efforts in the devastated areas – had acted as a vehicle for the fragmented initiatives of town planning, whereas the opposite had applied in the Netherlands, with housing structurally embedded within the town planning system since at least the 1901 *Woningwet* (Housing Act). As explained comprehensively in articles by Hilde Heynen, that contrast was hugely exaggerated by their differing wartime experiences, with Belgium emerging relatively unscathed and able to return rapidly to a market-dominated development system, but the significantly devastated and impoverished Netherlands resorting to even more extreme measures of collectivism and co-ordination than before, linked to distinctive built-form patterns of housing, including the astonishing rise to dominance of the "*galerijbouw*" system of balcony-access.[3]

"Socialist Flats" versus "Catholic Cottages": Postwar Housing in Belgium

Both countries' mass housing systems featured a sharp internal polarization between two different formulae of state-sponsored provision. But whereas, as we will see, the Dutch polarization was between two different forms of flatted rental housing, local authority and housing association, in Belgium the polarization was a far stronger one, between state-backed homeownership in detached suburban of rural houses with gardens – "*het huisje op het heide*," with the possibility of "right to buy" after fifteen years – and rental housing provided by social housing companies in urban apartment blocks, with homeownership expressly forbidden. Within popular discourse, the two patterns were stereotypically associated, respectively, with "Catholics" and "socialists": in 1953, for instance, Jeanne Van Der Veken of the *Socialistische Vooruitziende Vrouwen* (Socialist Visionary Women, SVV) argued that "a family of high moral standards … can live in a flat as well as in a single-family house."[4] Nationally speaking, power was generally shared through coalition governments, with the socialist BSP dominating up to 1949 and in 1954–1958, and the Catholic CVP otherwise, but with the Liberals also often involved in governmental coalitions (with the shorthand names "orange," "blue" and "red" used for CVP, Liberals and BSP). But equally important were other interest groups in society – trade unions, civil servants, employers, for example – who had in 1944 agreed a social insurance concordat, and others such as the Boerenbond and the SVV also made their contribution. However, all this fed rather imprecisely into built-form preferences and discourses: while predictably the CVP was a strong supporter of homeownership, arguing that "eigen haard is goud waard ('Your own hearth is worth its weight in gold')," equally the renowned communist-leaning architect Renaat Braem could hail the cottage in a garden as an optimum dwelling for families.[5] And Braem's well-known sardonic cartoons of "Catholic housing as seen by the Socialists" (a parochial jumble of discordantly gabled individual houses) and "Socialist housing as seen by the Catholics" (menacing "neo-slum" modernist slab blocks daubed with communist slogans) were arguably as much part of his own polemical campaign against the supposed ugliness of Belgian architecture as an accurate representation of a real architectural and ideological polarization.[6] In any case, in practice, most of the local housing companies in larger cities were managed by a balance of socialist and Catholic representatives.

The late 1940s and early 1950s, following an influential 1946 exhibition on housing in Brussels organized by the NMGW (renamed in 1956 the Nationaal Maatschappij voor de Huisvesting, NMH), saw a raft of measures that addressed postwar shortages, negotiating their way through the constraints of pillarization. The two most important laws, promoted by CVP Housing Minister Alfred De Taeye in 1948 and Fernand Brunfaut a year later, focused respectively on the stereotypical "poles" of Belgian housing, "conservative/Catholic" houses and "socialist' flats." The De Taeye Act's support provisions, including subsidies equivalent to up to 15% of dwelling costs, and mortgages covering the rest, were targeted especially at individual builders, but also Catholic housing companies, on the principle that, as De Taeye argued in 1948, "one's own yard is first and foremost the realization of a dream held dear by any worker; it is a form of small property. The small owner feels responsible for the continuation of his property, that is part of the national patrimony."[7] They were a roaring success, especially in urban Flanders, reaching over 100,000 beneficiaries, over twice as many as planned, within five years, and fuelling the country's vast suburban sprawl.[8] A range of other measures to support private building was introduced in the 1940s and 1950s, with government attitudes varying from the cautious support of CVP governments to a scaling-back by the Van Acker red-blue coalition government of the mid-1950s.[9]

The Brunfaut Act established a National Housing Fund, which was intended to cover all losses incurred by the social housing companies in building urban rental and rural homeownership housing, with the Ministry of Public Works covering road construction and services in social housing areas: it succeeded in briefly raising the social company share of total national housing construction to 25% in 1955, but the effects of the Korean War and rearmament, as in so many other countries, forced a temporary cutback. Output was also, arguably, impeded by the government's much-publicized endorsement of slum clearance in an act of December 1953 – the *Wet op de Krotopruiming*, or Second De Taeye Act – following a much-publicized visit by King Beaudouin to the Marollenwijk slum near the Palais de Justice a year earlier, at the instigation of yet another crusading Catholic priest, the Abbé Froidure, with Minister De Taeye also in attendance. The NMGW was encouraged to spend a portion of its subsidies on housing for slum clearance, and an experimental redevelopment got underway in the Marollen (Krakeelbuurt), with two phases of housing in multi-story blocks built by the Brusselse Haard HA in 1953–1963 and 1963–1975. Given the Belgian aversion to radical state intervention, these slum clearance efforts remained fragmentary, by comparison with the enormous output of De Taeye houses: year 1954 saw the foundation laying of the hundred-thousandth, in Warenghem, and the following year the hundred-thousandth NMGW dwelling.[10] Unlike the extreme cautiousness towards state intervention in housing at home, the last years of Belgian colonialism in Africa saw a far more forceful interventionism, steered by the government social housing organization, the Office des Cités Africaines (OCA), charged with building 40,000 dwellings in the Congo within eight years, targeted at *"évolués"* within the African population – all one- or two-story detached houses, the standard pattern of much colonial government-sponsored housing.[11]

By comparison with both France and the Netherlands, the place of town planning in Belgium was very restricted, focusing chiefly on road building and industrial development – the latter including new housing communities such as Nieuw Sledderlo, near Genk, where 650 terraced houses and three-story balcony-access flats were built in 1963–1970 to service a new Ford plant, by social housing company Nieuw Dak.[12] The De Taeye and Brunfaut systems each exerted their own consequential effects on city planning, with municipalities such as Antwerp laying out special zones for De Taeye housing, and social housing companies building houses "for sale" alongside their traditional rental *"huurpatrimonium."* Development of areas with both De Taeye and Brunfaut housing could bring aggregate financial benefits, combining the single-family housing subsidies of the one with the infrastructural support of the other – in the process further reinforcing the patchwork character of Belgian cities. Generally lacking, however, even under Brunfaut, was the massed slab building that increasingly prevailed in France, although the disparity was less obvious in the early 1950s, with French housing still making little progress. System building in Belgium was largely concerned with low-rise individual houses, with techniques such as the Danilith-Delmulle lightweight panel system for single-story bungalows, built from 1965 until the 1970s, often disguised with brick cladding.[13] Multi-story concrete-panel towers were very much the exception, including three very late towers built in 1972–1973 in Klein Heide, Hoboken, by the Vennootschap *"Beter Wonen te Hoboken."*[14]

More typically, experimental multi-story developments took the form of "one-offs" punctuating the suburban sprawl, as in the case of a thirteen-story slab block designed by avant-garde architect Willy van der

Meeren in 1953–1954 for the socialist housing company Ieder Zijn Huis ("Everybody's Home") in the outer Brussels municipality of Evere, responding to a call by socialist mayor Franz Guillaume for a "secular watchtower" landmark in the sea of petty-bourgeois Catholic small houses. Featuring access galleries every three floors and a reinforced concrete frame incorporating many prefabricated components, dimensioned in accordance with Le Corbusier's Modulor, the complex and idiosyncratic project was only completed in 1961.[15] In middle-sized cities, a pattern of isolated multi-story blocks equally prevailed, supported by a complex network of housing societies, and building contractors, often dating from the late 1960s and early 1970s, as in Gent and Bruges.

In the large cities, a more complex and ambitious approach applied, with large extension sites often divided between several locally based housing enterprises (*huisvestingsmaatschappijen*, or HVMs) for development. Even so, each phase of innovative housing design was generally represented by only a handful of estates in Belgium – several of the key examples being the work of Renaat Braem.

In Antwerp, three large NMGW-sponsored extension zones were all dominated by "socialist"-pattern flats, even though the societies themselves were pragmatically managed by a balance of Catholics and Socialists.[16] The earliest of these was the Luchtbal development of nine-story *Zeilenbau* "Langblokken" slabs, constructed from 1949 by the Onze Woning society to the designs of local engineer-architect Hugo Van Kuyck (later augmented with tall towers), followed by "De Goede Woning's" development, designed by Joseph Smolderen, in the Jan De Voslei from 1952. In the Kiel development area, controlled by the socialist SM Huisvesting-Antwerpen, the chief set piece was a characteristically monumental network of slab blocks of eight to twelve stories by Renaat Braem at Zaanstraat, 1950–1958, complete with extensive communal facilities and open access balconies: here Braem worked in a multi-political team with Catholic architect Hendrik Maes and socialist Victor Maeremans, in pursuit of an ultimately Constructivist concept of large urban buildings as social condensers (Figures 6.1 and 6.2).[17]

During the 1950s these Antwerp developments were only rivalled in scale by the multiphase Champ de Manoeuvre (Plaine de Droixhe), an 1,800-flat development in Liege, commissioned from architects Groupe EGAU by the cooperative society, La Maison Liegoise – including a row of thirteen-story slab blocks aligned diagonally to the existing road system, plus low blocks at right angles, all with a significant element of large panel prefabrication, and all at an overall density of 380 persons per hectare. Within Brussels itself, the only development on a scale equivalent to a French grand ensemble was the grandiose Cite Modèle/Modelwijk in Heysel, with its high slabs and lower blocks dispersed in rectilinear patterns in rolling greenery: another Braem project, whose protracted gestation and construction stretched from 1955 to 1974.[18] Subsequently, he designed a succession of smaller,

Figure 6.1 Luchtbal, Antwerp: four nine-story Zeilenbau slabs (langblokken) built 1949–1954 by the "Onze Woning" housing society: Hugo van Kuyck, architect – 1992 view before recladding. Photo: Miles Glendinning

Figure 6.2 Wooneinheid Zaanstraat, Antwerp-Kiel, 1950–1958, a boldly modernist project designed by Renaat Braem, Hendrik Maes and Victor Maeremans for the socialist-controlled housing society, Huisvesting Antwerpen – 2014 view. Photo: Miles Glendinning

Figure 6.3 Cité du Droixhe, Liège, commissioned from Groupe EGAU from 1954 by the housing society "La Maison Liègeoise": 2019 view. Photo: Miles Glendinning

more idiosyncratic social housing projects including landmark high blocks, as in the multiphase ex-urban Kreuskenslei development in Boom-Noord, south of Antwerp, built by the Boom Regional Housing Society, including two slender point blocks (Phase 2, 1963–1972).[19] The most idiosyncratic of all Braem's housing projects was the Sint Maartensdal development in Leuven, 1960–1971– the sole large-scale representative within Belgian social housing of the individualistic, organic late modernism of the 1960s. Stemming from Braem's own personal quest for the late 1950s for a more open "lively, eventful design approach," to encourage "personal and spiritual liberation," and co-designed with Albert Moerkerke and Jan De Mol,[20] the project broke from the rectilinearity of the Cité Modèle and Kiel, with its symmetrical arrangement of a twenty-story, 115 m hexagonal "condensed tower," crowned by a spire-like antenna, and flanked by herringbone-plan ten-story slabs. The project, a redevelopment of a redundant barracks, was made possible by the accession of a "red-blue" city administration in Leuven in 1953, and a reformist socialist mayor, Franz Tielemans, who steered the local HVM towards a wildly ambitious multi-story area redevelopment program – of which Sint Maartensdal was the only significant outcome (Figure 6.3).[21]

The Netherlands: Planned Housing and "Polder Politics"

Despite the apparent similarity of Belgium and the Netherlands in areas such as pillarization or brick row housing, the two countries' social housing policies headed in such different directions after the Second World War that the Netherlands ended up closer to a universalist system such as Sweden's, than to that of Belgium. The wartime privations hugely boosted the role of organized corporatism and communitarianism within the Dutch version of pillarization, which re-emerged after 1945 in a diluted form, with a slightly wider array of "pillars," lasting right up to the late 1960s, including the PvdA (Partij van de Arbeid; Socialists), the VVD (Liberals) and the KVP, ARP and CHU confessional parties. Echoing the many wartime schemes for modernization and creation of a welfare state, most working-class Catholics now strongly backed corporatism and modernization, as against Belgian-style family individualism.[22] Some of these schemes had been prepared in secret by modernist architect-planners, and others openly, under the aegis of the German-tolerated planning and building-industry management system consolidated by engineer Johan Ringers – subsequently the first postwar secretary for public works in 1945–1946.[23] The special interest groups within each "pillar" typically formed alliances with their counterparts in others – allowing a protracted period of "Rooms-rood" (Catholic-Socialist) coalition from 1946 to 1958, comprising the PvdA and the four religious parties and led from 1948 to 1958 by Socialist Willem Drees. Not only that but as the KVP (Catholic People's Party) was also central to the other main alternative coalition permutation (center-right), it was able to control the housing ministry for much of the period from 1951 to 1974 – Western Europe's chief rival to the continuity of social democratic rule in Swedish housing. From the 1960s onwards, in the wake of protest movements such as Provo, the old-style deferential pillarization increasingly fragmented.[24]

All of this was played out against an extraordinary demographic background of explosive population growth, unmatched in Western Europe, with 1920–1950 seeing a 48% population increase (crowned by the influx from independent Indonesia in 1949–1950), in contrast to 17% in both Britain and Belgium and only 7% in France. This boom accentuated the impact of wartime housing stock losses (4% totally lost, 25% damaged): even in 1950 there was still widespread billeting in under-occupied houses, and police controls of residence permits.[25]

To cope with this situation, one of the most highly controlled housing and planning systems in Western Europe emerged after 1945. The role of private and single-family houses was curbed, never accounting for more than 35% of output, and far less in the 1950s and mid-1960s. But housing played a key role in national planned investment: the 1946 national plan allowed 25% for housing and 55% for industry. The highly controlled character of the system stemmed partly from the strong powers of both central government (Rijk) and local authorities, building on prewar precedent. The central government was concerned both with quantity and quality. In the former area, it set national targets, manipulated regional distribution quotas for individual towns, controlled construction permits and regulated rent controls. Overall, its strategy until at least 1955 was to foster a low-wage economic revival with rather austere living standards, to max-imize national competitiveness – a strategy within which social housing played a central role.[26] In the latter area, building costs having increased by 350% compared with 1939, the most important central government power was its subsidies for *Woningwet* dwellings, which took the form of annual contributions, through block loans, towards the operating deficits of local authorities. With the average weekly cost of a *Woningwet* house in 1953 running at thirteen guilders, to achieve a weekly rent of seven to eight guil-ders a state subsidy of 5.50 was needed: for regulated private-enterprise houses, 30% of building costs were covered by government lump sum grants in the early 1950s.[27] Up to 1948, the *Woningwet* subsidy had been entirely covered by central government, and local authorities could at first decide whether to use it to build houses themselves or to pass it on to the *woningbouw vereningen* (WVs – housing associations), through construc-tion loans and annual contributions to management costs. As a result, the early postwar years in the Netherlands saw Western Europe's only direct nationwide equivalent to British municipal-controlled "council housing": of the roughly 200,000 dwellings built in 1945–1951, no less than 41% comprised council housing, 29% were built by WVs and 30% was built for owner-occupation (mostly regulated and with government assistance). This delegated subsidy was, in turn, a key power of the local authorities, but arguably even more important was their large-scale ownership of land and their planning powers, allowing them to regulate land disposal rates and prices to different tenures, social and private. By 1966, a foreign observer could remark simply that in the Randstad, the country's urban core region, municipalities "largely control the real estate market" – a position of power that would have been inconceivable in Belgium.[28]

Of course, multi-layered systems of regulation and control of housing-cum-planning also emerged elsewhere in the world in later years, notably in Hong Kong and Singapore. But unlike these territories, with their somewhat undemocratic political systems, in the Netherlands this was combined with the complex coalition wheeling and dealing required by pillarization. In the case of the nation's two largest cities, Amsterdam and Rotterdam, although the postwar years saw formidable strides in planned extension and social housing development, this achievement required constant cross-pillar nego-tiation, especially between KVP housing ministers and the PvdA-dominated municipal coalition administrations and *wethouders* (aldermen). Within the two cities, the fiercest clashes continued to be between technical/adminis-trative groupings, for example between the municipal planning authority (*Stadsontwikkeling*) and the output-dominated ethos of the housing de-partment (*Woningdienst*). But the KVP oversight of national housing policy ensured a gradual policy shift after 1948 away from open-ended central government subsidy of the local authorities' *Woningwet* activities, prodding the latter to borrow on the open market, or (after 1950) from life assurance societies, pension funds and the Bank for Dutch Municipalities.[29]

From 1950, too, the government specified increasingly comprehensively how many dwellings local authorities could build directly each year, and attempted to insist on economies in the approved building plans. At the same time, though, local authorities were granted new powers of land expropriation at controlled prices from the mid-1950s, to check land speculation.[30] There began a constantly rising succession of national house building targets to "solve the housing shortage." In 1949, following a panic that output was not rising fast enough, a 55,000 annual target was announced, to "solve the shortage" by 1965. In 1964, this was succeeded by a six-year plan to boost annual output to 125,000 and "solve the housing problem" by 1970 – combined with wild fluctuations in the means towards that end. In the late 1950s following the departure of the PvdA from the coalition, Housing Minister Johannes (Jan) van Aartsen made an initial attempt to direct subsidies exclusively to WVs, but his successor in the new confessional-Liberal coalition after the 1963 elections, Pieter Bogaers, a representative of the Labor wing of the KVP who was determined to keep the allegiance of the workers, struck out in a very different direction, towards a dogged pursuit of maximum output, racing up and down the country and harrying his civil servants and municipalities to press on. His plan was that the housing shortage should be tackled first, by a new six-year plan stretching from 1964 to 1970, and only then should the housing powers be transferred to the WVs. Unlike his predecessors, Bogaers also reversed the place of the building industry in his plans: rather than its existing capacity dictating the scale of the program, he decided it should be expanded to a level that would allow an annual output of 125,000 – a policy that would inevitably require adoption of industrialized building in one form or another. By the end of 1965, 148,000 dwellings were indeed under construction, and the years 1955–1961 and 1964–1965 saw significant over-fulfilment of the ministry's output targets. In the mid-1960s the emphasis shifted back to WV control of new social house building, combined with more area rehabilitation.[31] The years after 1973 also saw strenuous efforts to expand homeownership: year 1973 saw the highest overall completion level of all (155,000), but 65% of this was purely private enterprise. The percentage of *Woningwet* dwellings in national output also fluctuated radically, with peaks of 75% in 1949 and 54% in 1967, and the council-housing share of *Woningwet* completions dropped from 60% in 1951 to 49% in 1966 and 16% in 1973.[32] The percentage of social rental housing in the total housing stock increased steadily from 1950 (18%) to 1991 (52%), and the "millionth postwar dwelling" was formally opened in Zwolle in 1962.[33]

The post-1948 decline in the percentage of council housing was slowest to take effect in the Randstad, not least because of the messianic campaigning from 1948 of J. J. van der Velde, the socialist alderman for public works and social housing in Amsterdam, who relentlessly pushed forward a proposal for a massive 84,000-unit council-house building drive. His program sought to piggyback housing output onto the extensive extension plans of the prewar AUP (Amsterdam Extension Plan), and in eight years 33,000 dwellings had duly been completed.[34]

Despite the modest scale and budget of late 1940s and 1950s housing architecture in the Netherlands, it was the focus of impassioned and multifaceted debates, among designers, planners and politicians, relating both layout plans and block designs to elevated ideals such as the fostering of "community," or even national character: a Ministry publication of 1953 asserted that the Dutchman was "a great lover of his home," but the definition of "home" here was clearly quite different from that in Belgium! The addiction to contentious debate was, of course, a long-standing tradition within Dutch architecture and planning.[35] Despite attempts at a traditionalist, Catholic fight-back, led by Granpré Molière at the 1941 Doorn Congress, the 1940s and 1950s saw the inexorable, hegemonic rise of the modern movement concept of neighborhood planning. These began with wartime developments in Rotterdam, where 1941 had seen the publication by modernist architects of a report, "Urban possibilities in the new Rotterdam," and the proselytizing of a hierarchical neighborhood concept, or "*wijkgedachte*," by a multiagency committee chaired by city housing director Andries Wilhelm Bos: it envisaged an ascending hierarchy of neighbourhood and district sizes, from "*buurt*" to "*wijk*," "*stadsdeel*" and "*stadgeheel*." The concept was widely proselytized in a 1946 publication, "De stad van toekomst, de toekomst der stad ('The City of the Future, the Future of the City')." Key interwar modernists worked closely with Bos in the first attempt at large-scale realization of *wijkgedachte*, at Rotterdam's Zuidwijk "modern garden city," originally planned by Willem van Tijen in 1947 with only 16% flats, but eventually realized in 1954–1958 at much higher density, at the PvdA's insistence.[36]

It was arguably, in the design of *Woningwet* dwellings themselves, that the central government's influence over quality as well as quantity was most far-reaching. This was achieved through its vetting powers over new schemes, with detailed prescription of equipment and space standards in an official housing manual, the so-called "Voorschriften en Wenken ('Regulations and Suggestions')," first issued in 1951 by the Centrale Directie van de Volkshuisvesting; it resembled the contemporary "Westholms bibel" in Sweden and the INA-Casa "Suggerimenti" in Italy.[37] It was progressively updated: a 1953–1958 study group on "fundamental housing principles" by some old-timers of Dutch modern movement housing design – van Tijen, van den Broek, Stam, Merkelbach – eventually fed into a comprehensive 1965 update of the "Voorschriften en Wenken," hailed sardonically by van Tijen as "twenty years and a million dwellings too late." Overall, these "advances" in design coincided with a shift towards flats, accounting for 45% of all new Dutch dwellings in 1967; average dwelling area per flat reached a maximum of 646 ft.² the previous year.[38]

Overall, postwar Dutch housing design increasingly enshrined Modernist ideals of "need-fit" planning and standardization. An extreme example of "need-fit" was the emergency "Duplex" dwelling, of which 13,000 were built immediately after the war to house two large families, with the aim of subdividing each into two after ten years. Standardization was exemplified in the rigid egalitarianism of *"strokenbouw"* (parallel slab) layouts, first built prewar in Bos en Lommer and then incorporated in the 1940 plan for Slotermeer, which envisaged 11,000 dwellings entirely in *strokenbouw* (and mostly of four stories).[39]

In the field of housing construction, unlike the French emphasis on large-panel prefabrication, in the Netherlands the driving force was a combination of standardization and rationalization. Both of these were reinforced by the national coordinated reconstruction program shaped initially by Ringers, as well as by the use of Marshall Plan aid to boost research and innovation in constructional systematization, through measures such as the 1948 establishment of the Bouwcentrum in Rotterdam.[40] The late 1940s years saw an initial flurry of proposals for full prefabricated construction, with Zuidwijk again playing a central role: its first neighborhood was built using prefabricated systems at the insistence of PvdA councilors, but after costs were found to be 100% higher, construction reverted to traditional brickwork. At Kleinpolder (1947–1952), two contrasting systems were trialed, the BMB (Baksteen-Montage-Bouw) using large prefabricated panels clad in brick, and the Wijmer & Breukelman system (with prefabricated balconies included). By 1953, system building was well established within a smallish minority of the annual housing program – around 14% of total production, almost all flats and for low-income groups; between 1947 and 1964, 128,000 system-built dwellings were erected. From 1954, the central government tried to boost system building by exempting it from annual allocations (*"contingenten"*) and suggesting that municipalities should move to rolling, multi-year contracts. New systems had to be approved by the government-sponsored Ratiobouw Foundation: the most popular tended to be "rationalized-traditional" rather than fully prefabricated, including calculated brickwork construction.[41]

In contrast to France, in the Netherlands system building was only loosely connected to high building. In the latter case, the overall level of building followed a simple rise and fall trajectory, especially following a forceful pro-multi-story edict by minister Bogaers in 1963: *Woningwet* flats in blocks of nine or more stories soared from 18% of output in 1964 to 55% in 1967–1968 and then back to 40% by 1972. Overall, multi-story housing accounted for 21% of total postwar national output.[42] Rather as in England, a sharp turn against tall blocks began in 1967–1978, at the hands of conservative politicians reacting against their public unpopularity, but in the Netherlands the social housing program as a whole carried on unabated, in medium and low-rise form. Initially, multi-story construction had been deterred by the high cost, although the need for even low-rise dwellings to be piled in Amsterdam diminished the differential. Early high-rise schemes, such as Tijen and Maaskant's pioneering Zuidplein thirteen-story block of 1949 in Rotterdam, were very much isolated prestige projects, and 1948 saw lively debates about how to cut the cost of high blocks in Kleinpolder and make them affordable as *Woningwet* dwellings. One of the eventual solutions proposed was to adopt gallery access rather than internal staircase plans.[43] And it was, indeed, gallery access, or "galerijbouw," that was probably the most distinctive architectural feature of postwar Dutch flat-building – a building pattern that overrode distinctions between high and low blocks, and *Woningwet* and private tenure. The first use of this type at Spangen in Rotterdam around 1920 had provoked vigorous debates about its appropriateness in the Netherlands; but it was the late 1940s that saw its use suddenly explode, with fevered debates around 1948–1950 about the optimum planning of low-rise flats, the internal-staircase-access plan being steadily supplanted by *galerijbouw*. As late as 1952, journal reports on an experimental low-rise, concrete-frame *galerijbouw* block at Moerwijk, Den Haag, for WBV's Gravenhage, emphasized its still-experimental character, and commentator G. Westerhout argued that it had only "very gradually taken root in our country," facing distrust because of its excessive exposure to cold winds (Figure 6.4).[44]

Sometimes, the early *galerijbouw* projects were combined with two-story maisonettes, a combination largely unique to the Netherlands and England – as in the case of the Patrimonium Woonstichting Delfshaven's 1952 project in Mathenesserweg, Rotterdam, with its six-story blocks comprising three superimposed layers of maisonettes. By 1958, however, English housing specialists visiting Rotterdam's Pendrecht housing scheme referred to the galerijbouw flats there as an established, popular pattern, which "may seem rather curious to us, since we now rejected it as somewhat old-fashioned." And, by 1966, visitors from Britain found that while maisonettes were "on the way out," the dominance of *galerijbouw* was now unchallenged, and indeed referred to approvingly on grounds that Dutch people did not mind overlooking by passers-by, as "we have nothing to hide." The percentage of *Woningwet* flats in *galerijbouw* rose especially fast during the later 1960s, from 46% in 1964 to 98% in 1970: even more astonishing was that 87% of private dwellings completed in the same year were also gallery access. The terminology of multi-story building developed in parallel with that of galerijbouw, with the term "toren" being used for high towers, but "flat" used for gallery-access slabs: in 1958 in Amsterdam it could still be said that "even the word 'flat' is new."[45]

"Housers" versus "Planners" in Rotterdam and Amsterdam

Reflecting the strength of Dutch municipalities, there was a striking diversity of political, organizational and architectural patterns at local level, albeit with strong common elements – as emphasized in the two leading

Figure 6.4 Zuidplein, Rotterdam, a pioneering thirteen-story tower block including ground-floor communal facilities and early use of *galerijbouw*
access, designed by W. van Tijen and H. A. Maaskant with E. F. Groos-
man, 1945–1949: 2015 view. Photo: Miles Glendinning

cases of Rotterdam and Amsterdam. In both cases a diverse administrative
regime, politically dominated by the socialists and combining housing and
planning factions, pursued a staged program of peripheral city extension,
influenced but not dictated by national policies such as the Bogaers multi-story drive or the push for system building. But there were strong differ-
ences between the two, with Amsterdam featuring constant clashes between
different factions of public housing actors, and settling on sometimes bold

solutions, but Rotterdam following a more incremental, practical path towards housing "progress."

In Rotterdam, the Dienst Stadsontwikkeling (SO) incrementally developed the ideal of neighborhood unit community planning, with key figures such as architect-planner Lotte Stam-Beese playing a key role from the mid-1940s through to the mid-1960s. The city's early postwar reconstruction schemes had focused not just on neighborhood-unit planning but also on flatted development: the Opbouw group produced a "Rapport etagebouw Rotterdam" in 1942–1943. The consensual support for modernism in Rotterdam allowed the prewar avant-garde members of Opbouw and de 8 to help shape the city's policies, both via the housing department and via SO. At the same time, a new generation of modernist architects such as Lotte Stam-Beese embarked on projects such as Pendrecht (designed from 1948), advocating greater "differentiation" between dwelling and block types, and avoidance of single overriding patterns. The fevered argumentation reflected the early postwar controversies within CIAM, including the advocacy of greater complexity at the Bergamo CIAM 7 conference. Alongside this, however, in the early 1950s the former avant-gardes worked assiduously on city extension on behalf of the SO, whose director, Cornelis van Traa, in 1953 assigned Opbouw the Alexanderpolder development. Their initial response was a utopian proposal for a "vertische woonbuurt ('vertical neighborhood')," a "mammoth," "battleship" block of 350 flats, raised on columns: the built result was more prosaic.[46] In Rotterdam's northwest extension zone, open-planned, four-story *strokenbouw* predominated in SO's plan for Kleinpolder (1947–1952). In the north-eastern extension zone (Rotterdam-Oost), development was delayed until the 1960s–1970s, following a 1957 plan for two large areas, Ommoord and Oosterflank. Ommoord was initially designed by Stam-Beese in 1962 as a conventional mix of low-rise flats, but the Bogaers government drive for higher blocks and raised output prompted a radical boost in density and height, yielding 10,770 rather than 7,500 dwellings: as completed in 1977, the architectural form was highly differentiated, with a central cluster of twenty-story towers and angular "flats" of eight and fourteen stories, ringed by a belt of low-rise housing (Figure 6.5).[47]

In Amsterdam, by contrast, there were greater tensions between the housing and planning interests, including an early 1950s "turf war" between van Eesteren's SO and the WD (*Woningdienst* – Housing Department), focused on "quality versus quantity." The proliferation of competing factions was arguably a sign of the strength of the public housing and planning apparatus in the Netherlands, even if the practical urgency of housing output usually trumped the planners' airy good intentions, as in many other cases elsewhere, from New York or Glasgow to Hong Kong. The WD had an intimate working relationship with the Ministry of Reconstruction and Housing, which allowed some unusual working procedures, in the early 1950s, in areas such as the first phase of Slotermeer: the WD and the

Figure 6.5 Ommoord, a north-eastern extension of Rotterdam laid out from 1962
by Dienst Stadsontwikkeling (under the direction of Lotte Stam-Beese)
and completed in 1977: a cluster of towers and galerijbouw slab blocks,
ringed by low-rise housing: 2015 view. Photo: Miles Glendinning

ministry drew up the construction program, only informing the municipal
council retrospectively, for rubber-stamping purposes, and annoying the
planners, who felt that the housing development process was running ahead
of the official planning framework and bypassing the AUP. Year 1950 saw
a significant consolidation in the city's WV umbrella federation, the AFW
(Amsterdamse Federatie van Woningcorporaties; active since 1917) and the
instituting of a building agreement with the HD. To facilitate a shift away
from council housing to WP building in Amsterdam, 65% of output was
allocated to "neutral" associations such as AWV (Algemene Woningbouw
Vereniging), 20% to Catholic associations, Het Oosten and Dr Schaep-
man, and 15% to the two Protestant associations, Protestantse Woningbouw Vereniging and Patrimonium. This system would endure until the
1970s, while the role of the associations steadily increased. But the WD
was able to significantly influence their operations, for example by issuing layout plans, excluding "troublesome" architects and deciding which
developments should be system built. The SO fought its corner by stress-
ing the qualitative factor of "urban image" (*stadsbeeld*), and arguing for a

more differentiated cityscape, which inevitably foregrounded the question of multi-story towers.[48]

These issues of conflicting power bases and design ideas were repeatedly played out in Amsterdam's major postwar extension zones: the 1940s–1960s "Westelijke Tuinsteden" to the west, and the south-east extension from the 1960s onwards. The first phase of western development, Slotermeer, was a hybrid of garden city and *strokenbouw* patterns; Queen Juliana opened the "first dwelling" at Slotermeer in 1952. The clashes between SO and WD only really surfaced in the second Western development, Geuzenveld, where each WV had its own architect – van Tijen for Rochdale, Dudok for AWV. Complex disputes erupted about open versus closed layouts, high-rise versus low-rise, and van Tijen lined up with the WD against van Eesteren and the SO's complex parceling arrangements. In the final phase, Osdorp, development took a sharp turn "upwards," towards greater variety of building types in general and large-scale multi-story *galerijbouw* in particular. In the mid-1950s, when the first plans for the area were finalized, there was still general consensus that high blocks were unsuitable for families, and indeed for *Woningwet* housing in general. Accordingly, the first suggested use of tall slabs, adjoining the Sloterplas at the center of the Westelijke Tuinsteden, provoked the most complex debates in the years 1955–1957, with numerous alternative plans by architect Piet Zaanstra: after WD proposals for a single, immensely elongated slab were denounced by SO's van Eesteren as "a disaster," three diagonally aligned blocks were finally authorized, built not by the WD but by a private firm for higher-rental tenants – there was a strong correlation initially between high building and the middle classes. The first pile at Osdorp was driven in May 1957 by A. In 't Veld, director of Patrimonium and alderman of public health.[49]

Initial public reaction to the Westelijke Tuinsteden was rather muted. The Roman Catholic *Volkskrant* in 1954 attacked them as "an architectural monster," and in 1959 bemoaned the "anonymity" of Osdorp.[50] But by the 1960s, the old, disciplined social and architectural patterns of pillarization and early postwar modernism were dissolving under the influence of affluence and individualism. It was in this context of burgeoning affluence that the second major phase of postwar Amsterdam expansion, towards the south-east, was first proposed in 1959, and approved in 1964. Reflecting the economic bullishness of the times, the south-east expansion was now seen as not so much a "suburb" as a satellite "mini-city." The strategy was informed by a new kind of avant-garde architectural planning and debate, very different from the old, staid CIAM orthodoxies of Opbouw and the others – as was strikingly demonstrated in the "Pampus Plan" of 1964–1965 – envisaging the south-east extension as a linear city formed of ultra-high-density clustered nodes.[51]

Something of this utopian grandeur survived through to the more utilitarian development that was implemented as the first instalment of the strategy: Bijlmermeer – a 40,000-inhabitant development formed of a relentless honeycomb of nine-story industrialized galerijbouw slabs interspersed with higher towers. Along with Le Mirail, Corviale (Rome) and Alt-Erlaa (Vienna), Bijlmermeer was one of the few even partly built Western European realizations of the late-modernist utopian conglomerate vision of mass housing: many more developments of this scale were built outside Western Europe, in cities ranging from Belgrade to Hong Kong. Organizationally, Bijlmermeer looked backwards rather than forwards, towards the old WD-dominated output system, although the government-encouraged shift to WV control was well underway. No less than eighteen WVs notionally participated in this vast development, but their role was largely to take ownership of completed blocks: the project was laid out by the PWD and built to contracts organized by the WD, in close collaboration with the Ministry, which intended Bijlmermeer as a showcase of the latest (1965) iteration of the "Voorschriften en Wenken," "Woningen voor de jaar 2000." Bijlmermeer would also hopefully break from the past by including many higher-income, even middle-class residents (Figure 6.6).[52]

Figure 6.6 Bijlmermeer, Amsterdam's south-east city-extension, planned from 1965 onwards by the city's Public Works Department, developed by 18 WVs (each with its own architect), and completed by 1975: 1985 view from upper deck of Kempering Flat. Photo: Miles Glendinning

In 1965, Bijlmermeer's detailed development plan was fixed, overwhelmingly comprising family dwellings in multi-story blocks, with "open" ground floors, and extensive industrialized building. With the urgent political pressure to get started, the first 270 dwellings were built in 1965–1966, even before the city extension was approved. The first industrialized building contract, with Intervam, for 1,080 prefabricated dwellings, required construction of a precasting factory, and a second followed for later phases, in the "Indeco-Coignet" system. The giant development was finally completed in 1975, by which time government policy had turned decisively against mass housing. Far from appealing to higher-income tenants, Bijlmermeer was blighted by the same under-occupancy and poor maintenance as some other giant developments: by 1974 the turnover rate was 30% and ten years later 24% of the flats were vacant. Strenuous countermeasures were taken, including consolidation of all the fragmented housing associations (1983) and a general rehab and selective demolition program (from 1992).[53]

More generally, the years from the late 1960s saw a retrenchment from mass social building. With the retreat of austere pillarization, a limited shift towards home-ownership began, but swings in the profitability of private housing around 1980 allowed a dramatic revival of WV social housing in the 1980s: by 1994, 40% of the housing stock was still socially rented.[54] Architecturally, Dutch housing shifted sharply towards quirky solutions such as Piet Blom's "Kasbah" project of dense three-story blocks on raised podiums (1969–1974), and his even more wilfully eccentric Rotterdam-Blaak development of 1982–1984, garishly postmodern in its surreal forms, juxtaposing an eccentrically spired tower with rows of diagonal "cube houses" on stilts. The shift to conservation-neighborhood planning ("woonerven") in the late 1970s was accompanied by the first large-scale demolitions of social housing, as at Linnaeusstraat, Leeuwarden, where 430 flats were demolished in 1977.[55] The late 1980s and 1990s eventually saw the onset of a "new Modernism," reviving some forms of postwar Modernist housing and planning, including regional plans (Ijburg, Vinex) and galerijbouw, but in a radically different, market-led context – for example in the low-rise, ultra-individualized Borneo-Sporenburg dockland regeneration in Amsterdam by architect West 8, 1999–2002.[56] Despite these mounting pressures for commodification and individualism within Dutch housing from the 1990s onwards, the contrast between the pervasively planned system of the Netherlands and the equally entrenched laissez-faire attitudes in Belgium seemed as strong as ever – outlasting the "corporatist" welfare-state epoch in north-western Europe.[57]

Conclusion

In general, within postwar Western European countries, the drive for national modernization spurred the emergence of distinctive institutions, functionally differentiated in typical modernist fashion, which intervened in political crises when the private market was criticized for alleged ineffectiveness, and in turn helped shape the practices of individual states: in sociologist Anthony Giddens's words, "the structural properties of social systems are both the medium and outcome of the practices that constitute those systems.".[58] State-sponsored low-income housing became a prime example of this duality, as both an outcome and a vehicle of expanding state power, which also deeply reflected local cultural patterns – such as pillarization.

In both Belgium and the Netherlands, a "pillarized" social and political structure ultimately inherited from the religious conflicts of the sixteenth and seventeenth centuries formed the organizational foundation of postwar mass housing production, but the ways in which that foundation interacted with the planning systems and architectural forms of modern housing diverged sharply between the two. In Belgium, the split between "Catholic" and "socialist" pillars, between De Taeye and Brunfaut (despite the practical and financial overlaps between the two), seemed to echo, and amplify, the fragmentation of society and individualism of architectural design – whereas in the Netherlands, any fragmenting effects potentially stemming from pillarization were sharply counteracted by the nationally coordinated and municipally amplified preoccupation with planning control over of the built environment: the tokenistic character of WV "control" at Bijlmermeer exemplified the primacy of coordination at the expense of autonomy. Elsewhere in continental Western Europe, a similarly surprising diversity was found in other supposedly homogenous groupings of nation-states – for example within Scandinavia, between collectivist Sweden and individualist Norway – but nowhere was the sibling divergence as pronounced as in the pillarized Low Countries.

Notes

1 Gøsta Esping-Anderson, *The Three Worlds of Welfare Capitalism* (Princeton, NJ: Princeton University Press, 1990). See also Mark Swenarton, Tom Avermaete and Dirk van den Heuvel eds, *Architecture and the Welfare State* (Abingdon: Routledge, 2015).

2 NB: for convenience, in this chapter, the Flemish form will generally be used for Belgian national initiatives and institutions, and French for colonial matters.

3 Karina van Herck and Tom Avermaete eds, *Wonen in Welvaart: Woningbouw en wooncultuur in Vlaanderen, 1948–1973*, (Rotterdam: Uitgeverij 010, 2006), 272–278. On the Belgium-Netherlands comparison, see generally Hilde Heynen, "Belgium and the Netherlands: Two Different Ways of Coping with the Housing Crisis, 1945–70," *Home Cultures*, vol. 7, no. 2, 2010, 159–177.

4 Els de Vos, "Living with High-Rise Modernity: The Modernist Kiel Housing Estate of Renaat Braem, a Catalyst to a Socialist Modern Way of Life," *Home Cultures*, vol. 7, no. 2, 2010, 137; *Wonen in Welvaart*, 275; Michael Ryckewaert, *Building the Economic Backbone of the Belgian Welfare State: Infrastructure, Planning and Architecture* (Rotterdam: Uitgeverij 010, 2011);

Erik Buyst, *An Economic History of Residential Building in Belgium* (Leuven: Leuven University Press, 1992), 218. Politically speaking, the post-1945 bedrock of Belgian pillarization was the two main postwar parties, the Christelijke Volkspartij (CVP, or Christian Democrats) and the Belgische Socialistische Partij (BSP). See also *Wonen in Welvaart*, 4; Hilde Heynen and Janina Gosseye, "The Welfare State in Flanders: De-Pillarization and the Nebulous City," in Swenarton et al., eds., *Architecture and the Welfare State*, 51–68.

5 *Wonen in Welvaart*, 68, 110–127.

6 Renaat Braem, F Strauven, *Het Lelijkste Land Ter Wereld*, ASP, Brussels, 2010 (new edition; 1968 original).

7 *Wonen in Welvaart*, 68–78.

8 Buyst, 226–227.

9 *Wonen in Welvaart*, 54, 67–78; Heynen, "Belgium and the Netherlands," 167, 173; Heynen and Gosseye, "Welfare State in Flanders," 53.

10 *Wonen in Welvaart*, 147–164.

11 *Wonen in Welvaart*, 95–110.

12 *Wonen in Welvaart*, 203–216.

13 *Wonen in Welvaart*, 135, 231–248.

14 Klein Heide, https://inventaris.onroerenderfgoed.be/erfgoedobjecten/120667.

15 Maurizio Cohen, "Willy van der Meeren's 'Ieder Zijn Huis': Saving a Fragile Giant," *Journal / International Working-Party for Documentation and Conservation of Buildings, Sites, and the Neighborhoods of the Modern Movement (Docomomo)* vol. 54, 2016, 66–71.

16 Kevin Absillis and Katrien Jacobs, *Van Hugo Klaus tot hoelahoep, Vlaanderen in Beweging 1950–1960*, 497–507, Garant, Antwerpen, 2007.

17 https://inventaris.onroerenderfgoed.be/erfgoedobjecten/122126. *L'Architecture d'Aujourd'hui*, 1954, 66–69; Van Herck and Avermaete, *Wonen in Welvaart*, 10–11; G Segers, *60 jaar Luchtbal. Van polderlandschap tot moderne stadswijk*, Antwerpen, 1985, 31–32, 54–60. https://inventaris.onroerenderfgoed.be/erfgoedobjecten/302578; K Van Herck, "Wooneenheid Kiel," in J Braeken (ed), *Renaat Braem 1910–2001. Architect*, Relicta Monografieën, Brussels, 2010 (part 2). 89–102; Els De Vos, "Living with High-Rise Modernity," *Home Cultures*, vol. 2, 2010, 142–143. C Grafe and B Decroos (eds), *Linkeroever, Sprong over de Schelde* (Antwerp: VAI, 2017).

18 Absillis and Jacobs, *Van Hugo Klaus*, 50. Cité Modèle, Van Herck and Avermaete, *Wonen in Welvaart*, 178–193; *La Maison*, 5, May 1968, 236–237.

19 Karina Van Herck, "Woonwijk Kruiskenslei," in Braeken, *Renaat Braem*, 182–198.

20 Absillis and Jacobs, *Van Hugo Klaus*, 50.

21 Local HVM was the Samenwerkende Maatschappij voor Goedkope Woningen en Woonvertekken van Leuven (SMGWW): K Van Herck, "Sint-Maartensdal," in Braeken, *Renaat Braem*, 148–157.

22 Catholic party: KVP Katholieke Volkspartij; Protestant: CHU Christelijke-Historische Unie/ARP Anti-Revolutionnaire Partij; Liberal: VVP Volkspartij voor Vrijheid en Democratie.

23 Heynen, "Belgium and the Netherlands," 163–164; Liesbeth Bervoets, "Defeating Public Enemy No. 1 – Mediating Housing in the Netherlands," *Home Cultures*, vol. 7, no. 2, 2010, 179–195.

24 Michael Harloe, *The People's Home – Social Rented Housing in Europe and America* (Oxford: Blackwell), 244–247, 304–319; Friso Wiebenga, *A History of the Netherlands* (London: Bloomsbury, 2015), 230–236.

25 Information Department of the Ministry of Reconstruction, *Introduction to the Housing Problem in the Netherlands*, Ministry of Reconstruction, Den

Haag, 1953, 10; J Middleton, "Housing in The Hague," *RIAS Quarterly*, vol. 86, 1950, 53–55.

26 *Bouw*, 5 April 1970, 765–773; Harloe, *The People's Home?* 309–313; I Teijmant and F Martin, *Nieuw-West*, Bas Lubberhuizen, Amsterdam, 1994, 9–10; Information Department, *Rent in the Netherlands*, Ministry of Reconstruction, Den Haag, 1950.

27 Information Department, *Introduction to the Housing Problem*, 19; Central Directorate of Reconstruction, *Woningen 1946–1952 Nederland*, Den Haag, 1952.

28 Central Directorate, *Woningen;* Harloe, *The People's Home?* 300; R Rosner, "Housing and Planning in Holland," *Building*, 18 February 1966, 339–342.

29 Harloe, *The People's Home?* 309–313; Stadsontwikkeling Rotterdam, *Stedebouw in Rotterdam*, Van Gennep, Amsterdam, 1981, fold-out.

30 Stedelijk Museum, *Het Nieuwe Bouwen, Amsterdam 1920–1960*, Delft UP, Delft, 1983, 80–82; Information Department, *Introduction to the Housing Problem*, 19; Ministry of Reconstruction, *Revision of the Legal Measures Concerning Physical Planning*, Den Haag, 1953.

31 *Bouw*, 25 April 1970, 765–768, 771–772; Harloe, *The People's Home?* 306–308; Marjorie Bulos and Stephen Walker eds., *The Legacy and Opportunity for High Rise Housing in Europe: The Management of Innovation* (London: Housing Studies Group, 1987), 35–51. Both 1955–1961 and 1964–1965 saw significant over-fulfilment of the ministry's output targets.

32 Harloe, *The People's Home?* 313–317, 474.

33 Françoise Paulen et al., *Sociale Woningbouw Amsterdam Atlas* (Amsterdam: Amsterdamse Federatie van Woningcorporaties, 1992), 10–12. Paul Balchin, *Housing Policy in Europe* (London: Routledge, 1996), 90–91; Information Department, Ministry of Housing, *Some Data on Housing in the Netherlands*, Den Haag, 1974; *Bouw*, 5 April 1970, 771.

34 Ton Heijdra, *Amsterdam Nieuw-West*, Rene de Milliano, Amsterdam 2010, 75; Stedelijk Museum, *Het Nieuwe Bouwen*, 80–82; Teijmant and Martin, *Nieuw-West*, 9.

35 Information Department, *Introduction to the Housing Problem*, 10; R Blijstra, *Netherlands Architecture since 1900*, Amsterdam 1960, 6–14; Museum Boymans van Beuningen, *Het Nieuwe Bouwen in Rotterdam*, Delft UP, Delft, 1982, 109–121.

36 A Bos, *De stad van toekomst, de toekomst van de stad* (Rotterdam: Voorhoeve, 1946); Martin and Wagenaar, "Building a New Community," 147. Museum Boymans van Beuningen, *Het Nieuwe Bouwen*, 109–121; Frank Wassenberg, "The Netherlands," *Built Environment*, vol. 32, no. 1, 2006, 15–16; Blijstra, *Netherlands Architecture*; Heijdra, *Amsterdam Nieuw-West*, 66–75; Stadsontwikkeling Rotterdam, *Stedebouw*, 46–47.

37 *Atlas Sociale Woningbouw*, 12–13.

38 Ministry of Housing, *Some Data; Amsterdam – Wonen 1900–1970*, Amsterdam, 1970.

39 *Bouw*, 25 April 1970; Information Department, *Introduction to the Housing Problem*, 15; Museum Boymans van Beuningen, *Het Nieuwe Bouwen*, 80–82.

40 Heynen, "Belgium and the Netherlands," 165.

41 *Atlas Sociale Woningbouw*, 12–13; Museum Boymans van Beuningen, *Het Nieuwe Bouwen*, 89, 121–124; Stadsontwikkeling, *Stedebouw*, 44–45; Central Directorate, *Woningen;* Information Department, *Introduction to the Housing Problem*, 16; Middleton, "Housing," 53–55; Rosner, "Housing and Planning"; *The Builder*, 12 February 1954, 307–308; P C de Groot, "Maastricht bouwt Malberg," *Bouw*, 29 August 1964.

42 Bulos and Walker, *Legacy and Opportunity*, 35–51; Stedelijk Museum, *Het Nieuwe Bouwen*, 92–93.
43 Harloe, *The People's Home?* 307; Government Physical Planning Service, *Physical Planning in the Netherlands*, Den Haag, 1952; Museum Boymans van Beuningen, *Het Nieuwe Bouwen*, 109–110; *RIBA Journal*, September 1956, 455–456; Central Directorate, *Woningen*; "Nieuw flat-type te Rotterdam," *Bouw*, 1952, 362–364.
44 *The Builder*, 12 February 1954, 307–308; "Galerijbouw in de Haagse Moerwijk," *Bouw*, 1952, 476–480.
45 *Bouw*, 1952, 362–364; *Housing Review*, 7.4, Jul/Aug 1958, 118; Rosner, "Housing and Planning," 340; Heijdra, *Amsterdam Nieuw-West*, 106.
46 Museum Boymans van Beuningen, *Het Nieuwe Bouwen*, 110–122, 139–157.
47 Stadsontwikkeling, *Stedebouw in Rotterdam*, 44–57.
48 Stedelijk Museum, *Het Nieuwe Bouwen*, 54–74, 79–110; Amsterdamse Federatie van Woningcorporaties, *In Eenheid zit Kracht*, AFW, Amsterdam, 2007, 12.
49 Stedelijk Museum, *Het Niewe Bouwen*, 85–97: the multi-story percentage at Osdorp was much higher – 26.5% compared to 10% at Slotermeer, 1.5% at Geuzenveld and 8.3% at Slotervaart. A contemporary argued of Dijkgraafsplein that 'moeder-de-vrouw heeft op de hangbruggen namelijk overzicht en Pietje kan er buiten spelen' ('the housewife can keep an eye out from the balconies and little Johnny can play outside'): Heijdra, *Amsterdam Nieuw-West*, 75–77, 93–97, 114–117; Teijmant and Martin, *Nieuw-West*; *Amsterdam-Wonen 1900–1970*.
50 Heijdra, *Amsterdam Nieuw-West*, 114–147; Teijmant and Martin, *Nieuw-West*, 10, 43–45.
51 *Archis*, 9–1997, 'De nieuwe Bijlmermeer' (special edition); Directorate of Public Works, *Stedebouwkundige ontwikkeling en het grondbeleid in Amsterdam*, Amsterdam, 1967; *Bouw*, 7 November 1964; Cees Nooteboom, *Unbuilt Netherlands*, Architectural Press, 1985, 80–81; *Bouw*, 14 October 1967, 1476–1477.
52 One WV claimed, 'de Bijlmermeer is als het ware vóór en niet dóór de corporaties gebouwd' ('The Bijlmermeer was in effect built *for* rather than *by* the corporations'): *Bouw*, 19 June 1965, 946–950; H McClintock and M Fox, "The Bijlmermeer Development," *Journal of the Royal Town-Planning Institute*, July-August 1971, 313–316; *Archis*, 9–1997, 'De nieuwe Bijlmermeer'; *Atlas sociale Woningbouw Amsterdam*, 10.
53 *Bouw*, 14 October 1967, 1476–1477; *Archis*, 9–1997, 'De nieuwe Bijlmermeer'.
54 F M Dielman, "Social-Rented Housing," *Urban Studies*, vol. 31, no. 3, 1994, 447–463; Balchin, *Housing Policy in Europe*, 84–98; Harloe, *The People's Home?* 474.
55 ANWB, Royal Dutch Touring Club, "Woonerf," 1980; Dirk van den Heuvel, "The Open Society and its Experiments: The Case of the Netherlands and Piet Blom," in *Architecture and the Welfare State*, 133–154; Bulos and Walker, eds., 35–53.
56 Lidwine Spoormans, D N Carillo, H Zijlstra, T Pérez-Cano, "Planning History of a Dutch New Town," *Urban Planning*, vol. 4, no. 3, 2019. *De Architect*, 2–1988, 56–63; A Oosterman, *Housing in the Netherlands* (Rotterdam: NAI, 1996), 12–21; "Het woonmilieu Ijburg," *Archis*, 5–1995, 7.
57 A 2006 article argued that to Belgian reformists, the Netherlands seemed an ideal beyond reach – 'een perfect geordend, zeer net en modern land' ('a perfectly ordered, very tidy and modern country') – whereas Dutch policymakers

were uninterested in Belgium: Van Herck and Avermaete, *Wonen en Welvaart*, 272–278; see also Heynen, "Belgium and the Netherlands," 159–177.

58 Anthony Giddens, *Central Problems in Social Theory* (London: Macmillan Press, 1979), 69. See also Friedrich Engels, *Der Ursprung der Familie, des Privateigenthums und des Staats* (Hattingen: Swiss Popular Press, 1884), 58–59; Max Weber, *Politik als Beruf*, Lecture to the Free Students' Union, Munich, 1919.

Part III
(De)Segregation and the Housing Enclave

7 Housing the People Who "Lived Free"

Inhabiting Social Housing in the Tin-Can Neighborhood

Kıvanç Kılınç and M. Melih Cin

During a city council meeting in Izmir on June 9, 1965, three members submitted a written proposal advocating for the removal of the Ege neighborhood in the Kahramanlar district and the relocation of its residents to a district where "dwellings would at least be habitable."[1] Populated by a predominantly Roma community, most of whom lived in extreme poverty, the area in question was known as the "tin-can neighborhood" (*tenekeli mahalle*). It was situated in close proximity to the formally planned upper- and middle-class developments and state-run factories in Izmir, a coastal city in western Turkey. In their appeal to the council, the members characterized the place as "a bleeding misery wound" and urged the construction of new housing projects. This planned settlement, they argued, could be modeled on the recently completed social housing project in the Cumhuriyet neighborhood, on the opposite end of the city.[2] The latter was initiated in the early 1960s within the Izmir municipality's officially designated "squatter settlement prevention zone" (*gecekondu önleme bölgesi*) and consisted of minimally designed semidetached houses.[3] In the following years, it would be incorporated into "more developed and modern" housing projects, including fifty-three five-story apartment buildings (Figure 7.1).[4]

Despite their variations in form, most housing types implemented in the Cumhuriyet neighborhood in the 1960s and the 1970s followed an architectural diagram common in Turkey, which mirrored the earlier German *Siedlung* models.[5] Envisioning and catering to the lifestyle of an idealized, modern nuclear family, these plans were meant to provide a well-ordered and hygienic domestic setting by dividing the dwelling into clearly delineated private and public quarters.[6] However, built out of reinforced concrete and vertically stacked, these units could not meet the needs of larger extended families or be further expanded. Furthermore, the provision of social housing evoked, if not promised, the elevation of the impoverished residents of the inner city to a middle-class way of life. Yet in the use of smaller-than-usual floor areas and cheap construction materials, these projects failed to meet minimum standards.[7] Few common activities and spaces were on offer in the Cumhuriyet neighborhood beyond the parks and public schools planned in the vicinity. The participatory administrative

DOI: 10.4324/9781351182966-11

Figure 7.1 Izmir Karşıyaka Cumhuriyet Neighborhood Social Housing Project (1979). A contemporary view of the neighborhood surrounded by new settlements. Photo: Ahenk Yılmaz, 2020.

structure of social housing was altogether missing.[8] In short, the social remained noticeably absent from social housing.

After further deliberations the municipality decided against razing the tin-can neighborhood and, instead of displacing the community, undertook an on-site social housing project. What followed was a remarkable experiment that significantly departed from the housing models commonly employed in Turkey. This chapter tells the story of the Ege Neighborhood Social Housing Project in Izmir (1969)—hereafter referred to as ENSHP—which adopted an approach that sought to accommodate community life and user participation. Developed by the municipality, the project exemplified the localization of modernist architectural forms, which were creatively adapted by its inhabitants to respond to their dwelling practices and cultures. We argue that the gradual appropriation by the users of the project, which has almost seamlessly blended into the texture of the neighborhood, offers insights into the question of how locality and culture can better inform the design of modernist blocks. But more importantly, we seek to highlight the importance of reintroducing this project into the disciplinary memory of architectural history in Turkey as a place of architectural value.

Social Housing in Turkey and the *Gecekondu* Problem

Despite experimenting with various models, housing policies in Turkey have not been able to adequately address the question of housing inequality.[9] As Barış Alp Özden has shown, government policies encouraged instead home ownership in the 1970s by providing public subsidies to workers' cooperatives. According to Özden, these housing cooperatives often ended up building "... middle-class housing, which was far too costly for low-income workers, while unauthorized land appropriations and squatting became the primary mechanism through which the working poor could be incorporated into the urban fabric."[10] The wide-spread use, in the 1970s, of construction technologies for multistory housing blocks—tunnel-form construction and, to a lesser extent, prefabrication—did not make housing more affordable or accessible.[11] Furthermore, the industrialization and new job opportunities in cities accelerated the migration from rural areas and the proliferation of squatter (*gecekondu*) settlements.[12] Increasingly, the role of the central and local governments was limited to regulating the housing market and other fiscal priorities. Although legal frameworks were often in place, public agencies such as the General Directorate of Land Office (Arsa Ofisi Genel Müdürlüğü) rarely had sufficient funding to buy land preemptively to prevent land speculation.[13]

The situation in post-World War II Izmir was symptomatic of Turkey's prevailing housing question. According to Özden, "Between 1955 and 1965, rents in the three major cities of İstanbul, Ankara, and İzmir increased 150 percent." It became increasingly difficult for lower-income residents to find proper housing in major cities, and this increased the growth of informal housing settlements in the periphery of İstanbul and Ankara.[14] Added to this long list of problems was the low quality of available housing.[15] In short, the tripartite strategy adopted in the 1970s—through the combined efforts of the Real Estate and Credit Bank of Turkey (Türkiye Emlak Kredi Bankası), which supplied credit for developers but also undertook construction; small- and large-scale housing cooperatives; and the municipal administration (with funding secured by the Ministry of Public Works and Housing [İmar ve İskan Bakanlığı])—fell short of meeting the demand.[16]

Against this backdrop Turkish officials sought better, less expensive solutions, and two of them seemed to come forward. In the second half of the 1970s, at a time when the concept of "houses for the people" (*halk konutu*) was becoming more prominent in Turkish political and official discourse,[17] the new mayor of Izmir established the Social Housing Directorate (Sosyal Konutlar Müdürlüğü) as an integral part of the municipal government. The directorate included in its program two seemingly contradictory goals: building new social housing blocks, primarily to replace the *gecekondu*, and rehabilitating existing informal housing settlements.[18] As a result, in Izmir, as in other large cities in Turkey, certain areas were designated as squatter settlement prevention zones. Social housing at this time was considered a useful instrument to stop uncontrolled urban expansion. For instance, the Izmir municipal annual report of 1977 defined the *gecekondu* as "an oil-stain spreading through the peripheries of the city."[19] At the same time this building program went hand in hand with its absolute opposite: legalizing informal housing by providing title deeds to the residents and by extending public services (such as infrastructure, water, electricity, and transportation) to these neighborhoods.[20] These two policies, which seemed contradictory, were in fact directed toward the same goal. The supply of social housing was far from meeting the demand, and a more populist and practical formula was also put in place.

This approach had figured prominently in the writings of foreign city planning specialists who were invited to Turkey in the 1950s through the US-sponsored Marshall Plan (formally the European Recovery Program, 1948–1951) and prepared reports for low-cost housing developments in both urban and rural settings.[21] These experts redefined informal housing as an "opportunity" rather than an annoyance or blight, especially, because Turkey was a "developing" country and lacked the resources to fund large-scale housing projects. Therefore they suggested that the *gecekondu* could be adopted as a practical model for lower-cost housing through the "aided self-help method."[22] The idea behind this method was that, with financial and technical support and infrastructure provision, homeowners could build or repair their own houses. What were formerly considered illegal settlements could then become a viable solution to the growing shortage of affordable housing throughout the country. Such dwellings, which already housed large masses of people, could be produced more cheaply and with much more flexibility in terms of materials than comparable multistory modern housing blocks.[23]

Unlike other housing experts in this group, Bernard Wagner went beyond mere advising.[24] During his residency in Turkey between 1955 and 1956, he toured Turkish cities to examine living conditions, wrote lengthy reports, and recommended aided self-help as an efficient method of housing production. Wagner also outlined architectural plans for a workers' housing settlement in Bursa and made sketches for a larger urban proposal for Gerze, a coastal town in northern Turkey.[25] In Gerze his projects were actually built (with significant changes).[26] Popularly known as *yangın evleri* (fire houses), since they were built after a devastating fire that wiped out the town in the 1950s, they were not designed specifically for workers but as budget homes developed for various family and professional types. These rowhouses, in groups of four or six, followed the so-called garden city tradition, to a great degree popularized in Turkey by the German architects practiced there in the 1930s.[27] This choice was in line with Wagner's own reports; he had supported Turkey's transition from detached housing to both rowhouses and multistory apartment buildings.[28] In the first mass-housing experiments in Istanbul, Turkish architects had followed "American" models and designed multistory blocks, but Wagner's design for Gerze consisted of rowhouses that were tailored to the needs of diverse groups.[29] This hitherto unseen approach, which took into account the diverse lifestyles of the residents and followed a more horizontal plan, resurfaced some fifteen odd years later in Izmir.

Building for the People "Who Lived Free": ENSHP

In the late 1960s, two actors in municipal politics came to prominence in Izmir. The first was Osman Kibar, a leading public figure who initiated the development of ENSHP in the early 1970s as the mayor of Izmir (1964–1973). It is important to note that Izmir was one of the first cities in Turkey to make use of American aid, and numerous state-run factories and industry complexes were established there from the 1950s to the 1970s.[30] The Aegean Region Chamber of Industry (Ege Bölgesi Sanayi Odası, EBSO, 1954) was the first regional chamber in Turkey and the second one on the national scale. The first chairperson of its board was again Kibar.[31] Since the political climate was also favorable to the city at the time—İzmir was a stronghold of the ruling center-right parties—it seems that aid was more easily channeled to projects there.[32] The second major actor was İhsan Alyanak, the opposition Republican People's Party's (CHP) speaker in the city council, who fully supported the project, emphasizing the issue of social justice.[33] Alyanak was elected mayor of Izmir in 1973 and again in 1977, remaining in office until the military coup in 1980 violently disrupted democratic parliamentary politics in Turkey. The housing units produced by the Izmir municipality in his second term provided a widely imitated architectural plan.[34]

In 1968, while both Kibar and Alyanak were in power, the municipal administration brought the issue of the lack of decent accommodation in the Ege neighborhood to the attention of the council once again. The motion for providing social housing passed with considerable support, but there was a critical adjustment, which stirred further discussion among members: the act proposed the construction of new social housing blocks right in the neighborhood rather than at a remote site.[35] When a member complained that the proposed project would sit on one of the most valuable pieces of real estate in the city's possession and that the occupants would pay little in return, Mayor Kibar explained that the idea of living next to a Roma community received firm opposition from other local communities. Although he was not fully comfortable with the decision either, plans to build in a new location had to be dropped altogether.[36] Another reason for the decision was that "it was very difficult to dissuade these citizens [the Romani] from their habits and they would not move somewhere else" since "they did not want to live apart from one another."[37] According to the mayor, the Roma community had "made the habit of free living," and with the current proposal they would not have to leave the neighborhood to which they were accustomed.[38] He underlined that "it was not them who resisted" against their relocation and that he wanted to make sure both sides were satisfied and no disturbances occurred.[39] Then the municipality's project office (İmar Müdürlüğü Proje Şubesi) moved to prepare the blueprints and architectural models for the proposed social housing blocks. The aim was to "remove the extremely ugly tin-can shelters" and replace them with "healthy and social means for living."[40]

The tin-can neighborhood, where part of ENSHP was built, extends across about seventeen acres and was populated largely by the Greek minority in Izmir before the great fire of 1922 and the 1924 population exchange between Greece and Turkey.[41] The neighborhood today is also called by its residents *murtake*, a reference to the Greek *mortakia*, "the country of the dead," referring to a Greek cemetery that existed in the area. In interviews conducted in 2014–2016 some of the members of the Roma community traced their roots to migrants from Thessaloniki who arrived in Izmir during the population exchange.[42] Located close to a major city park (Kültürpark, 1936) and to primarily well-to-do areas such as the historical Alsancak neighborhood, the tin-can neighborhood is surrounded by small- and medium-scale industrial complexes to the north as well as a local train line to the west and the Melez Stream to the south and east. The neighborhood is home to around 5,000 people, most of whom live in small detached houses packed together along streets and passageways that do not seem to follow any regular plan.[43]

Historically Roma communities around the world have suffered from many forms of discrimination, poverty, and ghettoization.[44] In the Ege neighborhood the problem of social isolation was compounded by the lack of public transportation and easy pedestrian access to the neighborhood, which became closed off both physically and visually;[45] the proximity of state-run factories;[46] foul smells and nearby abandoned sites; and the absence of recreational facilities.[47] Prior to the 1970s most of the people lived in simple sheds made with both permanent and waste materials such as tin plates (hence the nickname tin-can neighborhood). Today many of the residents live in homes made not of tin plates but of more permanent building materials.[48] More than 90% of the existing housing stock consists of poorly built detached houses with a maximum of three stories, which are continually added to, annexed, and fitted to new purposes.[49] Some contain open spaces, such as small gardens. In 2015, around 2,700 people lived in 772 housing units, but only 582 of these inhabitants had title deeds.[50] The settlement is thus densely populated, as many individual houses share walls and, in some cases, even the roofs touch each other. The houses are surrounded by narrow passages allowing only pedestrian movement (Figure 7.2).

In 1969 the municipality of Izmir planned twelve social housing blocks in the neighborhood to accommodate 200 families, but only seven of them ended up being built.[51] The municipality owned the land, developed the architectural projects for ENSHP, awarded the contract, and was responsible for the surveying of construction until completion, but the project

Figure 7.2 A narrow passage between houses, Ege Neighborhood, Izmir. Photo: Kıvanç Kılınç, 2014.

was financed through Real Estate and Credit Bank loans supplied by the Ministry of Public Works and Housing.[52] Municipal officials estimated that a single unit in each housing block ("bloklu ev") with a floor space of forty-seven square meters would cost about 17,000 Turkish lira and the owners would pay this amount together with 3,000 lira in interest in a twenty-year period.[53] When the work came to an end in 1971, 118 families were provided with housing units.[54] All residents—except for those in one of the larger housing blocks, which remained unfinished except for the bare structural system—were given title ownership (provided a subsidized monthly rent was regularly paid). The unfinished building too was completed over time, as the people from the neighborhood carried out the rest of the construction and simply moved in (Figure 7.3).[55]

ENSHP consists of two types of housing blocks. Individual units have the same floor plan, but each type contains a different number of apartments. The first type was employed for the three larger blocks located on the main street. These contain eighteen units and six shops located on the ground floors. This is another aspect of the project that is social: providing job opportunities for the residents. The second type contains sixteen units. Planned behind the main street, these buildings do not include retail space.

Figure 7.3 ENSHP. The housing blocks with sixteen units. Photo: Kıvanç Kılınç, 2014.

While all the blocks were initially planned to be three-story buildings, on June 11, 1969, an additional motion was proposed in the municipal council for an amendment to the development plan, which increased the height from 9.8 meters to 12.8 meters and therefore to four stories.[56] The council agreed to the mayor's proposal, and it was then passed to the committee of public works. The committee agreed with the proposed change, commenting that three-floor blocks would fall short of meeting the housing need of all the residents.[57] We argue that in spite of this added floor, the overall horizontality of the building blocks played a significant role in allowing the project to blend into the existing urban fabric.

A Social Housing Project Localized

Most multifamily lower- and middle-income apartments in Turkey display a common plan type: each unit is accessed from a small entrance hallway—a niche that functions as a visual barrier that protects the privacy of the interior. The hall connects the kitchen, a living room, and a guest room, which is used for entertaining guests. A corridor (usually separated with a door) gives access to the private quarters where the bedrooms and the bathroom are located. If possible, a lavatory is provided near the entrance for the visitors, separate from the family bathroom.[58] In a typical mid- and high-rise housing block, all units share a main entrance to the building and a circulation core, but there are no common spaces where residents can meet and socialize. Even if the block is perceived to be horizontally arranged from the exterior, the units remain disconnected, accessed via separate vertical cores: a block typically comprises two or three vertical apartment buildings stitched together by common walls. A shared corridor and other communal spaces, which a horizontal organization would have allowed, are usually missing.

The design of ENSHP provides several interesting twists and alternatives to this plan. First, the layouts are atypical: the apartments share a semi-open circulation system adjacent to the front facade. These consist of stairwells and an open corridor, which are visually accessible from the street. They are used not only for circulation but also as balconies where residents can gather and hang clothes to dry outside.[59] Furthermore, from this communal space one directly enters the living room of an apartment. There is no entrance hall or short corridor, as in the more typical units described above. Instead, a small hall is located within the plan. But this hall serves to link the toilet, bathroom, and kitchen, all of which are minimally designed, rather than providing a visual barrier to the private quarters of the home. The bedroom is directly accessed from the living room and does not connect to this hall (Figure 7.4).

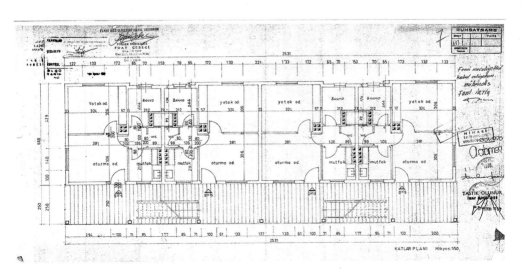

Figure 7.4 ENSHP. Type floor plans of the housing blocks with sixteen units. Konak Municipality Archives, Izmir, accessed in 2015.

Second, the response of the residents to this plan layout has not been to turn inward and add visual barriers to preserve each unit's privacy. In interviews conducted with the residents, none have cited the openness of the units to the outside as a shortcoming. Most houses have minimal gardens, and life is typically spent outside during day and night.[60] Beginning in the afternoon, street vendors are more frequently encountered, and outdoor spaces are more actively used; in a way, the main street where all the shops and coffeehouses are located "acts as the community center of the neighborhood."[61] Apart from the main street, as Melih Cin commented in his survey of the neighborhood, doorsteps serve as "small squares" customized by the residents. Here "the streets function as an extension of houses" and thus are always populated.[62] Both the main street and the small niches are most crowded late at night, when people return from work, including casual laborers, florists, and those who work in waste scavenging and trading recycled materials.

Specific forms of socialization and entertainment, such as the Spring Festival (*Hıdırellez*), when the rest of the city pours into various Roma neighborhoods, and three-day-long colorful wedding ceremonies all add to the extroverted use of the existing homes and continual interaction between the families. Some members of the local community point to the strong sense of solidarity and culture of collective living among neighbors, which becomes manifest especially in funerals and at wedding ceremonies.[63] The latter take place in the open space between four of the social housing blocks located behind the main street, and the celebrations are usually attended by 400–500 people.[64] Unlike regular weddings in the city, these offer entertainment beginning quite late in the evening and continuing until early morning. For the same reason it is difficult for the local community to rent a "proper" wedding hall (Figures 7.5 and 7.6).[65]

The residents offer mixed views about the current use of ENSHP, however. Multistory blocks do not provide individual courtyards or gardens, and some of the residents complain about the lack of such personalized space. When the flats are not regularly maintained or repaired, frequent utility failures cause quarrels among the tenants or owners. Detached houses with gardens (*müstakil ev*) seem preferable to some residents even if they are made of tin plates.[66] During the construction of ENSHP in 1969, the mayor had to respond to complaints in the council about the low construction quality. Criticism of the quality of construction—in the basement, walls, and staircases as well as coating and woodworking—and apparent lack of attention of the municipality's building inspectors came from multiple corners.[67] Recent interviews revealed that the apartments, although initially helpful in increasing the living standards of the residents, were no longer suitable: the minimally designed units were not spacious enough for larger and extended families.[68] These criticisms do not necessarily stem from a perceived lack of privacy in the units. Nor do the residents want to be shut off from their neighbors. On the contrary, as evidenced in Gönül İlhan's work, most feel less confined and "freer" living in single-family houses.[69]

Figure 7.5 The open space in between the housing blocks, where wedding ceremonies and *Hıdırellez* celebrations take place. Photo: Kıvanç Kılınç, 2014.

Figure 7.6 *Hıdırellez* celebrations on the main street of the neighborhood with the larger housing blocks seen in the background. Photo: Kıvanç Kılınç, 2017.

Conclusion: Learning from ENSHP and Its Lived Histories

In the fifty years that have passed since the construction of ENSHP, hardly any affordable housing initiative in Turkey has taken into account user-oriented models that respond to local dwelling cultures.[70] Considering the excessive standardization of mass housing production across the country in the last fifteen years under the aegis of Turkey's Mass Housing Administration (TOKİ), the official lack of interest in alternative and flexible types of housing, as well as the politics behind it, calls for a more extensive scholarly inquiry.[71]

Architects and planners can nevertheless still draw lessons by taking an interest in the afterlife of ENSHP. With the population increase in the last fifty years, new living spaces were added not only to the detached houses in the neighborhood but also to the social housing blocks. The concerns briefly mentioned in the previous section encouraged owners in most buildings to build extensions and to partially "occupy" the common circulation areas by incorporating them into individual apartments. In addition to the creative partitioning of the existing units, the shops were also converted to apartments: some of the owners gradually divided the spaces allocated for retail in the three blocks overlooking the main street and turned parts of them into living areas.[72] Furthermore, the flats are often painted in different colors, making it easier to identify them. The flexible nature of the reinforced concrete system and the horizontal planning of the blocks have made such modifications possible.[73] Today there are only a few shops in use—including kiosks, game rooms with foosball tables, and coffeehouses—while the rest seem to serve as extensions of the homes. Finally, in the case of the unfinished housing block, the practices of appropriation went above and beyond adding and subtracting parts; the local community played a significant role in its "informal" construction (Figure 7.7).

The significance of ENSHP as a housing experiment is further amplified when we consider its distinctive place in the history of affordable housing in Turkey. Whereas the majority of examples have reproduced downscaled and cheaper versions of generic typologies and with conventional spatial divisions well dressed in a seemingly modernist envelope, ENSHP emerged as a nuanced, localized design that has been more adaptable to the use and economic needs of the Roma community. But this was an experiment, whether by intention or not, that was ignored right from its inception. Its original, atypical plans and unusual process of production and occupation have not been widely acknowledged. Nor has it served as a model for the city's numerous social housing projects that followed. So, what does this "state of exception" in the history of social housing in Turkey and the silence in the afterlife of ENSHP mean? What can we learn from a "marginal" project that was built for one of the most marginalized communities in the city?

As many scholars have argued, the use of the category, the urban poor, like the term *slum*, is in itself problematic, as it homogenizes a vastly diverse set of conditions and people, caricatures the reality of impoverished

Figure 7.7 ENSHP. Housing units extended to the common circulation areas. Photo: Kıvanç Kılınç, 2015.

settlements, and reduces dwellers to certain stereotypes.[74] Shane Ewen writes that "slums are as much cultural artefacts and constructions of the journalistic imagination and the prejudices of municipal authorities as they are popular reflections of the limited life choices available to poor city residents."[75] Among the elitist constructions of the other, the Roma community is among those seen least favorably, and the most marginalized[76]— so much so that in the case of Izmir's Ege Mahallesi, the reluctance and resistance of their potential new neighbors dissuaded municipal officials from moving the settlement to another location in the city. Ironically, the territorial stigmatization of the Roma community "saved" them, for over five decades, from displacement and dispersal, contrary to the dominant tendency in Turkey and across the world to eradicate low-income inner city neighborhoods and replace them with luxury housing settlements and malls, and move their residents to the urban fringes.[77]

But the isolation and marginalization of the neighborhood continued in the following decades. More physical borders, such as the new suburban railway system, cut the neighborhood from the rest of the city. The divestment from Turkey's social welfare system has been felt especially with the privatization of the state-run factories nearby and the loss of almost all viable job opportunities in the formal sector. Interviews conducted with the residents in 2014–2016 revealed that unemployment reached 61.8% and the stigmatization of the neighborhood was a key factor in mass unemployment.[78] Furthermore, the description of the residents as people "who made the habit of free living," a phrase that was uttered in the abovementioned municipal council meetings, apparently referred to the "marginal" dwelling cultures of the Roma community, contrasted with a "proper" domestic family lifestyle. Could the fact that it was built for those who had such a "free" lifestyle anyway be the main reason why the architectural value of this project—with layouts that deviated from normative models, common living spaces, and an afterlife characterized by constant repair and readjustment—has failed to attract considerable interest?

To its visitors today, ENSHP looks like one of the most recognizable and familiar elements of the neighborhood.[79] It may be precisely because the project has been fully integrated into the texture and culture of this place that it has become equally marginalized and is no longer recognized by the canon either as "modern" or as "architecture."

The authors would like to thank the editors for their valuable comments and suggestions and for giving this chapter an inspiring new direction. We would also like to extend our thanks to the staff of APİKAM (Ahmet Piriştina City Archive and Museum) in Izmir for their kind assistance. An earlier version of this chapter was presented by Kıvanç Kılınç at The Housing Question: Nomad Seminar in Historiography, which took place at the University of San Diego on March 12–13, 2015, and a shortened, further revised version was published in Mimarlık, the architectural journal of the Chamber of Architects in Turkey. See Kıvanç Kılınç, "Teneke'den Öğrenen Modernizm: Ege Mahallesi Sosyal Konutları," Mimarlık 395 (May–June 2017): 72–77.

Notes

1 Izmir Municipality, 1965 City Council Meeting (Minutes of the 4th Meeting, 9.6.1965), 18. Ahmet Piriştina Kent Arşivi ve Müzesi (Ahmet Piriştina City Archive and Museum).

2 Ibid.; for the first phase of this social housing project, see İzmir Belediyesi Yıllığı 1963–1967 [Izmir Municipality Yearbook 1963–1967] (Izmir: Ticaret Matbaacılık T.A.Ş, 1967), 48–49.

3 For the squatter settlement prevention zones see *İzmir 1975 Belediye Çalışmaları* [Municipal Services in Izmir in 1975] (İzmir: Karınca Matbaacılık ve Ticaret Kollektif Şirketi, 1975), 71.

4 "Cumhuriyet Mahallesi'nde 400 Sosyal Mesken Daha yapılacak" [400 More Social Housing Units will be Built in Cumhuriyet Neighborhood], *Ege Ekspres*, May 6, 1966, Friday; for the mid-rise types built in the late 1970s, see Hülya Koç, *Cumhuriyet Döneminde İzmir'de Sosyal Konut ve Toplu Konut Uygulamaları* [Social and Mass Housing in Izmir during the Republican Period] (İzmir: DEU Mimarlık Fakültesi Yayınları, 2001), 129.

5 For some of these models, see Winfried Brenne eds. *Bruno Taut, Meister des farbigen Bauens in Berlin* (Berlin: Verlagshaus Braun, 2005).

6 Kıvanç Kılınç, "Imported But Not Delivered: The Construction of Modern Domesticity and the Spatial Politics of Mass-Housing in 1930s Ankara," *The Journal of Architecture* 17.6 (December 2012): 819–846. For a detailed discussion of the evolution of the typical apartment building typologies in Turkey, see Sibel Bozdoğan and Esra Akcan, *Turkey: Modern Architectures in History* (London: Reaktion Books, 2012), 148–169.

7 For an in-depth discussion, see also Gülsüm Baydar, Kıvanç Kılınç, and Ahenk Yılmaz, "Discrepant Spatial Practices: Contemporary Social Housing Projects in Izmir," in Kıvanç Kılınç and Mohammad Gharipour, eds., *Social Housing in the Middle East Architecture, Urban Development, and Transnational Modernity* (Bloomington, Indiana: Indiana University Press, 2019), 297–198; 311.

8 Housing complexes built within state-owned factories are an exception. See Ali Cengizkan, ed., *Fabrika'da Barınmak: Erken Cumhuriyet Dönemi'nde Türkiye'de İşçi Konutları—Yaşam, Mekân ve Kent* [Dwelling in the Factory: Workers' Houses in Early Republican Turkey – Everyday Life, Space, and the City] (Ankara: Arkadaş Yayınevi, 2009). For examples of postwar social housing in Europe, see Kenny Cupers, *The Social Project: Housing Postwar France* (Minneapolis: Univ. of Minnesota Press, 2014).

9 Aykut Namık Çoban, "Cumhuriyetin İlanından Günümüze Konut Politikası" [Housing Policies from the Proclamation of the Republic to the Present], *Ankara Üniversitesi SBF Dergisi* 67.3 (2012): 75–108.

10 Barış Alp Özden, "Health, Morality and Housing: The Politics of Working Class Housing in Turkey, 1945–1960," *New Perspectives on Turkey* 49 (Fall 2013): 57–86 (abstract). For instance, in the mass housing settlement developed by the Real Estate and Credit Bank of Turkey (Türkiye Emlak Kredi Bankası) in 1956–1957, some of the units were initially planned to be as large as 110–290 square meters, and individual flats had to be further partitioned and made smaller so that families could afford to live in them. "Türkiye'de Konut Sorununa Genel Bir Bakış," Report by the Chamber of Architects of Turkey, *Mimarlık* 115 (1973): 9–11. In 1963 the average size of a licensed apartment in Ankara was as high as 140 square meters. These generous figures were not on par with Turkey's level of economic development and were not paralleled in other countries in Europe or in the region, where most of the people lived in houses that ranged from fifty-eight to seventy-three square meters. Tekeli, *Türkiye'de Yaşamda*, 188.

11 For the prefabricated system, see İlhan Tekeli, *Türkiye'de Yaşamda ve Yazında Konutun Öyküsü (1923–1980)* [The Story of Housing in Life and Literature in Turkey] (İstanbul: Tarih Vakfı Yurt Yayınları, 2012), 282–283. Tunnel-form construction was first applied in the late 1970s by MESA Housing Industry, a private construction firm, and in large-scale cooperative housing projects such as Batıkent in Ankara. For the Batıkent project, see Murat Karayalçın, "Batıkent: A New Settlement Project in Ankara, Turkey," *Ekistics* 54.32 (1987): 292–299.

12 Tekeli, *Türkiye'de Yaşamda*, 107–110; *gecekondu* means "built overnight" in Turkish.

13 Ruşen Keleş, *Kentleşme Politikası* [Urbanization Policy] (Ankara: İmge Kitabevi, 2015), 481, 572, 576; Sümer Gürel et al., *Dar Gelirli Kesime Alt Yapısı Hazır Arsa Sunumu* [Sites and Services Schemes for the Lower-Income] (Ankara: Başbakanlık Toplu Konut İdaresi Başkanlığı, 1996), 22.

14 Özden, "Health, Morality and Housing," 79.

15 Ibid., 73.

16 Keleş, *Kentleşme Politikası*. In most of the earlier public housing projects built in the 1950s and 1960s, "costs have reached levels affordable only by upper-income groups," and most of the units were too large to count as social housing. Yıldız Sey, "To House the New Citizens," 172–173.

17 See Bozdoğan and Akcan, *Turkey*, 148.

18 *İzmir 1975 Belediye Çalışmaları*; *İzmir 1977 Belediye Çalışmaları* [Municipal Services in Izmir in 1977] (İzmir: Karınca Matbaacılık ve Ticaret Kollektif Şirketi, 1977).

19 My translation. See *İzmir 1977 Belediye Çalışmaları*, 96. The policy adopted was that informal settlements were to be demolished only when replacement housing was provided. Keleş, *Kentleşme Politikası*, 482.

20 Gülçin Pulat, *Dar Gelirli Kentlilerin Konut Sorunu ve Soruna Sosyal İçerikli Mekânsal Çözüm Arayışları* [The Housing Problem of the Urban Poor and Explorations into Socio-Spatial Solutions] (Ankara: Kent-koop Yayınları, 1992), 235. Some of the *gecekondu* areas in İzmir were rehabilitated with the support of the Marshall Plan as early as the 1960s. But these policies were much more rigorously followed in the late 1970s. See "Amerika – Marshall Yardımlarıyla Gecekondu Bölgelerinde Yapılan Islah Çalışmaları Hakkında Belediye Başkanı Osman Kibar'ın Konuşma Yaparken Görüntülendiği Siyah Beyaz Baskı Fotoğrafı." [A Black and White Photograph Featuring Mayor Osman Kibar's Speech about the Rehabilitation of Squatter Settlement by means of the American – Marshall Aids], A.İBB.İZFAŞ.Görsel.0000000049-18 25.04.2006. Ahmet Piriştina Kent Arşivi ve Müzesi.

21 These reports include Frederick Bath, "Report on Housing in Turkey," U.N. Technical Assistant Administration (Ankara, March 1960); Bernard Wagner, "Housing in Turkey," U.S. International Cooperation Administration (Ankara: 1956); Charles Abrams, "Memorandum to His Excellency Hayrettin Erkmen, Minister of Labor of Turkey" (October 19, 1954); Donald Monson, "Türkiye'de İşçi Evleri Hakkında Rapor" [Report on Workers' Houses in Turkey] (Ankara, 1953). This was by no means surprising since the 1950s was marked by Turkey's political alliance with the Western bloc and its economy was in great part fueled by foreign aid. See Burçak Keskin-Kozat, "Negotiating Modernization through US Foreign Assistance: Turkey's Marshall Plan (1948–1952) Re-interpreted," PhD Diss., University of Michigan, 2006.

22 Cevat Geray, "Türkiye'de Kendi Evini Yapana Yardım Yöntemi Uygulaması" [The Application of the Aided Self-Help Housing Method in Turkey], *Amme İdaresi Dergisi* 5.2 (1972): 42–73.

23 For an extensive discussion of the various positions that architects and planners in Turkey took in response to the *gecekondu* developments, see Bülent Batuman, "The Image of Urban Politics: Turkish Urban Professionals and Urban Representation as a Site of Struggle," *Journal of Architectural Education* 62.2 (2008): 54–65; also see Tekeli, *Türkiye'de Yaşamda*.

24 Bernard Wagner was the son of Martin Wagner, a renowned German city planner and architect who fled Germany under the Nazi regime in 1935 and spent three years in Turkey. Bernard Wagner had a post at the National Housing Agency and worked for ECA (Economic Cooperation Administration) in an advisory capacity, which initiated a series of design competitions to develop cost-efficient industrial housing in major West German cities. Bernd Nicolai, *Moderne und Exil, Deutschprachige Architekten in der Turkei 1925–1955* (Berlin: Verlag für Bauwesen, 1998); Jeffry M. Diefendorf, Axel Frohn and Hermann-Josef Rupieper, eds. *American Policy and the Reconstruction of West Germany, 1945–1955* (New York: Cambridge Univ. Press, 1993); Bernard Wagner, "More Homes for Germans," *Information Bulletin* (December 1951): 21–24. Apart from his active role in West Germany, Wagner contributed

to the writing of several books on housing in India, Guatemala, and the Philippines. See, for instance, Bernard Wagner, United States. Agency for International Development, *Housing and Urban Development in the Philippines* (USAID [Housing and Urban Development Division], 1968).

25 Bernard Wagner, "Gerze Kesin İmar Planı" [The Gerze Development Plan], *Arkitekt* 2.284 (1956): 68–70.

26 http://www.gerzeninsesi.com/guncel/gerze-yangin-evlerinin-korunmasi-icin-harekete-gectiler-h3721.html.

27 See Kılınç, "Imported But Not Delivered."

28 Geray, "Türkiye'de," 42–73.

29 Ayten Erdem, Rabia Özakın, "Yokolmuş Bir Kentin Yeni Simgesi: Gerze Yangın Evleri" [The New Symbol of a Destroyed City: Gerze Fire Houses], *Mimarlık* 365 (May–June 2012): 72–77.

30 Kenan Mortan, Osman Arolat, "İzmir Üstüne Düşünmek" [Thinking on Izmir], *İktisat ve Toplum* 35 (2013): 5–14, accessed February 10, 2015, http://www.iktisatvetoplum.com/wp-content/uploads/kenan-mortan-osman-arolat-izmir-ustune-dusunmek-s35.pdf.

31 Ege Bölgesi Sanayi Odası (Aegean Region Chamber of Industry): http://www.ebso.org.tr/en/about-ebso-/history.

32 Mortan and Arolat, "İzmir Üstüne."

33 Izmir Municipality, 1968 City Council Meeting, Minutes (Summary) of the 4th Meeting, 21.6.1968, p. 2.

34 The social housing blocks in the Cumhuriyet neighborhood were followed by similar projects in Esenler, Buca, Bornova, Çiğli, and Gaziemir, all of which were constructed in collaboration with the ministry and contracted in the second half of the 1970s. Please see Koç, *Cumhuriyet Döneminde*, 126–131.

35 The motion passed on June 21, 1968. *Izmir Municipality Working Reports* (1968), 57. Ahmet Piriştina Kent Arşivi ve Müzesi.

36 Izmir Municipality, 1968 City Council Meeting (Minutes of the 4th Meeting, 21.6.1968), 2–4 and 6. Ahmet Piriştina Kent Arşivi ve Müzesi.

37 One of the council members, Rüştü Şardağ, also supported this view. But Şevket Göknar complained about the allocation of valuable city land for the project and to the people "who resisted the state's authority." Ibid. 6.

38 "Serbest yaşamasını kendilerine adet edinen bu vatandaşlarımız" (our translation). Ibid., 3.

39 Ibid., 2, 3, 6.

40 "Re Development Plan Amendment," ibid., 5.

41 Handan Koç, interview with Gönül İlhan [Interview with Gönül Ilhan], January 14, 2012, *Biamag Cumartesi*, http://www.bianet.org/biamag/azinliklar/135439-izmir-in-tenekeli-mahalle-si.

42 Mehmet Melih Cin, "Urban Regeneration Strategies for Supporting Social Sustainability of the Roma Community: Izmir-Ege Neighborhood Urban Regeneration Project," Unpublished M.Sc. Thesis, Izmir Katip Celebi University, June 2016, 62–63. The neighborhood—among several others, namely Tepecik, Adatepe, İkiçeşmelik, Göksu, and Esendere—has since 1924 been home to a predominantly Roma community.

43 Cihan Baysal, "Markalaşan İzmir: Alaçatı'dan Ege Mahallesine" [Izmir in the Process of Branding: From Alaçatı to Ege Neighborhood], *Biamag Cumartesi*, August 2, 2014, http://www.bianet.org/biamag/toplum/157519-markalasan-izmir-alacati-dan-ege-mahallesine.

44 See, Duygu Gökçe, "Romanların Konut Sorunsalı: Zorunlu Tercih" [The Housing Problem of Roma Communities: A Forced Choice], *Mimarlık* 385 (2015): 71–75; and Egemen Yılgür, "*Teneke Mahalles* in the Late Ottoman Capital: A Socio-Spatial Ground for the Co-inhabitation of Roma

Immigrants and the Local Poor," *Romani Studies* 28.2 (December 2018): 157–194.

45 One of the residents commented that the modernizing of the suburban railway system (İZBAN) in Izmir has amplified the physical isolation of the neighborhood, since the new extensions cut off the neighborhood from other parts of the city. See Sinem Uğurlu, "Atları Barındıran Devlet Romanları 'Barındırmıyor'" [The Government That Accommodates Horses Does Not House the Roma Community], *Evrensel*, July 9, 2012: https://www.evrensel.net/haber/32306/atlari-barindiran-devlet-romanlari-barindirmiyor.

46 Erdal Onur Diktaş and E. İpek Özbek Sönmez, "Integration of the Formal and the Informal: The Case of Izmir Ege Neighbourhood and Alsancak District," *CUI '15 / III. International Contemporary Urban Issues Conference Proceedings*, November 19–21, 2015, İstanbul, eds. Hande Tulum (Istanbul: Dakam Yayınları, 2015), 48.

47 Cin, "Urban Regeneration," 84–89. Today the level of education in the neighborhood is low. The majority of the residents are primary school graduates or dropouts or have never received any formal education (though some are literate). Ibid., 65–66. Unemployment therefore remains high; the most common form of steady employment among the residents is to be hired by the Greater Municipality of Izmir as coachmen for the phaetons that ply the city's tourist districts. Other options are mostly part-time jobs that do not provide social security, such as working as street vendors or porters. For women the prospects are even scarcer. Other than helping with family businesses (such as the shops in the neighborhood), women usually work as house cleaners. Ibid., 67–74. In spite of these challenges, there are constant efforts by the civil society organizations in the neighborhood to change the negative image and reach out to the larger public. While they are looking for ways to create new jobs for the young people especially, fighting various stereotypes and biases against the Roma people is an everyday struggle.

48 Melih Cin's study found that in 2015 53% of the building stock was reinforced concrete and the remaining structures were built using the masonry technique. Ibid., 79.

49 Ibid., 68, 82.

50 The rest of the residents are not considered the rightful residents. Ibid., 64.

51 Koç, *Cumhuriyet Döneminde*, 124.

52 Izmir Municipality, 1969 City Council Meeting (Minutes of the 6th Meeting, 11.6.1969), 42. Ahmet Piriştina Kent Arşivi ve Müzesi; the amount of credit acquired from the Bank was 3,000,000 Turkish lira. See, Koç, "Cumhuriyet Döneminde," 124.

53 Izmir Municipality, 1968 City Council Meeting (Minutes of the 4th Meeting, 21.6.1968), 2–3. Ahmet Piriştina Kent Arşivi ve Müzesi. When the project was completed, the payment plan consisted of a down payment and ten yearly installments instead.

54 Koç, "Cumhuriyet Döneminde," 124.

55 The inhabitants of this particular block have no official title of ownership and, legally speaking, are considered "occupiers." Cin, "Urban Regeneration," 69.

56 Izmir Municipality, 1969 City Council Meeting (Minutes of the 4th Meeting, 6.6.1969), 10. Ahmet Piriştina Kent Arşivi ve Müzesi.

57 Izmir Municipality, 1969 City Council Meeting (Minutes of the 10th Meeting, 18.6.1969), 60. Ahmet Piriştina Kent Arşivi ve Müzesi.

58 For a detailed discussion, see Baydar, Kılınç and Yılmaz, "Discrepant Spatial Practices."

59 With the increased number of inhabitants over the years and additions made to the balconies, it seems that the use of these common areas for spending time

during the day is a less preferred practice today, as the placement of tables or beds would make it more difficult for neighbors to move around and reach their homes.

60 See Cin, "Urban Regeneration."

61 Diktaş and Sönmez, "Integration of the Formal," 43.

62 Cin, "Urban Regeneration," 64, 82.

63 Cin, "Urban Regeneration," 77; also see Diktaş and Sönmez, "Integration of the Formal," 46.

64 Ibid.

65 Ibid.

66 Gönül İlhan, *Bizim Mahalle Tenekeli Mahalle* [Our Neighborhood, the Tin Plate Neighborhood] (İstanbul: Heyamola Yayınları, 2011), 90. Furthermore, most of the residents, around 75%, preferred ownership to remaining as tenants. Cin, "Urban Regeneration," 81.

67 Izmir Municipality, 1969 City Council Meeting (Minutes of the 6th Meeting, 11.6.1969), 42. Ahmet Piriştina Kent Arşivi ve Müzesi.

68 Cin, "Urban Regeneration," 83.

69 İlhan, *Bizim Mahalle*, 68–69.

70 One of the exceptions was a large-scale housing project initiated by the municipality of Izmit (1974) to accommodate 30,000 people. The architects adopted participatory decision-making methods in design and developed prefabricated units, but the project was never realized. Tuncay Çavdar, "Toplum Bilinçlenmesinde Araç olarak Katılımsal Tasarım: 'İzmit Yenilikçi Yerleşmeler Projesi'" [Participatory Design as a Tool for Social Awakening: Izmit Innovatory Settlements Project], *Mimarlık* 154 (1978): 55–60.

71 Between 2002 and 2018 TOKİ produced more than 800,000 mass housing units nationwide, as well as housing settlements and social services outside Turkey. "Kenya 2030 Hedefleri için TOKİ'de" [Kenya (Delegation) Visited TOKİ for its 2030 Goals], *Hürriyet*, 10.05.2018, http://www.hurriyet.com.tr/kenya-2030-hedefleri-icin-tokide-40831857. Despite TOKİ's success on a global scale, its projects have also been subject to criticism within Turkey for their low quality of construction and inflexible layouts. For a detailed account of two such projects, please read Baydar, Kılınç and Yılmaz, "Discrepant Spatial Practices." For a discussion on various meanings and uses of "flexible housing," see Tatjana Schneider and Jeremy Till, "Flexible Housing: Opportunities and Limits," *Architectural Research Quarterly* 9.2 (2005): 157–166.

72 Cin, "Urban Regeneration," 69.

73 In 2012 such interventions caused conflict with the local municipality in Konak and the residents were evacuated by force. "Konak'ta Roman Krizi: 'Zorunlu' Tahliye!" [The Crisis with the Roma Community in Konak: 'Mandatory' Evacuation!"], *Ege'de Son Söz*, November 30, 2012, Friday.

74 Shane Ewen, *What Is Urban History?* (Cambridge; Malden, MA: Polity Press, 2016), 43–44.

75 Ibid., 46.

76 Özlem Akkaya and Egemen Yılgür's recently published research traces *tenekeli* neighborhoods to late nineteenth century, and in the case of Istanbul argues that Romani refugees and other urban poor were fused together. Please see, Özlem Akkaya and Egemen Yılgür, "Locally Confined Territorial Stigmatization: The Case of 'Gypsy' Stigma," *Idealkent* 10.26 (2019): 217–218. See also Loïc Wacquant, *Urban Outcasts: A Comparative Sociology of Advanced Marginality* (Cambridge; Malden, MA: Polity, 2008).

77 Ewen, 49. See also Mike Davis, *Planet of Slums* (London, New York: Verso, 2006). For a recent example of urban renewal from Turkey, see Ozan Kahraman

and Tolga Islam, "On the Dual Nature of Intra-Urban Borders: The Case of a Romani Neighborhood in Istanbul," *Cities* 29.4 (August 2012): 234–243.

78 Cin, "Urban Regeneration," 67.

79 In 2013 the Ege neighborhood was designated as an urban renewal and development site. The recent urban transformation project developed by the Greater Municipality of Izmir proposes to replace most of the existing building stock with mid-rise residential units as well as a high-rise residential and office tower, cafes, galleries, and a cultural center. While the municipality affirms that the on-site transformation model (*yerinde dönüşüm*) adopted at this project, which is based on a public-private partnership, will not lead to the forcible displacement of local communities, a number of other factors are likely to prove otherwise: smaller units provided by the project (as low as 31 square meters), rendering them less attractive for the residents who have economic hardship; possibly much higher rents; and increased overhead. Furthermore, the tenants are not eligible to purchase the new flats, and are instead offered to settle in TOKİ Uzundere, a mass-housing settlement which is located farther away from the city center. On October 22, 2020, the construction of the high-rise block was put out to tender. This will be followed by some of the mid-rise blocks, which also include affordable housing units. The project proposes to revamp and maintain 2 of the 7 ENSHP blocks as cultural facilities. Please see Cin, "Urban Regeneration," 74, 80–81; Izmir Greater Municipality, "İşte Yeni Ege Mahallesi" [Here is the New Ege Neighborhood], June 27, 2014: https://www.izmir.bel.tr/tr/Haberler/iste-yeni-ege-mahallesi/10484/156; https://www.izmir.bel.tr/YuklenenDosyalar/file/KENTSEL_DONUSUM/konut_proje/ege_29mb.pdf; http://www.izmir.bel.tr/YuklenenDosyalar/Ihaleler/encumen/23092020105313encumen.pdf.

8 Public Life and Public Housing

Charles Moore's Church Street South

Patricia A. Morton

On August 19, 1967, New Haven erupted in violence after a white restaurant owner, Ed Thomas, shot and injured a Puerto Rican-American resident, Julio Diaz, in the predominantly black neighborhood, the Hill. For five days, the city was the scene of clashes between the police and residents, firebombings, looting, and vigilantism by whites. Mayor Richard Lee declared a curfew and brought in the state police and the National Guard. Black community leaders demanded that the police be removed, arguing they were antagonizing residents, but Lee refused. The police used Mace, tear gas, and beatings to subdue and arrest blacks, whites, and Latinos who allegedly rioted or disobeyed the curfew. Residents fled inner city districts for the suburbs, fearing that the Hill would be burned down. Lee finally lifted the curfew on August 24, and the city returned to a state of superficial normalcy.[1]

At the beginning of that year, Charles W. Moore, chair of Architecture at Yale University, and his partner, William Turnbull, had begun design on a mixed-income housing project, Church Street South, for a site near the Hill (Figure 8.1).[2] Moore was an astute observer of changes in the postwar American public realm, articulated in his iconic essay, "You Have to Pay for the Public Life" (1965). Anticipating the emerging neoliberal regime of privatized space, Moore asserted that the public realm existed almost nowhere in the deracinated suburban landscape of places like California except in Disneyland, where you could have something like the public life if you paid the admission. For Moore, the public life entailed "giving up" something – "space or money or prominence or concern" – to the public.[3] Just who pays, and what is given up, for the public life was a central problem for Moore's work. In response to the alienating contemporary built environment, Moore and three colleagues had earlier elaborated a theory of "place." According to Moore, the responsibility of architecture was not the expressive use of materials and space, but the creation of place, the act of *"taking possession* of a portion of the earth's surface." Moore identified an absence of clearly demarcated edges as generating the chaotic, disordered spaces of the contemporary built environment, devoid of spatial delineation and composed of diagrammatic

DOI: 10.4324/9781351182966-12

Figure 8.1 MLTW/Moore Turnbull, Church Street South Housing, New Haven, Connecticut, 1966–1969, view of Station Court. Photo: courtesy of Lawrence Speck

buildings conceived in isolation from context or use. Boundaries formed by axes, landmarks, walls, or natural features would give order and produce a sense of place.[4]

Church Street South is a case study in Moore's attempts to learn from Disneyland and bring public life into architecturally defined places that would ameliorate the disorder of the privatized contemporary world. In response to increasing condemnation of high-rise public housing and out of their concern for creating "place," Moore and Turnbull designed a low-rise complex composed of "defensible spaces" that were intended to engender a sense of community identity for residents, individuate the dwelling units, and prevent the crime and vandalism found in public housing towers. As this chapter will show, its design was informed by contemporary critiques of high-rise, high-density projects built on CIAM principles and emerging social-science research into how design could prevent crime and nurture community. Located on a site close to the riots, Church Street South encapsulated then-current theories of how architecture could avoid the pitfalls of modernist planning while addressing the needs of residents.

This chapter analyzes Church Street South in terms of this imperative to create "place" and a public life for its low-income inhabitants and examines several larger questions. What is "public" in government-subsidized housing projects like Church Street South?[5] What type of "public life" could be produced in a public housing project whose residents had little choice in where they lived? How could architects create "public life" for low-income residents of a neighborhood that had suffered from racial and economic marginalization, compounded by a decade of urban renewal and dislocation? The case of Church Street South evinces the evolution of American public housing provision as well as its role in engaging social formations beyond the provision of decent shelter.

Church Street South: Site

Described by Moore as a "nowhere between two somewheres," Church Street South was located on an urban renewal site between the New Haven railroad station and the historic Green, adjacent to the Oak Street Connector that links to Interstate 95 and cuts off the site from downtown (Figure 8.2).[6] The district had been occupied by the wholesale market, which was demolished in the 1950s as part of the Church Street urban renewal project. It was proximate to the Hill neighborhood where the 1967 riots began, and had contained housing and businesses deemed blighted during the earlier clearance process. Always marginal to the central business district, the site had been the subject of several master planning exercises that attempted to integrate it into larger transportation, beautification, and renewal schemes.

The area was included in a 1910 Civic Improvement Plan by Cass Gilbert and Frederick Law Olmsted Jr., which envisioned a monumental, tree-lined City Beautiful boulevard stretching from a proposed new rail station toward the Green in New Haven's center. This grand promenade would have been lined by shops, restaurants, and hotels interspersed by a series of public squares. Gilbert and Olmsted's comprehensive master plan was prepared for the New Haven Civic Improvement Committee, which advocated for City Beautiful improvements to the city's infrastructure, street and transportation networks, and civic and park spaces. While their plan was not realized as proposed, Gilbert was commissioned to design the new Union Station in 1918.[7]

Aspects of the Gilbert-Olmsted plan were echoed in the 1942 Rotival Plan, created by French engineer, Maurice E. H. Rotival, and two Yale planning professors, Maynard W. Meyer and George A. Dudley.[8] For their New Haven plan, Rotival and his colleagues addressed economic development, population density, and traffic circulation, and proposed a massive new system of high-speed "parkways" and secondary routes within which they designated nine areas for redevelopment. Within the plan, they projected an extension of Church Street that took a route similar to Gilbert and Olmsted's elegant boulevard. This plan, revised in 1951, served as the basis for Mayor Lee's urban renewal programs.[9]

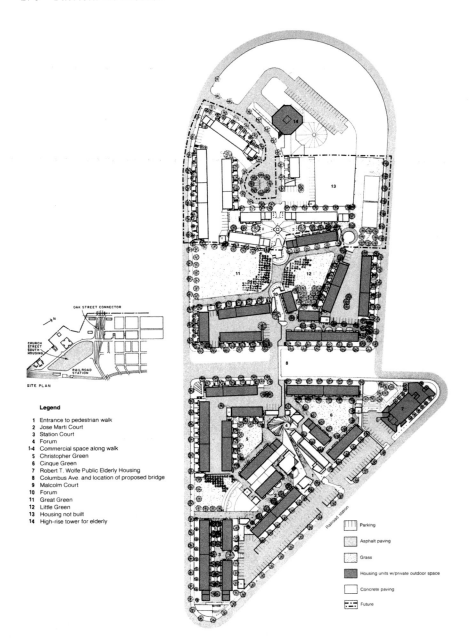

Legend

1   Entrance to pedestrian walk
2   Jose Marti Court
3   Station Court
4   Forum
1-4 Commercial space along walk
5   Christopher Green
6   Cinque Green
7   Robert T. Wolfe Public Elderly Housing
8   Columbus Ave. and location of proposed bridge
9   Malcolm Court
10 Forum
11 Great Green
12 Little Green
13 Housing not built
14 High-rise tower for elderly

Parking

Asphalt paving

Grass

Housing units w/private outdoor space

Concrete paving

Future

Figure 8.2 MLTW/Moore Turnbull, Church Street South Housing, New Haven, Connecticut, 1966–1969, site plan. Source: Sharon Lee Ryder. "Low-Moderate Baroque." *Progressive Architecture* 53 (1972): 77

After the demolition of the wholesale market, city planners envisioned two housing towers and a light-industrial commercial park on the Church Street South site, now included in the New Haven Redevelopment Agency's broader Church Street Project targeted at rebuilding the city's commercial core.[10] Church Street was extended south across Oak Street and formed a link between the central business district and the area near the rail station, although a less grand boulevard than Gilbert and Olmsted envisioned. In 1965, the city abandoned plans for commercial development on the Church Street South site after failing to attract investors for the proposed use. Mayor Lee invited celebrated architect Ludwig Mies van der Rohe to create a master plan encompassing 800 units of mixed-income housing, a school, a boys and girls club, and a new train station. Mies' plan, a modified "towers in a park" scheme, combined several high-rise buildings interspersed with low-rise bars of varying length set in open, landscaped spaces. In 1967, budget constraints, reductions to the program, and Mies' declining health caused him to withdraw from the project.[11]

Later that year, the Hill district adjacent to Church Street South exploded into violence, bringing into doubt New Haven's reputation as a "Model City" of renewal.[12] In the aftermath of the New Haven riots, *Progressive Architecture* published a report, "Urban Planning and Urban Revolt: A Case Study," that analyzed the causes of the riots and their connections to New Haven's vaunted urban renewal program.[13] Mayor Lee's fourteen-year-long redevelopment program had transformed New Haven, backed by a massive infusion of federal funding. Between 1954, when Lee took office, and 1967, New Haven garnered $120 million or $790 per resident in Title I funds, the largest per capita urban renewal program in the country.[14] P/A also recorded the deep distrust of residents of color toward the police, the New Haven Redevelopment Agency, the mayor, and city government generally as a result of their experiences with urban renewal. This state of affairs was not confined to New Haven. The Kerner Commission, charged with investigating the causes of the widespread urban violence that occurred across the US that year, asserted that,

> ... ghetto residents increasingly believe that they are excluded from the decision-making process which affects their lives and community. This feeling of exclusion, intensified by the bitter legacy of racial discrimination, has engendered a deep-seated hostility toward the institutions of government.
>
> In part, this is the lesson of Detroit and New Haven where well-intentioned programs designed to respond to the needs of ghetto residents were not worked out and implemented sufficiently in cooperation with the intended beneficiaries.[15]

Lee's much-lauded urban renewal programs had exacerbated the sense of disenfranchisement among New Haven residents, particularly those who were displaced by urban renewal.

P/A noted that Lee's programs produced infrastructure and developments calculated to attract suburbanites to shop or live in the city and benefit the business community or powerful institutions like Yale rather than the urban poor who were displaced. Over the fourteen years of redevelopment, 7,700 households (approximately 22,000 people) were displaced by the city's redevelopment programs, their neighborhoods replaced by commercial development or luxury housing.[16] Only 17% of the 5,291 housing units built and planned under urban renewal in New Haven were for low-income families.[17] Fred Harris, a Black community leader and president of the Hill Parent Association, asserted that New Haven had "more parking than apartment buildings" as a result of urban renewal.[18] Despite innovative antipoverty programs funded by the Ford Foundation that sought to counter structural inequality and the disruption produced by urban renewal, it seemed clear that disturbances would continue to occur, a prediction born out the following summer. A "cautionary exegesis of the ills of our cities and the noncurative aspects of most of our urban planning programs," P/A's report concluded that urban renewal and redevelopment were "not the panaceas they have been touted to be."[19] By decoupling physical planning from the social and economic conditions of the people renewal was supposed to help, the report called into question the fallacy of urban renewal's deterministic premise.

Church Street South: Housing

After Mies van der Rohe withdrew from the project in 1967, Moore was commissioned to design a new program focused on 710 units of low- and moderate-income housing, a change that had been prompted by local activists' criticisms that redevelopment had taken too many housing units out of the city's stock and displaced too many residents without rehousing them.[20] The project included a twenty-two story 217-unit tower of rent-subsidized elderly housing to be managed privately, an eight-story ninety-three-unit tower of elderly public housing to be operated by the Housing Authority of New Haven (HANH), and 400 units of low- and moderate-income family housing in low-rise buildings to be funded through the HUD/FHA Section 221 (d)(3) program and privately owned (Figure 8.3).[21] With the exception of the smaller of the elderly housing buildings, Church Street South did not consist of conventional "public housing," owned and managed by a municipal housing authority, but of privately owned housing intended for families receiving federal rent subsidies as well as housing for moderate-income families. The complex financing and subsidies that sponsored the

Figure 8.3 MLTW/Moore Turnbull, Church Street South Housing, New Haven, Connecticut, 1966–1969, Forum Court. Photo: courtesy of Lawrence Speck

Church Street South project would have consequences for the future of the housing.

The two buildings of elderly housing, anchoring the north and south ends of the renewal area, were designed, financed, sponsored, and constructed separately from the low- and moderate-income housing that took up the majority of the site. The twenty-two-story, 217-unit Tower One for the Elderly was financed under HUD's Section 221(d)(3) program and sponsored by the New Haven Jewish Community Council Housing Corporation. The tower has chamfered corners, "playing the role… of a poor relation" to Roche Dinkeldoo's monumental Knights of Columbus tower from the site across the Oak Street Connector.[22] The Robert T. Wolfe Public Elderly Housing contains 93 units, financed under Section 236 by HUD and constructed for the City of New Haven Housing Authority, making it the only conventional public housing in the complex.[23] It is an eight-story, brick building that steps down to four stories at its northern end, responding to the lower scale of adjoining structures at the intersection.

The low- and moderate-income housing was intended to be cooperative, integrating families on rent subsidies with middle-class families. This part of the project was sponsored by the Greater New Haven Jaycees, which received the FHA loans and hired a contractor, the Development Corporation of America, to build the housing. Design decisions, however, were made by the Redevelopment Agency. The strategy of mixing housing for different incomes was typical of Lee's approach, which opposed creation of high-rise, high-density public housing blocks as had been built in New Haven before his tenure as mayor.[24] The "scattered-site public housing" program was intended to avoid concentrating communities of color in large projects that perpetuated racial and income segregation, but it was viewed with distrust by Black leaders who saw it as a racist initiative to break up Black their communities.[25] A Black resident, Columbus Keinsler, testified before the Douglas Commission on Urban Problems in 1967 and pointed to the displacement caused by Lee's policies: "He's pushing us completely out. I want to know why he's pushing us all out of New Haven where nobody can see us."[26] In a 1967 proposal for projects totaling 848 housing units, including Church Street South, Lee declared that inclusion of low-rent housing in moderate-income cooperative developments, scattered in apartments and town houses where residents would not be identified as public housing families, "is a new approach that has not been tried anywhere."[27] The "scattered" approach was subsequently abandoned at Church Street South, according to Sharon Lee Ryder in *Progressive Architecture*, because middle-income families would not pay extra for a few amenities that did little to distinguish their units.[28] The ninety-nine units originally intended for moderate-income families were never built due to cuts in federal urban renewal funding, and the rest of the project was converted from cooperative to rental.[29]

Moore and Turnbull placed low-rise housing bars around a pedestrian spine that started at the rail station and turned toward the Knights of Columbus building and downtown beyond it (Figure 8.4). The spine was meant to compensate for the site's isolation, exacerbated when the Oak Street Connector severed it from downtown, by creating visual connections and an implied walkway to the city center. According to Moore, the planning process involved thirty-two site plans and agency reviews before a final scheme was approved. The final plan used only two building types while striving to form an urban fabric like the city. The pedestrian spine linked commercial spaces, landscaped green areas, and courtyards that were intended to form neighborhoods within the whole. The commercial spaces included a supermarket, a laundromat, a child care center, and small offices. To preserve access to the ground from every unit, parking was partly surface and exposed and partly located under one side of the

Figure 8.4 MLTW/Moore Turnbull, Church Street South Housing, New Haven, Connecticut, 1966–1969, view from New Haven Railway Station. Source: Sharon Lee Ryder. "Low-Moderate Baroque." *Progressive Architecture* 53 (1972): 78. Photo A. Wade Perry

four-story units.[30] Columbus Street, which bisects the site, was slated to be widened to four lanes as part of an Inner Ring Road encircling New Haven.[31]

Anticipating a wider street that would pose a barrier to pedestrians, Moore designed a bridge across Columbus to connect the two parts of the complex; his first scheme for the bridge included shops and housing in the manner of the Ponte Vecchio, an idea rejected by the FHA. The Ring Road never materialized, and the bridge across Columbus was never built.[32]

Because the complex was originally planned for construction in concrete planking that spanned precast wall slabs with brick end walls and wooden stairs, the facades of the units had to be completely standardized and uniform. Due to cost overruns, however, the developer substituted concrete block for the precast wall slabs and brick end walls at a point in the bidding process when it was too late to alter the facades, resulting in a relentless sameness among the housing bars.[33] Moore and Turnbull added textured block rustication around the windows, cantilevered cornices, and supergraphics around the entrances as a way of ameliorating the monotony of the facades (see Figure 8.1). The painting colors and shapes at the entrances were supposedly based on the window frames of Borromini's Collegio di Propaganda Fide in Rome.[34]

The units ranged from two to five bedrooms, including flats and duplexes, arranged in three- or four-story buildings of various lengths. The typology integrated two duplex units above a three-bedroom flat. On the basis of information gleaned from earlier Redevelopment Agency housing projects and consultation with the city's Relocation Agency, Moore was convinced that five-bedroom units would be needed, but HUD maximums did not allow extra funding for a fifth bedroom. Moore designated the fifth bedroom in certain units an "other habitable room," thereby gaining the extra bedroom. Every unit had access to a balcony or a garden space at ground level.[35]

To create "place" in a development employing minimal means, the architects used supergraphics, axial views, named courtyards, and physical addresses to allow residents to identify their units and to generate a sense of community. The courtyards were given names (Malcolm Court, Jose Marti Court, Station Court, Forum), to allow each unit to have a city street address, and supergraphics and distinctive color schemes to distinguish between the courts. The landscaping included four "greens" interspersed through the complex that provided relief from the hardscape dominant in the project. Paving patterns in asphalt and concrete further distinguished the open spaces; painted curbs and radial paving marked the units' entrances, defining the "territory" of each unit. Moore and Turnbull sought explicitly to bring the scale and vitality of the traditional street to a low-cost public project, an exercise in what they called "city-building." Mayor Lee and residents, however, felt the result looked more like a military barracks than housing, and it gained the nickname "Cinderblock City."

High-Rise versus Low-Rise

Church Street South reflected changes in thinking about the design of public housing in the 1960s and 1970s, particularly theories based on the presumption that correctly configured architecture could prevent crime and produce better social outcomes. Moore and Turnbull used a tower for the elderly housing building, but low-rise bars for the low-income units. This planning strategy accorded with other experiments in low-rise public housing that would supersede the Corbusian model of "towers in a park," which, for aesthetic and economic reasons, had been the preferred building type for subsidized housing. As Eric Mumford has shown, early twentieth-century American housing reformers, such as the Housing Study Guild, advocated for high-rises as the most economical form of rental housing where land values were high.[36] Under the impetus of postwar federal policy that set high density rates and low per-unit cost limits for public housing, high-rises were touted as the most efficient means for housing large numbers of poor residents.[37] The Housing Act of 1949 sought to provide "a decent home and suitable living environment" for all Americans and mandated the construction of 810,000 new units of public housing over six years, along with funds for slum clearance, urban redevelopment and public subsidies for mortgage insurance that underwrote the massive postwar boom in single-family home construction. As specified in the 1949 Act, public housing was subject to strict caps on federal contributions to local housing authorities, and the projects were forbidden to have "elaborate or extravagant design or materials," which pushed authorities to build more austere, cost-effective tower blocks.[38]

By the late 1950s, however, housing reformers were increasingly critical of public housing programs and the high-rise towers they had built in New York, Chicago, St. Louis, and elsewhere. In a 1957 article, prominent public housing advocate Catherine Bauer dissected the lack of widespread support for public housing and the problems with the program that had developed over the twenty years of its existence.[39] As Bauer saw it, public housing was caught in the "dreary deadlock" of inadequate funding, opposition from the real estate lobby, heavy-handed and rigid management, and a disconnection from the way American families wanted to live. The design of public housing – islands of high-density, monotonous superblocks – made its difference from middle-class life even more evident and stigmatized its low-income residents. Noting that suburban, single-family houses had become the norm in the postwar period, she decried the turn to stripped-down towers for public housing: "While everybody who had any choice was moving into a one-story home, the housing authorities were busily erecting high-density, high-rise apartments, with no private outdoor space whatever."[40] Bauer pointed to one of the most intractable issues around public housing: many of its residents had no choice of where to live because of racial discrimination. Displaced in higher proportions by slum clearance and highway construction, people of color made up the majority in many public housing projects.[41] Nevertheless, Bauer attributed part of public housing's failure to gain popularity to its formal qualities and modernist precepts: "in grasping for modern principles of large-scale community design, we embraced too wholeheartedly functionalist and collectivist architectural theories that tended to ignore certain subtler esthetic values and basic social needs."[42]

The social impact of high-rise public housing became a focus for critics of the "tower in the park." Local housing agencies had justified high-rise towers and slabs for public housing on economic grounds since cleared slum areas tended to have high land values, increasing their cost and making it difficult to stay within federal cost limits. Lawrence Vale and D. Bradford Hunt have demonstrated that the Chicago Housing Authority (CHA) had doubts about the efficacy of placing families in high-rises, but claimed it constructed them at Cabrini-Green (1941–1962) and other sites in order to meet federal density requirements and create open spaces in the projects that contrasted with dense surrounding street grids.[43] A *Chicago Sun-Times* reporter, Ruth Moore, predicted trouble when putting "some 400 children and 200 adults into one 16-story elevator apartment," problems the head of the CHA, Elizabeth Wood, acknowledged in a 1952 *Architectural Forum* article.[44] Criticisms of high-rises often alluded to the negative impact of their design and density on families and children. Mumford cites Philadelphia Housing Authority sociologist Anthony F.C. Wallace who, in

1950, warned against the dangers to family life posed by the "excessive social contact" produced by high-rise projects.[45]

By the mid-1960s, a growing body of research indicated that high-rise public housing buildings were "having disastrous effects on their occupants," as Oscar Newman asserted in his landmark book, *Defensible Space: Crime Prevention Through Urban Design* (1972).[46] Foremost among the "disastrous effects" was the ostensible link between high crime rates and high-rise public housing schemes, outcomes that Newman sought to combat through the design of spaces that could be surveilled and controlled by residents.[47] While Newman's book postdates Church Street South, it drew on research and journalistic accounts of high-rise housing and crime that dated to the early 1960s and strongly influenced the discourse on public housing. Jane Jacobs' criticisms of modernist planning and her advocacy of public safety through "eyes on the street" and around-the-clock activity were deeply influential on discussions of high-rise housing and crime, and Newman appropriated many of her ideas, unattributed.[48] Lee Rainwater's study of St. Louis' troubled Pruitt-Igoe housing project depicted the crime-plagued complex as filled with residents who were victims of the social pathology produced by their environment, which he referred to as a "federal slum."[49] Drawing on this discourse, Newman translated it into the formal theory of "defensible space" as a means for crime prevention and community safety.

The essential tenets of Newman's theory stressed design as a causal and, therefore, preventive factor in crime.[50] In analyzing high-rise public housing complexes such as Pruitt-Igoe in St. Louis and the Van Dyke Houses in Brooklyn, he associated features such as walkways lacking surveillance, communal areas, and shared external spaces with crime because they were not "owned" or controlled by residents. Newman believed the forms of residential areas "contribute to our victimization by criminals."[51] High-rise housing mitigated against the natural surveillance necessary for safety because residents could not observe entrances or outdoor spaces from units high above the ground.

While Newman was critical of public housing towers, his belief that form could modify behavior, prevent crime, and sponsor community derives from the determinism of modern architecture and town planning. He called for spaces designed to create a sense of territoriality in residents who could then control them through surveillance and positive control over activity. "Defensible space is a model for residential environments which inhibit crime by creating the physical expression of a social fabric that defends itself." He believed it was the responsibility of every person to participate in this collective policing, which ensured the functioning of the community. According to his theory, architects could strengthen civil society and preclude crime by creating "defensible spaces," clearly outlined territories that would encourage residents to police their own spaces. "Architectural design can make evident by the physical layout that an area is the shared extension of the private realms of individuals."[52] By means of good design, public housing could be made safe, but only by extension of the individual's private realm, not through generation of a public realm. While Newman sought to create community in public housing, his theory of defensible space emphasized private control over public life.

Newman's alternative to high-rise, high-crime public housing was low-rise housing organized according to a hierarchy of public, semi-public, and private spaces, creating security by establishing clear boundaries and thresholds. This approach resonated with Moore's theory of "place" as a bounded space with defined edges. While Moore and Trumbull did not refer to Newman's theories directly, I believe the decade-long discourse on public housing and safety had a clear influence on the project, as reflected in specific design elements. To help achieve defensible space at Church Street South, they gave many units a stoop at its entrance (Figure 8.5).

Figure 8.5 MLTW/Moore Turnbull, Church Street South Housing, New Haven, Connecticut, 1966–1969, stoop. Photo: photo courtesy of Lawrence Speck

The stoops allowed residents places to sit, watch over the courtyards, and socialize. Like their precedents in brownstone neighborhoods, these stoops were intended to function as intermediate spaces between the private residence and public space and were meant to encourage something like a public, urban street life. In accordance with Newman's precepts, the architects designed Church Street South with low-rise blocks that surrounded defined courtyards overlooked by windows from the units, creating the conditions for surveillance that Newman believed would make these spaces "defensible." "Designers can position units, windows, and entries, and prescribe paths of movement and areas of activity so as to provide inhabitants with continuous natural surveillance of the street and project grounds."[53] This strategy adapted Jacobs' principle of "eyes on the street" directly. Church Street South attempted to construct an ordered world, a place, with a hierarchy of spaces and a clear demarcation of public and private. With limited means, the architects worked to provide a territorial realm of defensible turf that would deter crime and sponsor a public life among its residents.

Design and Physical Determinism

As an exemplar of defensible space, however, Church Street South was not successful and it became known as The Jungle, a reference to its high crime rate. As documented in photographs taken by Larry Speck in the 1970s, Church Street South was already characterized by deserted plazas and graffiti-marked walls (Figure 8.6).[54] In the 1980s, David Littlejohn, Charles Moore's biographer, found empty courtyards, broken lamps, and black graffiti over the faded paint on the facades. "The lively outdoor scene Moore imagined has simply not materialized."[55] Once the supergraphics were painted over, the buildings lost the elements that Moore and Turnbull introduced to brighten the facades and resembled a barracks even more strikingly. According to architect Jonathan Hopkins, "Church Street South Housing became home to one of New Haven's most violent drug gangs of the 1980s and 1990s, the Jungle Boys," which was suppressed in the 1990s, but the crime rate in the complex remained high despite its proximity to the New Haven Police Department headquarters.[56]

Since its completion, a succession of owners and operators – from its original sponsors, the Greater New Haven Jaycees, to its current owners, Northland Investment Corporation – failed to maintain Church Street South; in the 1980s, the complex was given to private ownership.[57] Northland acquired the site in 2008 and was sued for failing to maintain the complex properly in order to justify its demolition and redevelopment.[58] When it became clear that Church Street South would be redeveloped, in 2011 the tenants, who had endured years of neglected maintenance and deterioration, organized to ensure that they would be given housing in the new mixed-use development replacing Church Street South. One resident expressed her dissatisfaction with the relocation plans: "I've lived here for

Figure 8.6 MLTW/Moore Turnbull, Church Street South Housing, New Haven, Connecticut, 1966–1969, end wall supergraphics. Photo: courtesy of Lawrence Speck).

25 years under crappy conditions. Now that they're building a new building, they want to throw me out." Another resident, Charleen Ortiz, voiced many residents' desire to return to the area: "I'd like to come back here."[59] In fall 2015, HUD rated it one of the worst public housing complexes in the country.[60] By June 2018, the last of the residents was relocated, and Church Street South was demolished to make way for a planned mixed-use development including 700–1,000 units of housing, 300 of which would be affordable, planned by Northland in partnership with the city.[61] Ironically, the two high-rise elderly housing towers sponsored by the Jewish Community Council and the public elderly housing block have fared better and were not demolished. The low-rise configuration of Church Street South neither determined its failure nor saved it from demolition to another cycle of profit-driven redevelopment.

A reliance on physical design to effect social outcomes and changes in behavior was integral to Newman's theory, as it had been for Jane Jacobs' valorization of the form and social life of traditional neighborhoods. In a 1962 review of *The Death and Life of Great American Cities*, sociologist Herbert Gans criticized Jacobs for equating what she saw as a lack of vitality in modernist urban renewal developments with their planning and for assuming that the "buildings, streets, and the planning principles on which they are based shape human behavior." Gans labeled this supposition the "physical fallacy" shared by Jacobs and the planners she attacked, which led them to ignore the social, cultural, and economic factors that contribute to urban vitality or dullness.[62] He charged that by extrapolating the social life of a working-class neighborhood into planning principles, Jacobs "in effect demands that middle-class people adopt working-class styles of family life, child rearing, and sociability," negating a preference for privacy and status over visibility and street life.[63] According to Gans, the real problems with urban renewal lay in racial discrimination, poverty, and the unwillingness of private enterprise to provide adequate low-cost housing.[64]

The 1967 New Haven riots put into focus the structural social and economic problems faced by nonwhite residents that had been exacerbated by urban renewal: discrimination in housing, lack of employment opportunities in a deindustrializing city where good jobs and housing were moving to the suburbs, and bad, segregated schools. Reporting on the riots and Lee's urban renewal schemes, Bernard Asbell noted that even the best built public housing created "nothing but transplanted ghettos where the poor are lost among the poor, the alienated among the alienated, unmotivated school children consigned to schools full of their own."[65] In this context, while Moore and Turnbull's design for Church Street South provided an alternative form for public housing than the red-brick towers of earlier projects, it remained enmeshed in the mechanisms of urban renewal and its deterministic fallacies. The structural problems of a deindustrialized, racially segregated city, amplified by real estate speculation, contributed more decisively to its demise than its design.

To return to questions posed earlier: what type of public is constituted by a public housing project? How can architects create "public life" for low-income residents in a project built to minimal means? Moore addressed these issues in regard to his own sense of inadequacy in providing a "place" for the residents of public housing:

> A dwelling should be the center of the universe for people who share it. To puzzle out a shape for the center of the universe with one interested family is a complex task. But to place dozens, or even hundreds, of these centers together for inhabitation by people whose identities are generally not even known to the designer approaches the hopeless.[66]

Moore's statement presumes that the architect-client relationship is based on personal connections, rather than a shared notion of public life. At Church Street South, he and Turnbull attempted to compensate for their distance from its residents by projecting a nostalgic vision of working-class urban life and giving it form as a set of defined spaces meant to produce security and a mythified public life. Their preference for places as coherent, bounded spaces intensified the constraints of site, budget, and demographics, resulting in a racially segregated enclave isolated from the rest of New Haven.

Notes

1 "Archives: 1967 Riots in New Haven," *New Haven Register*, August 13, 2017, https://www.nhregister.com/home/slideshow/Archives-1967-riots-in-New-Haven-160684.php [Accessed April 19, 2019]; Mary O'Leary et al., "1967 Riots: 4 Tense Days That Began 'Evolution' of Blacks," *New Haven Register*, August 14, 2017, https://www.nhregister.com/new-haven/article/1967-riots-4-tense-days-that-began-11813921.php.

2 They worked as MLTW/Moore-Turnbull, one of the variations on their original partnership with Donlyn Lyndon and Richard Whitaker. Marvin Buchanan and Donald Whitaker also worked on the project. Gerald Allen, "Church Street South," *Charles Moore. Monographs on Contemporary Architecture* (New York: Whitney Library of Design; 1980), 60.

3 Charles Moore, "You Have to Pay for the Public Life," *Perspecta* 9–10 (1965): 57–106. On Moore's early writings on place and the public realm, see my essay, "Charles Moore's *Perspecta* Essays: Toward Postmodern Eclecticism," in *Mediated Messages: Periodicals, Exhibitions, and the Shaping of Postmodern Architecture*, Véronique Patteeuw and Léa-Catherine Szacka, eds. (London: Bloomsbury Publishing, 2018), 159–174.

4 Donlyn Lyndon, Charles W. Moore, Patrick J. Quinn and Sim van Der Ryn, "Toward Making Places," *Landscape* 12:1 (Autumn 1962): 31–41.

5 For the purposes of this discussion, I here use "public housing" as a general term for government-subsidized housing. Conventional "public housing" is built, owned, and managed by public authorities, which was not true for all the housing built at Church Street South. See Joseph Heathcott, "The Strange Career of Public Housing," *Journal of the American Planning Association* 78:4 (2012): 360–375.

6 Sharon Lee Ryder, "Low-Moderate Baroque," *Progressive Architecture*, May 1972, 75.

7 Rachel D. Carley, *Tomorrow Is Here: New Haven and the Modern Movement* (New Haven: The New Haven Preservation Trust, 2008), 8–9.

8 A student of French planners Eugène Hénard and Henri Prost, Rotival had worked for the French colonial administration in Algeria. With Henri Prost and René Danger, he created a series of plans and studies for Algiers, culminating in a regional plan in 1931. Zeynep Çelik, *Urban Forms and Colonial Confrontations: Algiers under French Rule.* (Berkeley: University of California Press, 1997), 71–73. See Carola Hein, "Maurice Rotival: French Planning on a World-Scale (Part I)," *Planning Perspectives* 17:3 (2002): 247–265.

9 Albert R. Talbot, *The Mayor's Game: Richard Lee of New Haven and the Politics of Change* (New York: Harper and Row, 1967), 19.

10 Ryder, "Low-Moderate Baroque," 76. See *Redevelopment and Renewal Plan for the Church Street Project Area*. New Haven, 1957. http://hdl.handle.net/2027/mdp.39015070347664 [Accessed June 10, 2019].

11 Carley, *Tomorrow is Here*, 31.

12 On New Haven's urban renewal and antipoverty programs before and after the riots, see Fred Powledge, *Model City. A Test of American Liberalism: One Town's Efforts to Rebuild Itself* (New York: Simon and Schuster, 1970).

13 Peter N. Green and Ruth H. Cheney, "Urban Planning and Urban Revolt: A Case Study," *Progressive Architecture*, January 1968, 134–156.

14 *Progressive Architecture* cited a figure of $930 per capita. Green and Cheney, "Urban Planning and Urban Revolt," 139. Headed by Edward Logue, New Haven's Redevelopment Agency was aggressive in gaining federal redevelopment and highway funding. Jeanne R. Lowe, *Cities in a Race with Time: Progress and Poverty in America's Renewing Cities* (New York: Random House, 1967), 406.

15 *Kerner Commission Report: The National Advisory Council on Civil Disorders* (1967) (Princeton, NJ and Oxford: Princeton University Press, 2016), 288.

16 Based on numbers given by Alvin A. Mermin, the first director of New Haven's Family Relocation Office, Douglas Rae estimates that over 20% of New Haven's population was forced to move during Lee's administration, 1954–1969. Douglas Rae, *City: Urbanism and Its End* (New Haven, CT and London: Yale University Press, 2003), 338. On the displacement caused by urban renewal in New Haven, see Francesca Russello Ammon, *Bulldozer: Demolition and Clearance of the Postwar Landscape* (New Haven, CT and London: Yale University Press, 2016), 163–172.

17 Green and Cheney, "Urban Planning and Urban Revolt," 139.

18 Quoted in Mandi Isaacs Jackson, *Model City Blues: Urban Space and Organized Resistance in New Haven* (Philadelphia: Temple University Press, 2008), 112.

19 Ibid., 134.

20 Talbot, *The Mayor's Game*, 184.

21 The Section 221(d)(3) program was created under the Housing Act of 1954 to provide 100% mortgage insurance to non-profit developers (such as the Jaycees, in this case) and 90% to for-profit developers. The FHA-insured loans had a forty-year mortgage with a set interest rate of 3%, well below the market rate. Other portions of the 1954 Housing Act authorized FHA mortgage insurance for the rehabilitation and conservation of existing housing and for low- and moderate-income families, especially those displaced by urban renewal, to purchase housing. Andrew T. Carswell, ed. *The Encyclopedia of Housing*, "Housing Act of 1954" (Los Angeles: Sage Publications, 2012), 335; Talbot, *The Mayor's Game*, 177.

22 Ryder, "Low-Moderate Baroque," 76. In 1982, a second high-rise tower for elderly housing, Tower East, was built adjacent to Tower One.

23 "Church Street South, Housing for the Elderly," project description, Centerbrook Architects and Planners Records (MS 1844). Manuscripts and Archives, Yale University Library, A 23. Under Section 236 of the Housing Act of 1968, HUD provided mortgage insurance and an interest rate subsidy to private housing providers to enable below-market rents. "HUD-Subsidized and Project-Based Section 8 Programs," National Housing Law Project https://nhlp.org/files/multifamily_programs_info_packet.pdf [Accessed February 8, 2019].

24 See Rae, *City: Urbanism and Its End*, 274–280.

25 Green and Cheney, "Urban Planning and Urban Revolt," 151. The 1968 Kerner Commission Report recommended a similar strategy of decentralized housing developments and initiatives for increased ownership. See *Kerner Commission Report*, 28–29.

26 Quoted in Jackson, 111. The National Commission on Urban Problems, led by Senator Paul Douglas, had been empowered to study issues in US cities after the urban riots of previous years. It held public hearings in New Haven in spring 1967.

27 "$7 Million Co-op Tops 7 Plans for 848 Units," source unknown, stamped August 3, 1967. Centerbrook Architects and Planners Records (MS 1844). Manuscripts and Archives, Yale University Library, A 23.

28 Ryder, "Low-Moderate Baroque," 78.

29 From 1992, St. Basil's Greek Orthodox Church occupied a community center built on part of the site intended for moderate-income housing. A new building was completed recently and will remain during redevelopment. https://www. nhregister.com/news/article/St-Basil-s-Greek-Orthodox-Church-in-New-Haven-12204637.php - photo-14127640 [Accessed June 13, 2019].

30 Ryder, "Low-Moderate Baroque," 80.

31 Green and Cheney, "Urban Planning and Urban Revolt," 156.

32 Ryder, "Low-Moderate Baroque," 80.

33 Allen, *Charles Moore*, 65.

34 Ryder, "Low-Moderate Baroque," 82.

35 Ibid.

36 Founded in 1934, the Housing Study Guild was composed of Lewis Mumford, Henry Wright, Albert Mayer, and Carol Aronovici. In a study of urban housing, they concluded that high-rise housing was the cheapest alternative for the New York area. Eric Mumford, The "Tower in a Park" in America: Theory and Practice, 1920–1960," *Planning Perspectives* 10:1 (1995): 22–23.

37 Ibid., 25, 38.

38 Heathcott, "The Strange Career of Public Housing," 366–367.

39 The Housing Act of 1937 (Wagner-Steagall) created the first US Housing Authority and provided funding for capital, technical services, and oversight for the local housing authorities that would build public housing. Catherine Bauer had been instrumental in advocating for the Act and negotiating the compromises that allowed its passage. Heathcott, "The Strange Career of Public Housing," 363–364.

40 Catherine Bauer, "The Dreary Deadlock of Public Housing," *Architecture Forum* 106 (May 1957): 140.

41 On the national level, two-thirds of residents displaced by urban renewal were nonwhite. New Haven's black residents were 4.5 times more likely to be displaced by urban renewal or highway construction than white residents. Among those relocated, Blacks were three times more likely than white to end up in public housing. Amnon, *Bulldozer*, 164–165.

42 Bauer, 221.

43 Lawrence J. Vale, *Purging the Poorest: Public Housing the Design Politics of Twice-Cleared Communities* (Chicago, IL and London: University of Chicago Press, 2013), 219–222; D. Bradford Hunt, "Myth #2: Modernist Architecture Failed Public Housing," in *Public Housing Myths: Perception, Reality, and Social Policy*, Nicholas Dagan Bloom, Fritz Umbach and Lawrence J. Vale, eds. (Ithaca, NY and London: Cornell University Press, 2015), 52–55.

44 Ruth Moore, "CHA Planners Are Prisoners of Towers," *Chicago Sun-Times*, 4 September 1957, 4 cited in Vale, 222; Elizabeth Wood, "The Case for the Low Apartment," *Architectural Forum* (January 1952), 102–103.

45 Mumford, 36.

46 Oscar Newman, *Defensible Space: Crime Prevention Through Urban Design* (New York: Macmillan, 1972), xiii. Chapter 3 of Joy Knoblauch's dissertation provides a thorough overview of *Defensible Space* and its context in social science research of the time. Joy Knoblauch, "Going Soft: Architecture and

the Human Sciences in Search of New Institutional Forms (1963-1974)," PhD dissertation, Princeton, 2012.

47 See Fritz Umbach and Alexander Gerould, "Myth #3: Public Housing Breeds Crime," in *Public Housing Myths: Perception, Reality, and Social Policy*, Nicolas Dagen Bloom et al. eds. (Ithaca, NY and London: Cornell UP, 2015), 64–120.

48 Jane M. Jacobs, *The Death and Life of American Cities* (New York: Vintage Books, 1961). See Peter J. Laurence, *Becoming Jane Jacobs* (Philadelphia: University of Pennsylvania Press, 2016), 311–312, n. 7.

49 Lee Rainwater, a white sociologist, began his study of Pruitt-Igoe in the mid-1960s. Lee Rainwater, "Fear and the House-as-Haven in the Lower Class," *Journal of the American Institute of Planners* 32 (January 1966): 23–37; Lee Rainwater, *Behind Ghetto Walls: Black Families in a Federal Slum* (Chicago: Aldine Publishing Company, 1970).

50 For a review of Newman's theories and their legacy, see Graham Steventon, "Defensible Space: A Critical Review of the Theory and Practice of a Crime Prevention Strategy," *Urban Design International* 1:3 (1996): 235–245.

51 Newman, *Defensible Space*, xiii.

52 Ibid., 2.

53 Ibid., 15.

54 Larry Speck, "Looking at Church Street South Apartments," http://larryspeck.com/2011/05/10/church-st-south-apartments/ [Accessed August 16, 2016].

55 David Littlejohn, *Architect: The Life and Work of Charles W. Moore* (New York: Holt, Rinehart and Winston, 1984), 245.

56 Jonathan Hopkins, "Salimos de La Jungla: Renewing Church Street South Housing," https://newhavenurbanism.org/new-haven-architecture/renewing-church-street-south-housing. [Accessed February 12, 2018]. See "Jungle Boys," Southeastern Connecticut Gang Activities Group, http://www.segag.org/ganginfo/frjboys.html [Accessed May 31, 2019].

57 "After HUD foreclosed on the Jaycee Housing Corporation in 1980, Church Street South Housing came under the ownership or management of a series of private rental property companies from HRA Realty in 1983, to Colonial Realty, to Harbour Realty in 1992, to the Community Builders in 1998, to the most recent, Massachusetts-based Northland Investment Corporation, which has owned the property since 2008." Jonathan Hopkins, "Salimos de La Jungla: Renewing Church Street South Housing." https://newhavenurbanism.org/new-haven-architecture/renewing-church-street-south-housing/ [Accessed August 16, 2016].

58 In 2016, a class-action lawsuit on behalf of tenants was filed against Northland over its management of Church Street South; the suit contends it carried out "demolition by neglect" with repairs that covered up problems so the site would have to be razed and turned into a profitable venture. Mary E. O'Leary, "New Haven's Church Street South To Be Razed," *New Haven Register*, June 1, 2018. https://www.nhregister.com/news/article/New-Haven-Church-Street-South-to-be-razed-12961075.php [Accessed May 19, 2019].

59 "Church Street South Tenants Organize | New Haven Independent," May 18, 2011. http://www.newhavenindependent.org/index.php/archives/entry/church_street_south_tenants_organize/ [Accessed August 16, 2019].

60 Paul Bass, "Surprise! Now HUD Flunks Church Street South," *New Haven Independent*, January 21, 2016. http://www.newhavenindependent.org/index.php/archives/entry/church_street_south_reinspection/ [Accessed August 16, 2016].

61 Markeshia Ricks and Paul Bass, "City Teams with Northland to Rebuild," *New Haven Independent*, May 17, 2016. http://www.newhavenindependent.org/index.php/archives/entry/church_street_south_/ [Accessed August 16, 2016]; "New Haven's Church Street South, Before and After Demolition," *New Haven Register*, April 12, 2019. https://www.nhregister.com/

news/article/New-Haven-s-Church-Street-South-before-and-13763802.php-photo-17218681 [Accessed May 19, 2019].

62 Herbert Gans, "Urban Vitality and the Fallacy of Physical Determinism," *Commentary* (February 1962); reprinted in *People, Plans and Policies: Essays on Poverty, Racism, and Other National Urban Problems* (New York: Columbia University Press; Russell Sage Foundation, 1991), 36.

63 Ibid., 37.

64 Ibid., 39 and 42.

65 Bernard Asbell, "They Said It Wouldn't Happen in New Haven: Dick Lee Discovers How Much Is Not Enough," *New York Times Magazine*, September 3, 1967: 40. https://nyti.ms/2Zm1mZ9 [Accessed June 10, 2019].

66 Charles Moore, "Housing," *Architecture and Urbanism: The Work of Charles W. Moore* 5 (May 1978): 181.

Part IV

Land, Property, Colonization

9 Landing Architecture

Tropical Bodies, Land, and the Invisible Backdrop of Architectural History

Ijlal Muzaffar

One of the most expansive blind spots in modern architectural history has been that of land. We have talked about space, but not land. We have discussed architecture in the twentieth century as if it stood on some given, present, neutral, terrain, something readily available and uncontested, something we didn't need to discuss. To a certain extent, this was excusable in the Euro-American context. Here, the institutions that were presumed to secure land as property were actually present at the turn of the century, be it the state acquiring land through eminent domain or turning one form of tenure into another. But the myopia has been acuter, more consequential, when the projects discussed were in the decolonizing sphere. Here, the role of architecture was not only to provide an object but to legitimize a new set of institutions, from those securing dictatorships to international development. Here, land was not a given. Architecture served as a medium to secure, anchor, the legal and epistemological contours of land that such projects were to stand on. This was no light matter. Land defined as property differed from land defined as communal or public, and each variation excluded, framed, shaped the profiles of subjects who were to occupy it as well as justify the institutions that were deemed to have dominion over them.

This dimension of architecture, the shaping of land and its associated subjects, has been mostly absent from histories of modern architecture. And nowhere is this erasure more prominently apparent than in the works of British architects Maxwell Fry and Jane Drew for the colonial government in West Africa. Before Charles Abrams would propose self-made houses as an alternative for resettlement in Ghana, even before Otto Koenigsberger would be involved with the design of a new town and port around the proposed aluminum smelter on the heights of upper Volta in Nigeria, Fry and Drew were making their mark on how land was to be framed for the "native" populations in the late colonial period in the British colonies of Gold Coast and Togoland.

As planning advisors to the Governor's office, Fry and Drew produced a small but influential book called *Village Housing in the Tropics* that laid out best planning practices in these territories and proposed a plethora of

DOI: 10.4324/9781351182966-14

schemes under the Colonial Development Fund.[1] All of this would give their own practice a new lease on life after independence of Ghana in 1957. With their names becoming synonymous with the term "tropical architecture," they built schools, university campuses, as well as commercial buildings and houses for international and national clients. This late work, especially, has been discussed in detail in various publications, most often focusing on whether the principals of tropical architecture were a Western imposition or in line with African culture.[2] I have addressed elsewhere the limitation of that debate that presumes the two poles, West and Africa, as homogenous entities that have some sort of cultural essence against which appropriateness could be measured.[3] What I want to address in this chapter is how while giving shape to the idea of tropical architecture, their earlier work, parallel to *Village Housing*, framed particular ideas of land as well. We can discuss the merits of Fry and Drews' hurriedly drawn sketches in *Village housing in the Tropics*. But we must also pay attention to why these sketches float in the whiteness of the page. Here land, whose lack of articulation make it disappear into the white background, is presumed to be present as an aggregated entity, just there for the architects and planners to contemplate on (Figure 9.1).

We can find the implications of this erasure, as the well as the intensity of what it hides, most clearly in the two schemes the architects proposed in the small town of Tema on the outskirts of Accra in the 1950s. Tema was not an isolated scheme. The planning of Tema was part of the Volta River Project (VRP) that started in the late colonial period and turned into an ambitious national program under Kwame Nkrumah, Ghana's first prime minister and, later, president.[4] As Viviana d'Auria has discussed, from the onset, VRP was enmeshed in "conflicting objectives," from Cold War concerns to national objectives, to foreign industrial interests and transnational personal ambitions.[5] Yet, while these multiple strands could be unfolded to tell particular and contradictory stories of professional and institutional ambitions, they were nevertheless driven by a broader shift tying social change to economic development that produced critical change in the meaning of land. Looking back to Cold War inflected, post-WWII development theater, this coupling might appear unremarkable, but the emergence of VRP as an economic development project was a radical development in the 1950s.

After the WWI, the British colonial government had maintained political "maturity" as conditioned for independence. As independence movement combined with rising American pressures for decolonization mounted after the WWII, however, the British changed their tune of governance. Political maturity was now replaced with economic maturity as the proclaimed stepping stone for freedom.[6]

This produced immediate repercussions. We can see that initial proposals to tie various mineral and agricultural resources around the Volta River with economic development schemes were shunned by the colonial government.

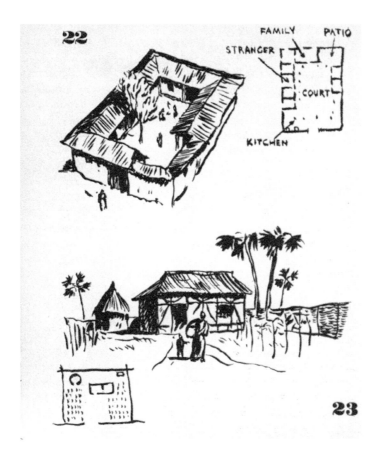

Figure 9.1 Maxwell Fry's sketch of a "traditional" compound house floating on a white background. Source: *Village Housing in the Tropics* (1948).

Soon after his arrival in the Gold Coast in 1913, Albert Kitson, an Australian-British geologist and the Director of Geological Survey of the British West African territories, had identified bauxite and manganese deposits in the Atewa Range in the north. Kitson was an ambitious thinker. In 1915 he proposed a dam at Akosombo on the Volta River that would allow generate electricity to turn bauxite into aluminum (a proposal that would later become the signature piece of the VRP under Nkrumah). He also imagined it being the source of transforming the economic makeup of the countryside. Even before arriving in the Gold Coast, he had proposed cultivating North American wheat to Nigeria, replacing the "less-valuable" millet, cassava, yams, and maize that were grown there. But Kitson's plans didn't gain any traction at the time. The colonial government saw more value in simply expunging raw materials from West Africa for the war effort.[7]

The change only came later, after WWII, when the Colonial Office set up a Colonial Development fund. Though its budget was meager compared to its professed scope, the fund undertook certain high-profile social and economic development projects that could be advertised well at home and abroad. With the rest of the VRP still largely undersigned, Tema initially was imagined as one such project. As Accra developed from a small fishing village to the colonial capital in the late nineteenth century, Tema was planned as a nearby harbor town with accompanying housing to accommodate displaced fishing communities in the region and give colonial rule the new frame of economic development.

Stepping Stones of Tema

Though a showcase example, Tema's planning was not just propaganda. It was mean to accommodate rising challenges to colonial control of land through new models of ownership and design. Fry and Drew's previous work came in handy to give them a new role in this changing political and administrative landscape. When the planning of Tema was in full swing, Fry and Drew were running an established practice in Accra, together with a host of compatriot colonial architects who had similarly found a sustaining clientele in both the indigenous elites and multinational firms clamoring for a share of Ghana's resources as they were being released from the colonial hold under national and international pressures.[8] But Fry and Drew had a leg up among the competition. Their name was synonymous with the term tropical architecture, thanks, as was mentioned earlier, to the handy little book, *Village Housing in the Tropics*, they had written soon after landing in West Africa as the leader and staff member, respectively, of the planning office of the governor of West Africa.[9] Their initial Tema scheme was a faithful implementation of the principles outlined in the book.

The two had roamed the West African British territories with their colonial entourage, documenting the mishaps of existing approaches to rural planning and development undertaken by the colonial government. *Village Housing*, a result of these travels, was described as a "handbook" for colonial officers, printed in small pocket size to be zipped out of one's khakis at any suspicious site. One of the key offenses, the authors claimed, was the iron grid, implemented on any unsuspecting location without consideration of topography, wind direction, and location of trees, among other things. Of this there was no dearth of examples in the African countryside. Small towns laid out by colonial planning authorities followed the thousand years old model of Roman garrisons like lost outposts who never received the word that time had moved on. Funny things happened when a planner placed a grid plan on a sloping site. Long buildings that found themselves in the direction of slope resigned to its contours like limp carrots lying lazily on the ground. The second most common crime, which was a direct consequence of the first, was latching the grid directly onto the main highway.

Instead of one or two, all parallel streets opened onto the main thoroughfare. This resulted in the village market overflowing onto the highway, producing congestion, and danger for life and property of the villagers.

The solutions were presented as simple and commonsensical, eluding only, the architects asserted, the rigid colonial mind obsessed with preconceived notions of what order looked like. Thus, all the main streets, the two argued, should move horizontally with the contours of the land, relieving the houses and the loaded backs of the villagers from the need to climb the hills. The settlement should be placed downhill from vegetation, giving it protection from rainwater and floods. Such a placement also prevented land erosion by preserving planting on critical areas of the landscape. Once the form of the town followed the contours, only one or two streets should connect to the highway. The entrance to the town should open up to a market and a lorry stand, with the houses further away from traffic.

Fry and Drew were convincing in their recommendations, no doubt. The principles laid out in *Village Housing* were later develop into a full-scale textbook, *Tropical Architecture in the Dry and Humid Zones* (1964), that continues to serve as required reading on countless courses across the world.[10] But to see these principles as simply outlining good planning is to ignore the political relationships in which and for which they were produced. And here the context is not just a question of providing background, but introducing a stratum of meaning that alters the meaning of the projects themselves. Architectural history has taken *Village Housing* to be a book about space and planning. But it is more importantly a book about changing the meaning of land and the legal and administrative structures around it. For example, limiting village access to the main road to one or two entrances doesn't just expedite traffic, it outlines a transformation of property relations. The infrastructure, the road, is now marked as exclusively state-owned, and the village as "communal" land (Figure 9.2).

These are not accidental propositions. Rather, the separation articulates the separation of the two legal spheres, the "native" and the colonial. In this regard, *Village Housing in the Tropics* draws on another book for the "tropics," Frederick Lugard's *The Dual Mandate in British Tropical Africa*, published in 1922, that summarized the quintessential model of governance used by the British colonial government in its territories in East and West Africa: Indirect Rule. The model employed a substructure of chiefdom and native authorities with penal, judicial, and administrative powers to implement British policy on the ground.

Lugard was no distant armchair commentator on colonial affairs. Born in India to parents in colonial service and raised in Worcester, England, he had been Governor of Hong Kong, and then Governor General of Nigeria. His implementation of Indirect Rule in these areas was an administrative response to an ethical and managerial dilemma that had long been sounded in the British parliamentary debates under the rubric of the "native question": how can a small white minority rule with a moral and physical

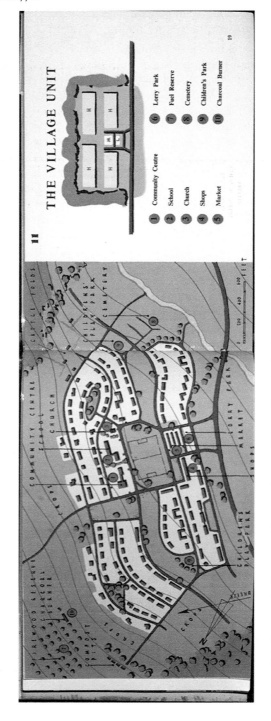

Figure 9.2 Corrected village road layout. Source: *Village Housing in the Tropics* (1948).

authority over a large indigenous majority in expansive territories? As Mahmood Mamdani has argued in *Citizen and Subject*, Lugard's answer to this dilemma was to construct what he called a dual mandate, a separate set of laws for "the native" and the European, marking the native body, rather than the native space, as distinct from the European.[11] This allowed for the indigenous population to serve in the same colonial spaces—the city, the factory, the bungalow—yet be subjected to a different set of laws than the Europeans.

This distinction along racial lines allowed for the movement of populations from the village to the mines to the factories, depending on the needs of the colonial economy. But, as Mamdani highlights, the native laws were not framed as authoritarian measures—as they actually were under an oppressive system of native chiefs operating without any historical checks and balances. Rather, the dual mandate was put forward as a cultural preservation proposal, as a measure to preserve indigenous culture in the face of rapid modernization. This imbued Lugard's dual mandate with a moral authority that any other "direct" rule approach would have lacked. It is often forgotten that the apartheid in South Africa, a model drawn from the dual mandate, was not a right-wing conservative measure, excluding natives from the space of modernity because they were seen to be inferior. Rather, as Mamdani stresses, it was a liberal argument, emphasizing the need for separate laws for the native for the protection of their own "cultural heritage."[12]

Indigenous populations were thus excluded along racial lines from the protections of civil society under the cover of cultural preservation. They were then included, or incorporated, into the highly exploitative economic system of colonization through the backdoor of Indirect Rule. The civil society therefore existed, without having to declare it so, only for the white colonizers.

We can add a particular framing of land to the system of power identified by Mamdani, a dimension that is betrayed in Fry and Drew's book. If the native was excluded from civil society on racial grounds but included in the economic system of Indirect Rule, then that economy of exclusion and incorporation was built on the distinction between land and property. Here we must keep in mind that land is different from space. Lugard's dual mandate indeed differentiated the "native" and the colonizer along racial lines, as Mamdani has shown, but it was not shy about tying those racial identities to different understandings of land. The native's racial identity was defined in terms of a set of perceived relationships with land, not property.

A series of colonial legislations between 1877 and 1920 defined land as a "communal" resource of the "natives." This resource included not only the land one resided on but also those who occupied it. The idea that land was a shared resource that extended rights over both terrain and people allowed the colonial government to imbue the chief with the powers to not only pay taxes but also move people from the field to the mine at will. As that economy shifted, from extrapolation of resources to management of capitalist markets, so did the need to change the meaning of land from inalienable communal land, in which rights over people overlapped with right over land, to communal land where these interests could be identified as intermingled but distinct and separable into new forms of ownerships if required.[13]

It is this accommodation that we witness in Fry and Drew's proposals. The demarcated boundary of the village still defines the village as communal land. But this communal land is of a different order than that shaped under Indirect Rule, where rights over people and rights of land were indistinct. The demarcated village of *Village Housing* is land defined, in both legal and physical terms, as something in between communal and property, as no-longer-communal and not-yet-property. And as such a land in waiting, the demarcated village comes to be defined by the colonizers as a land in *transition*, something that is in the process of translating communal holdings into property form. Under Indirect Rule, the rights over people and rights over land were intentionally rendered indistinct to keep communal land apart from civil law regarding property. The communal property demarcated under new planning proposals of Fry and Drew, however, is imagined as sum of distinct parts, where rights over people and rights over land are rendered as separate ingredients, ingredients that were together for the moment in communal land but could be separated through design in later stages.

Not-Yet-Property

The land being organized in and around Tema was no idle terrain. Its indistinct sketches by the architects in their little book had heavy consequences. The territory was a part of the Gold Coast that had come to be known, in midst of competing claims of ownerships, as Ga country, named after the migrating groups that had come and settled there from the east. The region however was quite contained. It composed of a stretch of some forty miles of grassland between Densu River on the west, the Laloi Lagoon, just south of Tema, on the east, the sea on the south, and the Akwapim Range rising onward from Aburi in the north. These geographic restrictions framed the growth of Accra as it developed from a small fishing village to a colonial town in the nineteenth century, making the land both highly valued and highly contested. Tema shared those pressures of legal contention and change.

To avoid competing with other "native" and colonial contestants, British had used the policy of setting up "chief" and "stool" lands in the region with large portions defined as forests and wastelands that could be acquired quickly through decree from the crown under the premise that they were vacant or unused.[14] This confiscation of land, however, quickly came to be challenged as competition for land development rose, with many independent European firms looking to get a foothold in the expanding mining industry.

To mitigate the situation British introduced a series of land ordinances, first in the 1870s and then in the 1890s, to set up procedures for compensation for land acquisition in and around the city, including in Tema, in a way that would ward off the rising criticism from home and abroad that the crown was confiscating indigenous land outside of any legal framework. As Naaborko Sackeyfio has argued, the Public land Ordinance of 1876, for example, created rules and procedures on how the "value, acquisition, and disposition; and compensation for" land was to be established. But in setting up procedures for monetary compensation, it introduced a new language of "certificates, tides, conveyances, receipts and surveys into the language of land,"[15] opening the flood gates for further conflict. Who was owed how much, and for how long? How did the value of land change over time? The Native Jurisdiction Ordinance of 1878 tried to answer some of these concerns. But, the new legislations had already transformed the very social makeup of Ga country, preparing the ground for the immense wave of property disputes that swept Accra in the first half of the twentieth century:

> Intrafamily conflicts over inheritance also evolved as social relations were reformulated with the introduction of colonial courts and new challenges to old forms of authority. Ga mantse Taki Tawia began to convey land outright to influential allies and to followers in the 1880s and conflicts began to arise over the control of land in Accra's Alata and Asere quarters. Individuals, chiefly authorities and other office-holders, and the wulomei (priestly authorities) all sought to maintain control over property as urban land underwent commoditization...Indeed, as chiefs faced a decline in their judicial powers and revenues with the introduction of colonial courts, they embraced their roles as distributors of urban and rural land.[16]

Yet despite these unintended setbacks, the ordinances reintroduced an idea that had been the bedrock of Indirect Rule into the emerging legal landscape: that native land was a communally held entity and thus had no inherent procedures of buying or selling. It needed outside quantifying measures and legalizations to make it exchangeable. To the extent that such efforts failed, they only reinforced the inalienable nature of communal land in the legal discourse.

Once these assumptions became accepted in the new legalized landscape, communal land came to be seen as one more thread in the knot of land rights and people rights that, presumably, required the guidance of the colonial government to be untangled. In the proceeding decades, the government tried to solidify the procedures of setting value to land that had been demarcated earlier. Previously, when the government needed the land for "absolute purchase" for the colony, it sent out colonial surveyors to both demarcate land and also establish its value. In due course, both the boundaries and the deemed value were greatly contested. Under two new ordinances in 1894 and 1897, surveying land was separated from its valuation and made part of the district administration.[17] The Governor could call for any colonial land to be surveyed and demarcated under a new "trusteeship" clause, whether it was required to be purchased or not, and its boundaries were to be marked permanently. The chief or a family then couldn't allocate the land to additional benefactors nor change the boundaries without notification to the District Commissioner and permission from the Governor.[18]

These powers, legitimized on a new scale, however, were immediately seen by the Accra elite as threatening to their interest in land speculation and mining boom. Seeing their assets under threat, the urban property holders cast themselves as protectors of native right and formed Aborigines' Rights Protection Society (ARPS) and establish alliance with various European firms to challenge crown's control of land. The challenge took on public dimension with articles in newspapers employing the language that the British had used to codify the language of property, challenging the colonial criteria of ownership and authority itself. A revised bill was presented in 1897, but that didn't let up the heat. In 1899, crown gave up all claims to confiscate land.

But all was not lost for the crown. What is important to note in these contestations is the legitimization of the claim that land relationships were not a matter of politics or commerce but of planning. The separation of spatial and legal dimensions of land resulted in recasting the role of the administrators as managers of a sequence. Any decision to transform a particular parcel of land was now justified through a logic of pace. Under the new framework, the management of land thus changed from a question of political oversight to now a problem of design. The term "transition" became a shorthand for recasting politics as design. The native land was in transition. "The [main] problem is to provide suitable houses…" asserted Fry and Drew in Village Housing, "answering present-day needs in the *transitional* stage of their development."[19]

In the proceeding years, the government further strengthened its positions as managers of land by framing it as a question not just of property and rights but also of trust and transition. The crown was repeatedly framed as the trustee of "native land" and the native elite and chiefs framed as clamoring for its theft. In 1911, the colonial office appointed Henry Belfield, an administrator with years of experience managing similar conflicts in Malaysia, who was soon to be appointed Governor of East Africa in 1913, to write a report on the land situation in the Gold Coast.[20] Belfield squarely put the blame on profiteering both native and European. European capitalist interest in mining, Belfield asserted, had met with local speculative greed, resulting in unauthorized land sales and embezzlement of funds. If the trend continued, he cautioned, it would lead to delegitimizing the structure of chieftaincy in the rural areas and property in the urban that Indirect Rule had sought to establish.

The accruing effect of this posturing was the building of a narrative of land as something in transition and, through her relationship with land, the native too that resided on it. The transformation of the meaning of land was necessary for the regime of Indirect Rule to chart a path through the forest of contestations that had grown around land rights if it was to remain a viable model of rule. Fry and Drew recommendations are also strategies for extending the life of Indirect Rule into new forms. Their designs present an argument for setting the pace of turning land into property, and thus make it plausible and sustainable in a rapidly transforming political and capitalist context.

A New Flatness

Fry and Drew proposed two plans for Tema. Both of them draw from the same playbook of framing land as a sum of people rights and land rights that appeared rearrangeable through different architectural proposals. The two plans, however, imagine this separation and their rearrangement in drastically different ways (Figures 9.3 and 9.4).

The first plan closely follows the principles laid out in *Village Housing* (Figure 9.2). The main road opened onto a market square, with residential areas extending from it along the contours. The town was placed closed to the water, with the houses going downhill from the market, rather than uphill, to give the inhabitants closer access to their fishing boats. Though the houses were grouped in the form of "clusters," nodding to what Fry and Drew saw as the traditional housing patterns of the *Ga*-community, each house was designed for a single family with its own individual courtyard. In this regard, the arrangement followed more closely the "neighborhood unit" model in vogue in British planning circles at the time than the village housing it referred to.[21] With this arrangement, however, Fry and Drew proposed a particular model of combining people rights with land rights: give land rights first and the people rights would resolve themselves in time.

It is easy to forget that the single-family house was a highly improbable proposition in a region where large extended patriarchal tribal family structure was prevalent. But the architects fathomed, as recounted earlier, that the house itself was a device for "transitioning" the tribal family into a modern one. These transition-producing qualities are evident in the transitory nature of the houses themselves. While their second proposal would profess intermingling of the "environment" and architecture, such overlap is missing from the first proposal. Terms like house and "environment," or the relationship between object and context, do not point to an indistinct overlap of boundaries but to articulation of distinctions. The house figures as an object and the surrounding environment only as background. If we look closely at the plan we see that the house is articulated to the extreme, while the background, the environment, figures only as a black box. And the term "black box" is not farfetched here. Fry and Drew described their

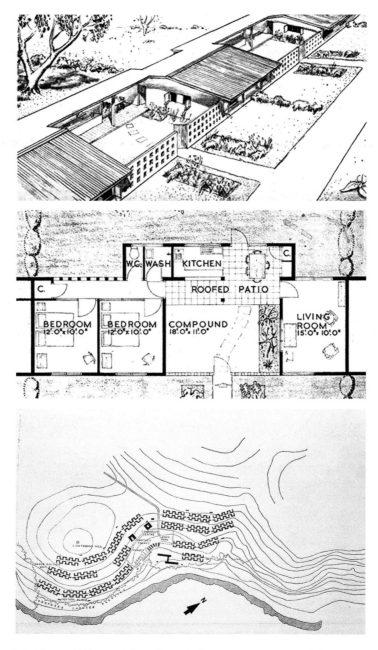

Figure 9.3 Maxwell Fry and Jane Drew's first "open compound housing" scheme for the village at Tema, with a dividing line of shrubbery trailing off from the house (seen in both perspective and plan), emphasizing the individualized nature of the property, Source: *Overseas Building Notes* (Garston, Watford, UK), no. 87, May 1963.

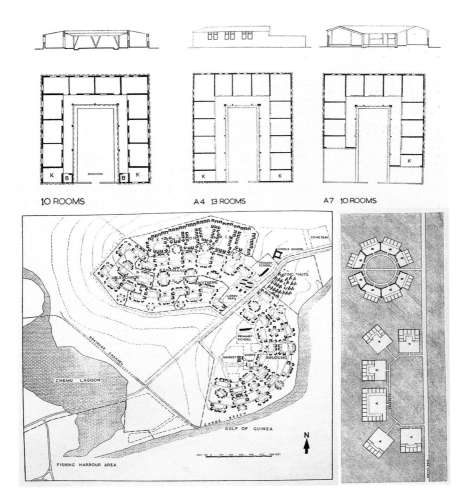

Figure 9.4 Maxwell Fry and Jane Drew's second "flexible" compound housing scheme for the village at Tema, showing unspecified arrangement of rooms, reflecting unspecified structure of property control. Source: G.W. Amarteifio, D.A.P. Butcher, David Whitham, *Tema Manhean: A Study of Resettlement* (Accra: Ghana Universities Press, 1966).

proposals as "systemic" arrangement of particular forces, be they environmental or human. As Katherine Hayles would tell us, if there is a system, there is a black box, that which lies outside the logic of the system.[22]

A system, arguably, is an argument for a set of relationships between finite parts that form a whole. The parts could be infinitely expanded, but they can't be infinite in themselves. A system, to be a system, has to have an identifiable set of relationships that produce identifiable set of results, or "states."[23] In other words, a system must assume a boundary. Beyond this boundary the rules that govern the relationship between parts of a system don't apply. Even open systems that imagine a system to the embedded in another one ad infinitum, assume that the logic of those that are nested does not extend to those that nest them, making the enclosing system invisible from the point of view of the enclosed. That space beyond, or sometimes even within, the boundary, whose behavior cannot be judged from within the enclosed universe of the system, is the black box.

To borrow a phrase from Hayles again, the system of the house Fry and Drew present in their first plan for Tema is not any system, but a "flat" system, where all parts that form the whole are visible at once.[24] What you see is what you get. Everything is assigned a place in this system. It is a system because everything has a place assigned to it. In this framing of the house as a system, the environment figures as a black box, a sphere that lies beyond the logic of the house. All focus is on how the house reacts to the environmental forces, how it receives the imprint of these forces, not on how the environmental forces interact with each other or are produced.

This erasure of the environment is necessary to advance the notion of a speedy transition of land under the Indirect Rule. Turning the environment into a black box, exhorting of the possibility that whatever this "environment" might be, it might already be a crosshatching of other systems. With the denial of that "texture," the environment is also made available as a receptive future. With its time and space ridden of any historically produced restrictions, it is available to the logic of the transition that the house delineates. This logic is, above all, of turning land into property, or seeing land as only not-yet-property.

Here the climatic dimension of the house, a key dimension of the architects' design vocabulary, is deployed in a particular way. Climate erases from the environment and, consequently, from land, the texture of all historical and politics forces. The very idea of thinking of land through climate, as only a composite of wind, heat, sun, shade, turns it into an abstraction outside of history, and its politics. Climate depoliticizes.

In the first Tema plan, the wind brings news from nowhere. The purpose of the house is not to make the inhabitants comfortable in hot climate, but how to use the house as a stepping stone in their own "development." The houses are only transitory stops in an inevitable journey to the city, toward urbanization. Weather and climate play a particular role in the design. Every inch of the house is mapped according to this climatically driven performance toward modernity and development. The plans are kept deliberatively thin in their depths to facilitate cross ventilation. The courtyard walls are porous, with open brick grillwork, to receive hot air and cool it as it enters the courtyard. Even the placement of furniture in the plan responds to light and air. The house has a mechanistic logic where distinct but interrelated parts work together to produce a result, to the extent that even details like where you dry your clothes and wash your dishes supposedly make a difference.

But, again, the purpose of this climatic performance is not to improve living with the climate. Rather it is to transcend it. The house employs climate as a performative index to make visible the contours of a new and efficient life. Two bedrooms, four beds, nine chairs, and a table are all signposts along the trajectory of modernization reaching beyond the house. The plan outlines necessary set of movements that, with each repeated performance, inscribe new patterns whose sole purpose is to overlay, erase the traces and habits of past life.

The house, then, is a challenge to the logic of Indirect Rule. Instead of imposing, legitimizing, an idea of "native culture," it presents climate as transitory hinge to move beyond it. The courtyard points to a recreational or utilitarian space for an individual family, not to a gender bound space of the multifamily, polygamous, tribal household. The "traditional" family structure, changed as it did under the Indirect Rule, still had no place, Fry would argue later, in modern Ghana, a sentiment shared by country's independence leader and first prime minister, Kwame Nkrumah as well.[25] The function of the courtyard was to activate a transition from traditional to modern living. These transitory spaces form the mechanism of achieving property ownership, to change the structure of the family itself, transform it from a shared, though still hierarchical, arrangement to an individualized, private one.

This performative dimension is evident not just in the over articular of the house but also in the manner the environment is erased around the house by thin lines of plantation leading off at a tangent into the backyard. The planting marks individual property lines. The purpose of transition set up by the house is to frame the inhabitant as an individual property owner. With this projection, the plethora of ongoing, complex, and contested notions of property being litigated in Accra courts for almost half a century is erased, packed into the confines of a neatly defined idea of tradition and sent off to a past claimed to be over with equal certainly. How can such an equation be proposed on such contested land? This was not just mere wishful thinking on behalf of the architects, but was part of the ongoing efforts to open a new strategy of management, of governance and political maneuvering, that picked up where the land ordinances of the late nineteenth century had left off.

Parallel or Sequential Change?

In 1956, the governments of Uganda, Kenya, and Tanganyika issued a combined report.[26] The report was a response to another, one issued a year earlier by a Royal Commission sent by the Colonial Office, Fry's original employer in London that had set up him for the post of the planning advisor to the Governor of West Africa.[27] The exchange between the governments and the Royal Commission betrays two different approaches to the transformation of land being considered at the moment. Even though the exchange concerns British East African colonies, it pointed to similar complications concerning transformation of land in British West Africa, the territory traversed by Fry and Drew in their writing of *Village Housing*.[28]

It also sheds new light on how Fry and Drew's proposals were very much immersed in, and contributed to, resolving this debate.

The transformation of land into exchangeable property was a major concern for colonial office after WWII. Without such transformation Britain's colonial holdings could not be made to participate in the new Bretton Wood financial system. But both the Commission and the governments were keen on ensuring that the advantages of Indirect Rule translate into the language of governance for a new era.[29]

For this purpose, the Royal Commission proposed that "native" land, divided under a complicated and layered system of stools and chief lands, should be consolidated by promising individuated titles. The very promise of the title, the Commission report asserted, would resolve the overlapping people and land rights that were the backbone of Indirect Rule and transfer them into a new system of individual and property rights now needed in the postwar economic environment.[30] The governments were suspicious of such a streamlined process imagined from afar. For the governors of Uganda, Kenya, and Togoland, such an approach, which imagined dismantling of communal rights and the emergence of individual ones as simultaneous and parallel processes, would not result in a simple transfer of one kind of system into another. Rather it would result in the explosion of one that would forever cloud the establishment of the another, losing the benefits of both for the colonial government.[31] A parallel process of resolving and issuing rights would tangle the new system with complications of the previous one. The governments countered that the question of rights and claims should be separately settled and "extinguished" before the process of issuing titles was ever started. Linear approach instead of a parallel one.

But difference between the two point of views was more than a matter of sequence. The Royal Commission was driven by economic expediency, or, more precisely, the idea of economics as expediency. From its perspective, the promise of profit and property would itself resolve questions of power. For the governments, however, at stake in moving from one model of governance, Indirect Rule, to another, market administration, was the stability of governance itself. What to the Royal Commission appeared as a slow and outdated arrangement, wasting economic potential in the rural countryside, ensured for the governments the percolation of one administrative model into another:

> The Government does accept that titles should be issued and interests registered for anything less than an economic unit. The Royal Commission believe that the registration of title should be used to encourage consolidation; but the Government thinks that the time and effort involved should be spent first on encouraging consolidation. The procedure envisaged by the Government is thus: first, scheduling; then adjudication of interests and extinction of other rights; then demarcation and record therefore of; then survey; and finally registration proper and the issue of a title.[32]

In other words, culture and custom first, law later. If "encouraging consolidation" entailed "waste," slowness, delay, that was precisely what made the system tick. Quick profit was all well and good, but it was of no use if it was going in someone else's pocket. Thus, two notions of transition appear in these reports. In the Commission's report, transition is set in motion by individuated property itself, while in the governments' response, transition was already under way, it only needed to be managed, slowly.

The generous employment of the same term, "transition," in these reports parallels its use by previous ordinances as well as by Fry and Drew's themselves to describe transformation of land. The governments' insistence to see their territories under transition frames change once again as a matter of pace and sequence. Thus, like the ordinances of the 1890s, it turns transformation of land into a problem of design, rather than politics. But in framing it as such, the politics, and especially the politics of Indirect Rule, don't disappear, but are rather rendered invisible, and displaced onto new registers. If forced labor was extorted indirectly through "native" authority's appointment in the name of cultural preservation under Indirect Rule, in the new transitory phase that labor and the value it produced were now to be procured through generational and patriarchal authority, with older male members of the tribe favored by the government to control property as well as the income of younger members and women who relied on that property for resources. The governments' insistence that rights over people be "extinguished" before rights over land was a euphemism for excluding contesting claims from minority stake holders from civil law. Once the first phase was declared over, all contesting claims to land were rendered illegitimate, extinguished. Transition serves as translation, translating public cultural authority into private generational authority marked along gender lines.

Fry and Drew's two plans for Tema were drawn at the same time when the Royal Commission and governments' reports were issued. They betray not only how their proposals were entrenched in this debate, but, by virtue of their site in Tema, also the intensity these concerns had acquired in specific "transitory" theaters. There is a certain correlation between the flatness of Fry and Drew's first scheme and the change imagined as a linear progression by the Commission. One cannot exist without the other. Only a plan like Fry's—and it's a project in plan with houses being simple extrusion of lines stretched in two dimensions—could be proposed in the wake of the Commission's report. The plan imagines life as a flat system, where interrelated parts work to push the inhabitants toward more and more urban styled living, single family, and private property. This transition, rushed into the inhabitants' life by the house, its wheels systematically pushing them toward modern living every time they wash their dishes and dry their clothes in proper places, creates a narrative of land in which past litigations become moot and illegitimate. All claims meet the response: the inhabitants have a house, they have property, they need to move on.

A Glorious Retreat

But moving on is one thing that the inhabitant didn't do. This systemic understanding of interaction with the environment in this decolonizing context was untenable. The clarity, the distinction of parts and their boundaries, the articulation of input and outputs came to haunt the imagined system. In laying out the fiction of what was needed to fill the intermediary steps of modernization, which might have worked well in the other contexts, here forced the architects and planners to display their hand too soon. It was simultaneously too much and too little.

For the authorities, Fry and Drew's proposal for the village at Tema could only be a model, a one off. The houses were simply too costly. You couldn't provide such houses for the entire population that was being displaced without articulating where the money was going to come from. The more privileged inhabitants disliked them because the houses didn't appear good enough. They appeared to be a step down in the social hierarchy, rather than a step up. With their single sloping tin roofs, they resembled the notorious factory and mining hostels. And no one was ready to forget the oppressive history of forced population movement to those places. A youth group burned down a model house, the elders walked out of meetings, budgetary planners shook their heads.[33]

Fry and Drew added another angle to the roof to appease the critics. But, the scheme moved one incline too many away from the modernist ideal of the flat roof they cherished. Fry and Drew had only recently presented the singular slope roof at a CIAM conference as an example of how modernist ideals could be adapted to different climatic and cultural scenarios without losing their purity.[34] Adding another angle was just going too far. But the inhabitants willing to move to Tema wanted precisely that another angle, for the double sloping roofs resembled the roof of the colonial bungalows, and constituted a sign of upward social and economic mobility.

At the first glance, the second plan seems to appear to have been scared up the hill by all the uproar (Figure 9.3). Instead of following the contours of the shore line, the houses are coiled up on the hill. But this change is more than a change of heart about the benefits of being near water. It is a change, we will contend, in the definition of the system that makes the house, a change in the kind of system the houses are supposed to be.

The linear string of houses of the first plan is scrapped away and replaced with what was originally discarded: the courtyard house. It is as if modernism resigns in the face of tradition and relinquishes itself to surface dressing. The outside wall is straightened up, the entranced placed symmetrically on one of the now blank walls. Some new windows are introduced but they are neither in the direction of wind, nor particularly shaded from heat. Cleaned up, visually and materially, the native house with a line of rooms around a central courtyard returns.

Yet more than the design itself, what is unusual is the manner in which this return takes place. Unlike the houses in the first plan with interiors showing all the details, from furniture to plants, here the interiors of the house are nothing but a void. There are also no property lines, shrubbery, and trees, showing the house in relationship to the "environment." When we see the houses in the new site plans, their interiors are blacked out.

We see their blacked-out shapes in the site plan too, but there seems to be a disconnect between the site plan and the plan of the house. The idea of the system laid out in the first plan seems to have been inverted in the second. Now it's not the environment that is the black box, but the house, the system itself. The previous plan allowed for a certain viewing distance from which the boundaries of the system could be seen, its working observed. The architect stood outside, while the inhabitant remained inside. In the new iteration that distance, that security of a neutral, objective view, is no longer possible. The architect and the inhabitant occupy the same space. Both are inside the system whose workings are opaque to them. We have shifted from one notion of a system to another, from an enclosed one, whose performances could be measure by the inputs and outputs entering or leaving its identifiable boundaries, to an open-ended system, whose boundaries cannot be observed, in which the observer and the observed occupy the same space, not being able to see what inputs or outputs are being manipulated by the systemic interaction of different parts.[35] Being inside the system, the observers don't know if their observation is part of the system or not. They cannot predict where one part ends and where the next one starts. When embedded in the system, it's not possible to see it as a system, parts making up a whole working toward a collective goal. If we are inside the system, how do we know what is its nature? The system itself turns into a black box whose workings are opaque to us.

Spatializing Race, Culturizing the Body

With this immersive system, Fry and Drew render invisible the boundary between private property and communal land. The houses in the second plan are still private, but cast in communal form. This overlap is not without consequences. In bringing back the indistinct boundaries of Indirect Rule into the emerging nationalist and decolonizing context, they translate its exploitative structures into a language that can function in these contexts.

The houses preserve the generational and patriarchal hierarchy of Indirect Rule in a market-driven arrangement. This gives the structure of native authority put in place by Indirect Rule a new lease on life, only in terms that are now palatable in the new context. Instead of demarcating communal space on racial grounds, it is demarcated on cultural grounds. The house borrows the shape of "traditional" houses because this is what is claimed to be culturally desired. But there was nothing culturally inherent in Indirect Rule. It manufactured a system of preserving culture on racial grounds so the native population could be subject to a separate set of laws without being subjected to a separate set of spaces.

Now when the same multifamily-polygamous-patriarchal-traditional house is reproduced as individuated privatized property, the elders who previously had legal protection as members of the native authority are given financial assets and legal protection as private property owners. As a bonus, they are given this property in a form in which they can still exercise generational and patriarchal control on all those who are now reliant on this property. The new houses, and the new industrial agriculture and mining economy it is part of, are indeed meant to function in a market economy. But in reproducing the structure of communal land under Indirect Rule into this new arrangement, it allows the money earned in this economy to be still controlled by the previous members of the native authority, an Indirect Rule, indeed.

The house is rendered as a black box in Fry and Drew's second Tema plan because the designers cannot acknowledge how it overlaps with the radicalized contours of Indirect Rule. By rendering the relationship between previously communal and now private property indistinct, the black box allows the racialized definition of tradition to continue into a new language of culture. Architecture here spatializes race. It reproduces the racialized body, as well as the structures of control over it, by now presenting it through the culturized house. The second plan turns communal land not in private property. The first plan tried that and failed. The second plan turns communal property defined in racialized terms under Indirect Rule into the perpetual purgatory of no-longer-communal and not-yet-property.

To ask in this context whether the houses are modern or culturally appropriate, or see them as "critically regional" is to miss the point; the point that architecture is here deployed to render invisible the racial structure of authority of a supposedly bygone era into new forms. And it does so silently—not through the climatic performance or through the traditional symbolism of the architectural object, which have been the focus of architectural history in the main, but by deploying the qualities of the object to change or preserve the meaning of land. To confront this translation, we have to land architecture.

Notes

1 Though Fry and Drew had a third author, a colonial planner named Harry Ford, he remained largely unknown in academic discussions. The book is attributed largely to Fry and Drew's field observations. See, Jane B. Drew, E. Maxwell Fry, and Harry L. Ford, *Village Housing in the Tropics* (William McLean, 1948).

2 This argument, that modern architecture formed a Western imposition preventing the "native" culture from developing its own modern expression, is advanced by Rhodri Windsor Liscombe in "Modernism in Late Imperial British West Africa: The Work of Maxwell Fry and Jane Drew, 1946–56," *Journal of the Society of Architectural Historians*, Vol. 65, No. 2 (June, 2006), pp. 188–215; and Monique Eleb in "An Alternative to Functionalist Universalism: Écochard, Candilis and ATBAT-Afrique," in *Anxious Modernisms: Experimentation in Postwar Architectural Culture*, Sarah Williams Goldhagen and Réjean Legault eds. (Cambridge, MA: MIT Press, 2000).

3 See Ijlal Muzaffar, "The World on Sale: Architectural Exports and Construction of Access," in *OfficeUS Agenda*, the catalogue of the US Pavilion at the Venice Biennale, 2014 (Lars Müller, 2014).

4 See Viviana d'Auria "More Than Tropical? Modern Housing, Expatriate Practitioners and the Volta River Project in Decolonising Ghana," in *Cultures of Decolonisation: Transnational Productions and Practices*, 1945–1970, Ruth Craggs, Claire Wintle, eds. (Manchester University Press, 2016).

5 d'Auria argues that VRP's continuation after decolonization should not be seen simply as Neo-imperialism in a different form. Even if the project's goals were set up from particular perspectives, they produced unforeseen effects

that were subverted and utilized for different ends: "Professional mobility and trans-cultural knowledge production, encouraged by the prominence of internationalism and UN-induced development, can therefore hardly be understood as merely old colonial relations living on in post-colonial linkages." For a detail study of how many of these strands played out against each other on a professional level, for instance, "Ghana Institute of Architects (GIA) [competing] against the Gold Coast Society of Architects," see Viviana d'Auria "More than tropical?" op cit., p. 201.

6 This shift is explored by Suke Wolton in charting the career of Malcolm Hailey, the British colonial governor of the Punjab from 1924 and 1928 and, later, the author of influential colonial social science compendium, The African Survey, in Lord Hailey, *The Colonial Office and the Politics of Race and Empire in the Second World War: The Loss of White Prestige* (New York: St. Martin's Press, in association with St. Anthony's College, Oxford, 2000).

7 Kiton had also identified rare diamond deposits along Volta. Bauxite and diamonds become the critical fuel for running Britain's military during WWI. See N. R. Junner and F. A. Bannister, *The Diamond Deposits of the Gold Coast with Notes on Other Diamond Deposits in West Africa*, GCGS, Gold Coast, 1943.

8 See Rhodri Windsor Liscombe, "Modernism in Late Imperial British West Africa: The Work of Maxwell Fry and Jane Drew, 1946–56," *Journal of the Society of Architectural Historians*, Vol. 65, No. 2 (June, 2006), pp. 188–215.

9 Fry had secured the appointment in the Colonial Office during WWII when work had grown scant in Britain. Initially, he worked in London, but in 1944 he was presented with the chance to serve as the town planning advisor to Lord Swinton, the resident minister of British West Africa. He had already become involved with Jane Drew, both professionally and personally, at the time and made her appointment on his staff as a condition for his acceptance. See Maxwell Fry, Autobiographical Sketches (London: Elek, 1975).

10 Maxwell Fry and Jane Drew, *Tropical Architecture in the Dry and Humid Zones* (New York: Reinhold Pub. Corp., 1964).

11 See Mahmood Mamdani, *Citizen and Subject: Contemporary Africa and the Legacy of Late Colonialism* (Princeton, NJ: Princeton University Press, 1996).

12 Ibid. p. 15.

13 The shift in the relationship between rights over people and rights over land is noted by Martin Chanock in "A Peculiar Sharpness: An Essay on Property in the History of Customary Law in Colonial Africa," *The Journal of African History*, Vol. 32, No. 1 (1991), pp. 65–88.

14 See "South Africa and Land Policy in South West Africa up to 1952. Note from British Embassy in Washington, DC, 4 March 1964, Enclosing Article Written by Dr John H. Wellington" (Foreign Office, The National Archives London, UK). Ref. FO 371/177115. Also see A.F. Mockler-Ferryman, *Imperial Africa: The Rise, Progress and Future of the British Possessions in Africa* (London: The Imperial Press, Limited, 1898).

15 Naaborko Sackeyfio, "The Politics of Land and Urban Space in Colonial Accra," *History in Africa*, Vol. 39 (2012), pp. 293–329. Also see Richard Roberts and William Worger, "Law, Colonialism and Conflicts over Property in Sub-Saharan Africa," *African Economic History*, Vol. 25 (1997), pp. 1–7.

16 Ibid. p. 30.

17 See, Kwaku Nti, "This Is Our Land: Land, Policy, Resistance, and Everyday Life in Colonial Southern Ghana, 1894–7," *Journal of Asian and African Studies*, Vol. 48, No. 1 (January 20, 2012), pp. 3–15.

18 The newly established "Concessions Court" had the power to allocate what it saw as forest and "wasteland" to the crown under a new "trusteeship" clause. See Thomas Shaw, "The Integration of Multiple Layers of Land Ownership, Property Titles and Rights of the Ashanti People in Ghana," *Urban Forum*, Vol. 24, No. 1 (March 2013), pp. 155–172.

19 Fry and Drew, Village Housing, op. cit. p. 30.

20 Henry Belfield, Report on the legislation covering the alienation of native lands in the Gold Coast Colony and Ashanti, with some observations on the Forest Ordinance, 1911 (London: H. M. Stationary Office, 1912).

21 For the influence and use of neighborhood planning model in Fry and Drew's proposals, see Iain Jackson, "Maxwell Fry and Jane Drew's Early Housing and Neighbourhood Planning in Sector-22, Chandigarh," *Planning Perspectives*, Vol. 28, No. 1, (2013), pp. 1–26.

22 Katherine Halyes, "Toward Embodied Virtuality," in *How We Became Posthuman: Virtual Bodies in Cybernetics, Literature, and Informatics* (Chicago, IL: University of Chicago Press, 1999), pp. 1–24.

23 Ibid. pp. 18–19.

24 See Katherine Hayles, "Print Is Flat, Code Is Deep: The Importance of Media-Specific Analysis," *Poetics Today*, Vol. 25, No. 1 (2004), pp. 67–90.

25 For a detailed history of Volta River resettlement scheme, see Iain Jackson, Ola Uduku, Irene Appeaning Addo and Rexford Assasie Opong, "The Volta River Project: Planning, Housing and Resettlement in Ghana, 1950–1965," *The Journal of Architecture* Vol. 24, no. 4 (2019), pp. 512–548.

26 Commentary on the despatches [sic] from the Governors of Kenya, Uganda and Tanganyika and the Administrator, East Africa High Commission, on the East Africa Royal Commission 1953–1955 Report, Presented by the Secretary of State for the Colonies to Parliament by Command of Her Majesty, July 1956 (London: Her Majesty's Stationary Office, 1956).

27 The Report of the Royal Commission on Land and Population in East Africa (London: Her Majesty's Stationary Office, June 1955).

28 This parallel is also betrayed by the reach of Lugard's Dual Mandate, the instigator of Indirect Rule, in both Eastern and Western colonial territories.

29 See Commentary, op cit., p. 3. "All the Governments agree with the emphasis" the report stressed, "which the Commission has placed on the need for a guided revolution in African agricultural methods based on a departure from subsistence farming and the entry of the African cultivator into a modern exchange economy."

30 See Report of the Royal Commission, op cit., Chapter 23, Para. 1. On the one hand, the Commission stressed that "Tenure and Disposition of Land: Policy on land tenure and disposition should aim at individualizing ownership and at a degree of mobility which will enable access to land for its economic use without ignoring existing property rights." The government "accepted" this position because it talked about the pace, the "degree of mobility," of change. But on the other, the Commission proposed in Para. 16 that "Legislation must be enacted to empower governments to dispose of all residual interests in land which has been subject to adjudication and registration." This clause was accepted by the governments but with a telling exception: "It is clear that must be a provision, either by statute or through native law and custom, for the extinction of such interests, though not necessarily by the Government [emphasis added]." See Commentary, op cit., p. 93. As we'll argue below, it is in this exception that generational patriarchy is mobilized under the cover of custom to extend the life of Indirect Rule into "modern exchange economy."

31 Ibid.

32 Commentary, op cit., p. 94.

33 These details are recounted Iain Jackson and Rexford Assasie Oppong, in "The Planning of Late Colonial Village Housing in the Tropics: Tema Manhean, Ghana," *Planning Perspectives*, Vol. 29, No. 4 (2014), pp. 475–499.

34 Ibid.

35 See Katherine Hayles, "The Second Wave of Cybernetics: From Reflexivity to Self-Organization," chapter 6 in *How We Became Posthuman*, op cit. pp. 131–159.

10 The Rise and Fall of California City

Shannon Starkey

A marketing photograph from 1958 depicts California City in the expanse of the Mojave Desert: a couple dozen buyers and sellers milling around under the harsh desert sun, cars parked indiscriminately on the sand miles from the nearest paved road, a cluster of A-frame signs, blue and gold flags, folding tables, and mountains looming in the distance, all surrounding a new billboard in the center of the frame exclaiming "California City Sales Office" (Figure 10.1). The photo evokes a postwar fantasy-minded culture, and, more than that, the ambition and wherewithal of California City's charismatic developer, Nathan Mendelsohn, to transform over 80,000 acres of remote desert into an urban oasis that would rival Los Angeles 100 miles south.[1] At the start of the 1960s, the development boasted thousands of landowners and investors, tens of millions of dollars in revenue, a main boulevard lined with commercial buildings, 10,000 trees dotting a new green park, and a twenty-six-acre artificial lake. California City appeared poised to become the city for 1 million projected by Mendelsohn and his architectural team, Community Facilities Planners (CFP).[2] By the end of the decade, roads were beginning to show their age, the plastic-lined lake was slowly shrinking from evaporation, new development had all but ceased, the population barely surpassed 1,000, and an overwhelming majority of the desert looked the same as it had on day one, marked with nothing more than the occasional foot print or tire track.

At first glance, California City appears to be just another case of ambitious postwar desert development attempting to profit off Westward migration that ultimately failed to materialize. As a protégé of the prolific West coast developer, M. Penn Phillips, Mendelsohn learned to:

> [s]ecure land, build homes on it, put in the minimal amount of infrastructure to make the homes inhabitable, bring in a population that creates the basis for a community that includes momentum for establishing some form of a jurisdictional governmental agency, sell all of the parcels acquired, take a profit and move on to the next development elsewhere.[3]

DOI: 10.4324/9781351182966-15

Figure 10.1 Opening Day, California City, 1958. Source: *American Heritage New Pictorial Encyclopedic Guide to the United States.* New York: Dell Publishing, Co. Inc., 1965.

The widespread logic of development outlined above was exemplified by Phillips who engaged in the creation of more than twenty developments from Baja California to Oregon. In 1956, after a joint development venture in Hesperia, California, Mendelsohn struck out on his own, acquiring the desert land that would become California City. He hired the Pasadena-based collaborative Community Facilities Planners (CFP)—architects Whitney Smith and Wayne Williams, landscape architect Garrett Eckbo, and urban planner Simon Eisner—to plan his development.[4] Proposing a slight alternative to Southern California's tract housing, the architects conceived a master plan with a green downtown surrounded by garden cities and a greenbelt that was still infilled with hundreds of tracts of single-family lots. The ensuing development inverted conventional practice. Rather than build homes, the company prioritized the construction of highly visible public spaces and common recreational facilities that signaled to investors and potential buyers the existence of a new and thriving public entity. Whereas the planning of suburban subdivisions typically negotiates a balance between for-profit speculative housing development and public infrastructure and subsidies, in the case of California City both public and private aligned to produce a mutually reinforcing and endlessly deferred mirage. A collective suspension of disbelief enabled, and was enabled by, the proliferation of landowners on the one hand, and the development of recreational spaces and facilities on the other hand. However, the oasis centering on a glittering, glistening body of water was funded by and built for largely absentee landowners spread across the country and around the world. They represented an investment community linked financially by deeds and bonds, and socially by the *California City Sun*, the company magazine masquerading as an independent press that accelerated land sales while promoting the illusion of a thriving community. California City illuminates, by exaggeration, the financial mechanisms of postwar American housing development, and the expansion of architectural services to connect land to forms of paperwork to generate financial value. California City was packaged, circulated, and stored on multiple forms of paperwork including deeds, bonds, and newspapers/publications. California City and its mediations facilitated the global circulation and local accumulation of thousands of documents and tens of millions of dollars structured on a collective illusion of housing.

CFP provided services to the California City Development Company for nearly a decade, designing everything from signs and architecture to infrastructure, and even the environment itself. "Total design" and Mendelsohn's grand vision, however, were first structured on the systematic evacuation of the land of any defining feature, resource, and population.[5] The expanse of the desert was highlighted and used as the basis for claims of isolation and a lack of site specificity. California City was imaged as an empty and undefined surface, boundless and remote, setting the stage for total design and a new land market designed to attract middle-class consumers.[6] Its previous history was suppressed, including its use as farmland for cotton and alfalfa and its role in the nineteenth-century borax trade.[7] In marketing material and articles, Mendelsohn dismissed existing cities while framing California City as empty by implication: "In the first place, most cities—whether large or small—have historically sprung up around some dominating influence such as a large industrial complex, or, perhaps, a strategic geographical location along an important river or waterway."[8] The denial of history and external forces was even extended to the land's natural resources, seemingly counter-intuitive considering the desert location: "Other cities have focused on... a single natural resource which in some cases dictates or limits the city form and the experience of living there."[9]

Located 100 miles from Los Angeles, California City was only accessible by a single two-lane road at the time of its founding.[10] Los Angeles became a stand-in for a broader indictment of existing cities and their planning and development strategies. Mendelsohn hired Charles Clark, an outspoken city planner who claimed cities suffered from a lack of central planning, and laid problems of traffic circulation, land crowding, and slums at the feet of subdividers and developers.[11] Total design was offered as the solution to the perceived failures of piecemeal development and poor planning encapsulated in the early twentieth-century city of Los Angeles, described by Smith and Williams as a mishmash of "construction, automobiles, expansive asphalt parking lots... billboards... and flickering signs."[12] In early advertising, Mendelsohn proudly boasted that "Mr. Clark's plan for California City has been on the drawing boards for over six years."[13] For Mendelsohn, California City would succeed where Los Angeles had failed because it was a blank canvas with a comprehensive plan: "What would Los Angeles be like if we could sweep away everything and start from scratch—a new plan with all new buildings, utilities and streets?"[14] Overlaying this new blank canvas, CFP proposed a collection of six distinct and interdependent towns anchored by a large downtown located in the southwestern tip of the property to welcome visitors and potential buyers. With an initial projected population of 400,000, the downtown and satellite towns filled out the entirety of the development, connected by a massive new transportation system.

Both Williams and Clark emphasized the importance of large-scale transportation frequently neglected by piecemeal developers.[15] California City was designed around two new crisscrossing freeways.[16] Designed to move people through the city, a number of major highways would then deposit visitors into the individual towns making up California City. Secondary highways, collector streets, and finally local streets rounded out the transportation system within each town. The organization of the road system reflected the different development conditions. In order to accommodate efficient development in town, the roads adhered to a rigid grid system. Between towns, where development was restricted to parks or large-scale industry, roads broke free of the grid to achieve what Williams described as "pleasure transportation," of which cars were only considered one mode alongside walking, horse riding, cycling, boating, and even swimming.[17] Finally, between the curb of "auto design" and the sidewalk of architecture, the master plan proposed street furniture, graphic signs, public fountains, and lighting to encourage recreation and "the feeling of living within a large park rather than in blocks of houses."[18]

The extensive transportation system provided access to the primary product on sale: hundreds of single-family residential tracts of land (Figure 10.2). The development company boasted forty miles of roads in the first year.[19] As roads stretched across the empty desert, parcels were released to the public for sale. Pavement was often no more than an inch thick and produced from the desert sand through which it ran.[20] Many roads were simply graded, differentiated only from the surrounding property for sale by street signs and tire ruts. Nevertheless, once established and graded, parcels were sold to a network of buyers that began in Southern California and grew to encircle the globe.

At the scale of the individual lot, architectural services were redefined. Rather than attempt to inflate the speculative value of land by representing possible future improvements, i.e. the design of different housing types,

Figure 10.2 Aerial View, California City, date unknown. Courtesy of Architecture and Design Collection, Art, Design & Architecture Museum, University of California, Santa Barbara, CA

Smith and Williams proposed design restrictions written into the deed that delimited speculation. The usual separation between real estate and the design of architecture was collapsed into the deed. The restrictions helped to accelerate sales by setting up artificial distinctions in the sea of otherwise undifferentiated lots, and additionally, according to the development company, protect buyers' land investment.[21] The lack of infrastructure, however, discouraged subsequent development. Further, the company formed an Architectural Review Board (ARB) to review and approve all development. The measures set up to protect investment were also essentially obstacles to the development of housing. From opening day in 1958 well into the 1960s, thousands of land deeds were issued, but just a few dozen homes were built.

Despite millions of dollars in sales, scant few landowners moved to California City to build a house and take up residence. And while designs for public, communal, and recreational facilities were conceived, and some even built, designs for houses were more frequently conceived as written guidelines rather than drawings. Few residential types were designed beyond a handful of single-family homes and a concept sketch for a low-rise housing block, all designed to nestle into a new green landscape. Reacting against homogeneous tract developments, CFP proposed a variety of housing densities to create more diverse communities in terms of "interests and abilities, of races and religions, of varying family compositions and living patterns" and "discourage the large-scale massing of persons of similar age, marital status, and economic levels."[22] Even though Smith and Williams generated a few models, most projects were designed on a case-by-case basis for evaluation by the ARB. "In addition to the building itself, design control also extend[ed] to exterior colors, materials, textures and major landscaping. (Every tree has its place) Standards would be set far in advance..." The ARB operated under the direction of Mendelsohn and in consultation with Smith and Williams, and required approval for all proposed development.[23]

Locating design within the deed as a set of restrictions, combined with the formation of the ARB, effectively situated architectural services between land and its conversion into property. Smith and Williams used architectural design to aestheticize property, rather than building. The aestheticization of real property, as a result of efforts to control every aspect of the master planned community, produced the specter of housing that never quite materialized beyond scattered and isolated cases. Real property and the real conditions of the land were concealed with the aesthetic of housing, however negatively defined through restrictions, that aided both the sale of land and its inflated value. Mendelsohn noted with surprise how restrictions helped the sales efforts by articulating artificial distinctions. Further, the architectural aesthetic, produced from guidelines both inscribed in the deed and outlined by the Architectural Review Board, implied a virtual, seemingly immanent, future of massive, widespread residential development. For the dispersed community of absentee landowners and potential buyers, however, property was sold on the implication that development would be undertaken by others. Land was not so much paired and sold with the house, or even the design of a house, but with the mechanisms for controlling and envisioning a thriving and well-designed future. Development was, in effect, presumed, shifting focus to the nature and quality of design.

On opening day in 1958, the first tract of residential lots sold out, totaling half a million dollars in revenue. Land that the developer had acquired, in some cases for pennies an acre, was put up for sale as quarter-acre lots starting at $990.[24] With a five-year loan financed by the development company, a lot could be purchased with a down payment of just 10%. Real estate developer and investor, Max Derbes, characterized this kind of market as follows:

> Created markets occur where the individual promoter attempts the marketing of speculative lands, usually as a 'paper subdivision.' High pressure salesmanship promotions, low down payments, and even

misrepresentation may cause values and activity to rise beyond reason in particular areas while similar properties remain at a low level.[25]

California City represents a more extreme case; with relative geographic isolation, monumental size, and the development company acting as sole owner, seller, and financier, Mendelsohn effectively created a line in the sand preventing any external market forces. Therein, Mendelsohn adjusted the value of land. As land sales increased, so too did the price of land, which had the dual effect of generating more income for the company and propping up an illusion of increasing value to landowners. The isolated and inflated market was reinforced in a few rare cases where landowners tried to sell; the company reacquired the lots at their own inflated market price.[26] Control of the built environment extended to its financialization.

By the end of 1959, total sales surpassed 12 million dollars, and by 1963, total sales after cancellations and repossessions reached nearly 30 million dollars.[27] The company's operations increased along with its revenue. What began as a small corporate headquarters in Hollywood and a sales office in California City spread across California, the West, and ultimately internationally. Dozens of branch sales offices opened across California, Illinois, Washington, Kansas, Hawaii, and later Mexico, Germany, and the Philippines.[28] The company traveled to fairs and conventions across the country.[29] California City attracted international buyers, prompting sales trips.[30] As early as 1960, plans for offices in Kuala Lumpur, Bombay, Madras, and Antwerp were explored to such an extent that the company's public relations spokesperson, Fred Beck, boasted that "Mosques, minarets and pagodas may some day (sic) outnumber plain houses in California City."[31]

While Mendelsohn maintained a relatively small corporate office in Hollywood, the salespeople who worked with the company numbered in the hundreds. The company blurred the distinction between salesperson and buyer, as advertisements for new recruits rivaled ads for buyers.[32] In many cases, sales were generated from employees, rather than by them. New recruits were heavily pressured to purchase land, and encouraged to reside in the city to show their commitment to the company. As a result, a majority of the city's residents were directly or indirectly employed by the development company.[33] At the start of 1963, the company reported more than 14,000 individual investors, but only 203 "registered voters."[34] By 1969, it was reported that the California City Development Company had generated revenue in excess of $100 million.[35]

CFP's master plan for California City was explicitly comprehensive: "The plan calls for virtually total design control."[36] While total design was claimed by the developer and architects as a way to avoid the pitfalls of incremental design, when combined with the formation of a community services district, it helped shift financial responsibility from the developer to a new public of individual landowners. The design of houses was eschewed in favor of the design of public infrastructure and community recreation facilities. The latter was mobilized to bolster the creditworthiness of the district to sell general obligation bonds, issued and backed by the full faith and credit of the district. The insertion of the bond as a financial instrument into the process of private development had significant impact on the development of the town and its finances. Restricted from funding private enterprise, bond issues were directed toward the development of public facilities. Further, because bonds are secured by taxes rather than assets, physical development was rendered unnecessary and irrelevant. Architectural services were redirected away from building and towards the production of imagery that bolstered creditworthiness. The ability to attract investment surpassed the use of that investment. This is most explicit in the creation of an origin myth for California City, the representations of which served not to build architecture but to illustrate a marketable fabricated history.

Shortly after California City was opened to the public, the county received a petition to establish a community services district. California's Community Services District Act of 1951 authorized the formation of independent governing bodies empowered to develop public facilities, provide services, tax residents and landowners, and issue bonds to provide public services to residents in rural areas.[37] The legislation required that petitions come from residents of the proposed district. As Mendelsohn employed most of the earliest landowners and residents, he was able to both orchestrate the petition and select the new district's board. Only nine residents petitioned to create the special district. The California City Community Services District's (CCCSD) enumerated powers included:

> to supply the inhabitants of the district with water for domestic use, irrigation, sanitation, industrial use, fire protection, and recreation; the collection, treatment or disposal of sewage, waste and storm water of the district and its inhabitants; the collection or disposal of garbage or refuse matter; protection against fire; public recreation by means of parks, playgrounds, swimming pools or recreation buildings; street lighting; the equipment and maintenance of a police department or other police protection to protect and safeguard life and property; to acquire sites for, construct, and maintain library buildings, and to co-operate with other governmental agencies for library service.[38]

The special district thus took over many of the responsibilities that would typically be provided by the developer of an unincorporated territory. At the direction of Mendelsohn, one of the first acts of the CCCSD was to purchase the water system and rights from the development company. The board arranged to take ownership for the price of $1,350,000 with payments deferred for the first ten years.[39] The district then voted to approve a bond issue for $1,000,000 to build a large park, several recreation facilities, and more public roads.[40] With the board under his control, Mendelsohn continued to design and develop California City with little personal investment.[41] Bank of America, an early investor, purchased nearly half of the initial bond issue.[42] However, contrary to a construction loan secured by a developer with the resulting building serving as collateral, bonds issues are secured by the residents and landowners of the issuing district and re-paid through taxation. Not only did bonds shift the financial burden of de-velopment onto the residents/landowners, they also relieved the developer from an obligation to deliver physical development. The special district—and Mendelssohn's ability to access and issue bonds through the CCCSD—enabled the cycle of speculative investment and profit without the need for building. The profit of productivity through housing, in the vein of KB Homes and any number of other postwar developers, was eschewed for the valorization of private undeveloped land with public facilities.[43]

In his 1957 analysis of special districts in the United States, political scientist John Bollens identified nineteen community services districts in California. California City was the first district to provide recreation and community facilities.[44] It precipitated and was emblematic of a shift in Cal-ifornia governance in the postwar period: the decline of new town incorpo-rations and the rise of non-school special districts. Nationwide, the decade from 1942 to 1952 saw municipalities grow by just 3.5% while non-school special districts grew by 50%. Special districts became so rampant in the 1950s that by 1955 their budgets rivaled cities, and well exceeded coun-ties and towns.[45] And unlike school districts that typically received their funding from property taxes, non-school special districts received more than 75% of their funding from bond issues. Indeed, this was the case in California City, where, in effect, the development company was able to design and build public community and recreational facilities by indebting the landowners and residents through bonds. The ramifications of this pro-cess became overwhelmingly apparent in 1965 when the district formally incorporated with an estimated $7,500,000 in public debt and a recorded population of just 617.[46]

Since the original 1951 Act stipulated that only those who reside within the proposed district may petition the county, the development company pressured its salespeople to purchase land and take up residency. In 1961, the Act was amended to allow absentee landowners to petition the county to form community services districts.[47] In the ensuing years, developers exploited the law to such an extent that scrutiny and investigation was swift. Writing in 1965, Thomas Willoughby, as part of the Joint Assembly Subcommittee on Premature Subdivisions convened by the California state legislature, called out California City specifically when he asserted:

> Although the use of special district to finance development projects is obviously advantageous to potential developers, as a matter of public policy it bristles with danger. In the first place, the use of a public agency to perform an essentially private and proprietary service provides no guarantee that any lasting "public interest" is served thereby. Subsequent land owners have no real voice in such a shadow agency. It will have in-curred its major indebtedness and concluded its principal activities prior

to their residence in the district. Yet these homeowners, not the original developer, become responsible for repayment of district indebtedness.[48]

The financial mechanisms of general obligation bonds and developer-financed deeds combined to suppress privately funded development including houses and industry. At the same time, the sale of land and the issuance of bonds fed each other, the latter used to develop a collection of public recreation and communal facilities. The conventional development logic of the period was inverted. Private property and individual rights did not engender a public sphere; rather a public sphere was conceived to sell private property.

Like cities emblematic of California modernism—Palm Springs and the Salton Sea—California City, too, was oriented toward recreation and leisure, rather than production. However, anticipating the flawed logic linking post-industrial production with the availability of increased leisure time, the development company presented leisure facilities as investments to attract a labor force and productive enterprises.[49] The company spokesperson claimed in 1960: "Industry requires labor and labor requires good family living conditions and good recreational facilities."[50] Development centered on a public road system, congregational church, recreation and community center, public parks, pools, a golf course, and—perhaps the largest physical transformation of the design—a twenty-six-acre artificial lake. Prioritizing recreation over housing as a development strategy resulted in an expansive but largely unused recreational zone. Heavily documented and reproduced in the pages of the *California City Sun*, it primarily functioned as advertising for the sale of land. In title, format, content, audience, and operation, the *Sun* blurred the line between an in-house company magazine, a local independent newspaper, an investor report, and a long-form advertisement. Pairing photographs of the development in the city and drawings of proposed projects with narratives of local activity and events, the publication projected the image of a thriving town that communed a network of buyers, potential buyers, employees, investors, residents, and architects. Distributed across the country and around the world, the publication packaged, distributed, and sold California City.

The first facility to be completed was a community center, a small, one-story building on Randsburg-Mojave Road, the main downtown boulevard.[51] Located at the far west edge of the downtown loop adjacent to a small commercial strip, it welcomed visitors arriving from the Los Angeles area. Although the building appeared quite large from the street, a significant portion was simply a roof elevated on wood posts, with a wall along the street giving the illusion of enclosed space.[52] The construction of the commercial strip followed, anchored by two buildings for the development company, a sales office and an administration building (Figure 10.3). The sales office, a low-slung, single-story building, featured a low gable roof, stucco walls, and scant windows. As the first stop for visitors, the sales office turned inward, focusing potential buyers' attention not on the

Figure 10.3 Smith and Williams, Architects and Engineers, *California City Shopping Center*, Date Unknown. Courtesy Architecture and Design Collection, Art, Design & Architecture Museum, University of California, Santa Barbara, CA.

city outside but its carefully curated representation: architectural renderings, charts, and staged photographs. The location of the buildings and the boulevard itself reveals the grand scale envisioned for California City. Randsburg-Mojave Road was conceived as a four-lane boulevard with center divider, flanked by surface parking lots, pushing the buildings more than 200 feet from the curb.

The remainder of the strip comprised three buildings separated by vacant lots. And while the development company frequently referred to the strip as the first phase of a "shopping center," the initial plans by CFP reveal that the primary item on sale was the development itself. Beyond a small supermarket and variety store, most of the storefronts were either commercial entities related to the development company or communal and public facilities: local realty offices, the non-profit California City Club, a design center for the Architectural Review Board, local post office, library, and nursery providing landscaping services to the development company.

The jewel of the development was California City Central Park (Figure 10.4). Named after its New York counterpart, Central Park constituted sixty acres of public land with an additional 100 acres of public-oriented private

Figure 10.4 Smith and Williams, Architects and Engineers, *California City Central Park*, 1962. Courtesy of Architecture and Design Collection, Art, Design & Architecture Museum, University of California, Santa Barbara, CA

land to visually increase its size, and contained a congregational church, recreational facilities, a golf course, and an artificial lake.[53] Most of the land was transformed from dry desert into a green landscape with a "natural canopy" of 10,000 new trees and other greenery.[54] Central Park served as ground zero for a new "natural" landscape designed to spread throughout California City, designed to put leisure and recreation zones within just a few blocks of every resident.[55] Several pavilions and buildings for communal gathering and public use were dispersed across the park. The first building, located just outside the entrance of the park, was a congregational church with adjacent education building (Figure 10.5).[56] The open plan included a pulpit at one end and moveable pews. Slanted stucco walls with no windows stood independently of the roof. The roof, a series of upside-down clamshells, rose from within and extend beyond the walls of the church. Each section of the modular roof was built out of a set of eight plywood fins spanning twenty feet across from a single six-inch steel column. The top

Figure 10.5 Smith and Williams, Architects and Engineers, *California City Congregational Church*, 1962. Courtesy of Architecture and Design Collection, Art, Design & Architecture Museum, University of California, Santa Barbara, CA.

half of the fins were then covered with bent plywood.[57] The roof appeared to float above the walls. The same modular bent plywood roof was used in a pavilion located at the end of a long pier in the lake, and its image became the logo for the development company. The lake-side pavilion was complemented with two others located in a small island in the middle of the lake. Loosely programmed, they served mostly to provide shade.

The emphasis on park recreation extended even to the road system, where the development company quickly abandoned the construction of neighborhood roads in favor of a new parkway. With no apparent destination, the proposed 150-foot wide parkway restored the nineteenth-century Borax trail as a 300-acre communal recreation zone with parks and picnic areas in addition to paths for cars, bicycles, and horses.[58] In 1963, the parkway was realized as a two-lane automobile road with none of the accompanying pathways, wagon trail, or parks.[59]

The largest development was the artificial lake.[60] It featured prominently in marketing material and was celebrated by Mendelsohn as a crowning achievement. Containing 30 million gallons of water, the lake was the first step in Mendelsohn's dream of transforming the dry desert into a lush landscape, lined in plastic.[61] Just a few years later, Reyner Banham visited Central Park, remarking that "in the newer and remote instances, an artificial body of water is almost mandatory… California City's central lake seems, in its improbable desert setting, both ludicrous enough to be a joke, and welcome enough to be a blessed miracle" (Figure 10.6).[62]

Despite the significant developments in Central Park, they were experienced primarily through the *California City Sun*. Published monthly, its first issue was released before there were any residents, and even before opening day.[63] With a recurring column by Mendelsohn, the *Sun* was fairly transparently a company publication despite the inclusion of news articles as if it were an independent free press. As a marketing strategy, the distribution and coverage of the newspaper were reversed in California City. As implied by the conception of the newspaper before a single investor or resident, the newspaper enjoyed widespread distribution, while largely limiting its coverage to California City. Even as the city began to accumulate residents, however scant, the audience for the newspaper remained absentee and potential landowners scattered across the world.[64] In the pages of the *California City Sun*, buyers and investors were apprised of the progress and future of the development; stories created the appearance of a thriving development in their absence.

The lake, in particular, was leveraged as an image, representation, and illusion of water, implying a thriving and resource-rich development. Just months after the first lots were released to the public for sale, Mendelsohn claimed the existence of "a vast underground lake under the sands of the Mojave Desert" capable of providing 20 million gallons per day.[65] Despite numerous claims, the California Department of Water Resources (DWR), the Long Beach United States Geological Survey Office, and the California Association of Engineering Geologist immediately debunked the claim, asserting it "is bound to appear to any disinterested man with scientific training as utterly fantastic nonsense."[66] In 1961, the DWR admitted that "California City [was] certainly in no danger of running out of water soon… [b]ut… the original claims of having water in perpetuity were 'absolutely fraudulent'."[67] By contrast, the lake served as a compelling mirror image of the supposed underground lake and abundant water availability.[68] It was christened on the fourth birthday of California City with buckets of water claimed to be from the lake in New York City's Central Park, spectacularly dropped by Mendelsohn from a helicopter hovering overhead.[69]

The most explicit evidence that California City was positioned as a stage set distributed through images and publications was its origin myth. A Hollywood illustrator, Stan Repp, was hired to produce a series of drawings that represented California City simultaneously in the past and the future.

Figure 10.6 Smith and Williams, Architects and Engineers, *California City Central Park Lake Pavilion*, 1962. Courtesy of Architecture and Design Collection, Art, Design & Architecture Museum, University of California, Santa Barbara, CA.

Rampant development and a transformed landscape coexist with horse-drawn wagons, all under the watchful eye of cowboys and ranchers on horseback. Early versions even included animal skulls scattered across the trails that run alongside paved freeways. The images reveal not only future projections but also a mythologized past that intermingles with the modern metropolis. Further, the incorporation of Native-American imagery illustrates how indigenous peoples were simultaneously eliminated from modern maps only to be re-introduced to lure tourists and investors as a kind of cultural preservation project not unlike the Twenty-Mule Team Parkway.[70]

The flurry of large-scale development largely stopped by the end of 1961, just four years after the city's founding. The folding tables and A-frame signs from opening day had become a small green recreational oasis with a bustling sales office that, by the end of the 1960s, generated over 100 million dollars in revenue from nearly 50,000 landowners. However, California City became not so much a thriving community but a compelling proxy for it. Communal areas and recreational facilities were largely empty save for scant potential buyers that visited through a vacation program. Instead, a majority of the tens of thousands of individual landowners and potential buyers were spread across Southern California and around the world. As much as California City existed as an oasis in the desert, it also circulated as paper around the world. It continues to circulate. Recently retired city manager, Tom Weil, reported that people still arrive in town in search of a plot of land that they inherited or were willed by an original landowner.[71]

On the one hand, it's easy to dismiss California City as a massive failure of postwar development. On the other hand, California City reveals that failure, or the promise of a future deferred indefinitely, is part of the late capitalist discourse of development. Total design and development, in the form of recreation and leisure facilities, landscapes, and most explicitly, the artificial lake, not only articulated the promise of a future thriving metropolis, but concealed aspects of the present that might threaten that future, namely the lack of water. That is to say, physical development was pursued less as a future realized and more as strengthening the promise of some greater future forthcoming, namely, thousands of individual landowners arriving and building housing. The concerted effort to create a public in the desert was used to benefit the monopoly capital of private investors, while shifting the burden of failure to that new public. Development undertaken by Mendelsohn had to be oriented toward the promised future metropolis as it was funded by borrowing against absentee taxpayers. Housing was positioned as a phantom facilitating a mutually reinforcing cycle of land sales and public debt registered in the company magazine/ free press. The *California City Sun* operated as a marketplace where the future was established, bought, sold, and traded. Land was purchased on financed deeds, while investors purchased bonds to finance recreation-themed developments. But physical development was pursued less as the resulting product of risk and more as a way to keep the dream alive. California City evidences this shift away from the profit of production to the credit to exercise it.[72] Architectural services were mobilized to set up a market for the exchange of credit where physical development was eschewed for the valorization of the land.

The financialized development practice at California City, where supply and demand move in sync, created an inherently unstable financial situation. While the company boasted 100 million dollars in revenue, that translated to significantly less cash flow, as many buyers defaulted on their loans. Inquiries by the FTC and the Attorney General of California at the end of the 1960s punctured the credit bubble. The entire company and its assets were sold to a national conglomerate for just 30 million dollars, most as stock, which might be considered a last attempt to maintain the creditworthiness of the development. By the early 1970s, the development company was spun off and ultimately dissolved. When the dust settled, not only had nearly all of the financial value disappeared, but the town's residents were more than 7 million dollars in debt.

The population has seen some increase in the fifty years since. Today, the population of California City is just under 15,000. But the collision of total design and attempts to control a master planned community comprising 100,000 acres, with market forces and housing built on an as needed basis, by individual buyers, produced the surreal image of California City today. Dispersed homes dot the landscape. Roads weave through the empty desert. The downtown commercial strip is a multi-lane boulevard with landscaped dividers. From the air, California City's comprehensive master plan sharpens into focus. On the ground, a journalist summarized the scene concisely as "an immense jigsaw puzzle with most of the pieces missing. There are houses with no neighbors, boulevards with no cars, streets that end abruptly and reappear blocks or miles away."[73]

Notes

1 Al Johns, "Down to Earth: Former Teacher Plans New City," *Los Angeles Times*, February 28, 1960.
2 Manuel Jimenez, "The California City Plan: A Cure for Urbanitis?" *Los Angeles Herald-Examiner*, December 11, 1966.
3 Mark Gutglueck, "Hesperia Entrusting Next Phase of City Administration to Police Chief," *San Bernardino City Sentinel*, January 9, 2016.
4 John Chase, "Coda: 1414 Fair Oaks Avenue," *arcCA* 5, no. 3 (2005): 116.
5 Marc Reisner, *Cadillac Desert: The American West and Its Disappearing Water* (New York: Penguin, 1993).
6 Eduardo Gruner, "The Intellectual's Journey into the Desert: A Critique of the Postcolonial Notions of 'Third Space' and 'In-Between'" (paper presentation, CongressCATH 2002: Translating Class, Altering Hospitality, Leeds Town Hall, England, June 2002).
7 On borax, *Romantic Heritage of Upper Mojave Desert: A Saga of Pioneer Discoveries and Modern Achievements* (Victorville, CA: California Interstate Telephone Company, 1961). In the media, Richard Lingenfelter, *Death Valley*

and the Amargosa: Land of Illusion (Berkeley: University of California Press, 1986).

8 "We're Only 5 Years Old," *Los Angeles Times*, March 29, 1963.

9 "Land Investment is the Sure Road to Future Wealth" (Hollywood: California City Development Company, 1961).

10 "Ribbon-Cutting to Cut Miles, Time," *California City Sun* 6, no. 6 (1963).

11 Charles D. Clark, "Land Subdivision," in *Los Angeles: Preface to a Master Plan*, edited by George W. Robbins and L. Deming Tilton (Los Angeles: Pacific Southwest Academy, 1941), 160.

12 "Smith and Williams, Architects and Engineers, "California City: A Planning Approach" (Pasadena: Author, 1968).

13 "California City: Largest Community in U.S. Launched in Boron Valley," *Independent* (Long Beach, California), March 29, 1958.

14 "A Plan for the City of Tomorrow," *Los Angeles Examiner*, January 22, 1961.

15 Charles D. Clark, "Subdivision Plotting and Map Filing," in *Subdivision Principles and Practices*, edited by Harrison R. Baker (Los Angeles: California Real Estate Association, 1936).

16 The architects aspired to design public vehicles including buses and "electrically powered tricycle cars." Community Facilities Planners, "California City 1980" (Pasadena: Author, 1961).

17 Community Facilities Planners, "California City 1980."

18 Community Facilities Planners, "California City 1980."

19 "You and Your Money," *California City Sun* 4, no. 3 (1961): 4.

20 "East Kern Unit Moves to Preserve Part of Twenty Mules Team Road," *Bakersfield Californian*, September 8, 1962; "California City: Huge Bunko Operation," *Los Angeles Underground* 1, no. 13 (1969).

21 The developer noted with surprise at the time that the restrictions did not hinder sales but accelerated them. Community Facilities Planners, "California City Story: Three Short Years of Dynamic Growth" (Pasadena: Author, 1961).

22 Community Facilities Planners, "California City 1980."

23 "A Plan for the City of Tomorrow."

24 "California City: 2nd Unit Launched After $500,000 1st Unit Sell-Out." *Valley News* (Van Nuys, California), April 27, 1958.

25 Max Derbes, "Use, Development, or Speculation of Real Estate," *The Appraisal Journal* 32, no. 2 (1964): 219–229.

26 Robert Fellmeth, *Politics of Land: Ralph Nader's Study Group Report on Land Use in California* (New York: Grossman Publishers, 1973).

27 "Property Sales Top $8 Million," *Los Angeles Times*, January 17, 1960; Paul Weeks, "Take a Good Look Before You Buy Piece of Desert Tract," *Los Angeles Times*, April 29, 1963.

28 "East is East, West Is West, Twin to Meet," *California City Sun* 5, no. 3 (1962); "First Seattle Day," *California City Sun* 11, no. 10 (1968); Fellmeth, *Politics of Land: Ralph Nader's Study Group Report on Land Use in California.*

29 "Growing Vacation Program Boosting Population Here," *California City Sun* 11, no. 10 (1968): 4.

30 "Calif. City Lures Philippine Business Interests," *California City Sun* 1, no. 8 (1965).

31 "In California City with Fred Beck," *Los Angeles Times*, March 21, 1960.

32 "2000 Attend Cal City Awards Meeting," *Los Angeles Times*, September 21, 1968.

33 Fellmeth, *Politics of Land: Ralph Nader's Study Group Report on Land Use in California.*

34 Frank Lee Donoghue, "Former Professor Designs Community Master Plan," *Los Angeles Herald-Examiner*, November 29, 1963.

35   Fellmeth, *Politics of Land: Ralph Nader's Study Group Report on Land Use in California.*

36   Community Facilities Planners, "California City Story: Three Short Years of Dynamic Growth."

37   Advisory Commission on Intergovernmental Relations, *A Commission Report: The Problem of Special Districts in American Government* (Washington, D.C.: Author, 1964). *Statutes of California, 1954–1955, Volume 1* (Sacramento: California State Printing Office, 1955): 322.

38   "Land Investment is the Sure Road to Future Wealth."

39   "An Open Letter from Your Community Services District," *California City Sun* 6, no. 6 (1963).

40   "$400,000 of New Recreational Developments," *California City Sun* 1, no. 7 (1965).

41   The developer subsidized the district just enough to keep its debt from becoming more excessive than allowed by law. Thomas Willoughby, "The Quiet Alliance," *Southern California Law Review* 38, no. 1 (1965): 72–79;

42   "B of A Buys California City Bonds," *Los Angeles Herald & Express*, September 15, 1960.

43   California City is early evidence of the widespread displacement of profit through productive enterprise for the appreciation of credit that characterizes late capital financialization. Michael Feher, *Rated Agency: Investee Politics in a Speculative Age* (Cambridge: MIT Press, 2018).

44   John C. Bollens, *Special District Government in the United States* (Berkeley: University of California Press, 1957).

45   Bollens, *Special District Government in the United States.*

46   "California City: Huge Bunko Operation."

47   Willoughby, "The Quiet Alliance."

48   Willoughby, "The Quiet Alliance."

49   Daniel Bell, *The Coming of Post-Industrial Society: A Venture in Social Forecasting* (New York: Basic Books, 1976).

50   See, Fred Beck, "In California City with Fred Beck," *Los Angeles Times*, February 12, 1960.

51   It was later renamed California City Boulevard.

52   Williams also created a "Social Advisory Committee" to organize "socials, dances, 'town hall' meetings, community improvement projects," movies, "visiting lecturers from UCLA, [and] art exhibits." Community Facilities Planners, "California City Story: Three Short Years of Dynamic Growth."

53   Community Facilities Planners, "California City Story: Three Short Years of Dynamic Growth."

54   Community Facilities Planners, "California City Story: Three Short Years of Dynamic Growth."

55   Frederick Belden, "Recreation Is a City: City Builder Recalls When Park Trip an Event," *California City Sun* 1, no. 3 (September 1967): 3, 10.

56   "Church Fund Drive, Just Begun, Already Nears Its $20,000 Goal," *California City Sun* 5, no. 4 (June 1962): 2.

57   "Plywood: New Shapes Yield New Strength," *Architectural Forum* (April 1964): 126–127.

58   "We're Stubborn About Saving 20-Mule Road," *California City Sun* 5, no. 5 (1962); "He Didn't Exactly Enjoy the Walk But the Muleshoe Was Worth it," *California City Sun* 5, no. 11 (January 1963): 5.

59   "20-Mule Road Plan Set for County Action," *California City Sun* 5, no. 8 (1962).

60   Dana Cuff, "Collective Form: The Status of Public Architecture," *Thresholds* 40 (2012): 55–66.

61 "Artificial Lake at Desert Development Being Filled," *Los Angeles Times*, April 9, 1961.

62 Reyner Banham, *Los Angeles: The Architecture of Four Ecologies* (Berkeley: UC Press, 2009), 142.

63 Nathan Mendelsohn, "Looking Forward," *California City Sun* 3, no. 1 (1960).

64 A nearly complete set of issues in Konrad Wachsmann's archive shows addresses following Wachsmann across the U.S.A. and Europe. See Konrad Wachsmann Archiv, Akademie der Künste, Berlin.

65 "Underground Lake Reported," *Redlands Daily Facts*, January 23, 1959; "California City: Largest Community in U.S. Launched in Boron Valley."

66 California Department of Water Resources, Report (Sacramento: Author, 1960).

67 Howard Gingold, "Desert Promoters' Claims Produce Varied Reactions," *Los Angeles Times*, June 9, 1961.

68 "In California City with Fred Beck," *Los Angeles Times*, May 24, 1960.

69 "Parties Improve With Age," *California City Sun* 5, no. 4 (1962).

70 Gwendolyn Wright, "Building Global Modernisms," *Grey Room*, 7 (2002): 124–134.

71 Mike Anton, "A Desert City That Didn't Fan Out," *Los Angeles Times*, August 14, 2010.

72 Feher, *Rated Agency: Investee Politics in a Speculative Age*.

73 Campbell, "Like Its Layout, California City Politics is Confusing," *Bakersfield Californian*, March 5, 1984.

Index

Note: *Italic* page numbers refer to figures and page numbers followed by "n" denote endnotes.